Fawning

Also by Dr. Ingrid Clayton

Believing Me:
Healing from Narcissistic Abuse and Complex Trauma

Recovering Spirituality:
Achieving Emotional Sobriety in Your Spiritual Practice

Fawning

WHY THE NEED TO PLEASE MAKES US LOSE OURSELVES— AND HOW TO FIND OUR WAY BACK

Dr. Ingrid Clayton

G. P. PUTNAM'S SONS
NEW YORK

PUTNAM
— EST. 1838 —

G. P. Putnam's Sons
Publishers Since 1838
An imprint of Penguin Random House LLC
1745 Broadway, New York, NY 10019
penguinrandomhouse.com

Book design by Kristin del Rosario

LIBRARY OF CONGRESS CATALOGING-IN-PUBLICATION DATA
has been applied for.

Hardcover ISBN: 9798217045327
Ebook ISBN: 9798217045334
International ISBN: 9798217178964

Printed in the United States of America
1st Printing

The authorized representative in the EU for product safety and compliance is
Penguin Random House Ireland, Morrison Chambers, 32 Nassau Street,
Dublin D02 YH68, Ireland, https://eu-contact.penguin.ie.

To my clients presented within these pages,
and those who are written between the lines,
I have learned more from you
than all my education and training combined.

And to everyone who sees themselves reflected here:
You were never broken. You make perfect sense.
This book is for you.

Contents

Contents

A Note on Client Stories

There are seven clients highlighted in this book. They each get their own story, and I additionally refer to their experiences throughout the text. These are real people I care about deeply and whom I've seen in my private practice for between one and sixteen years. There is no way to do them and the entire arc of our work together justice—and yet, as it relates to fawning, I aim to try.

It's important to note that each of these individuals can identify themselves as fawners and have at least some space from it. They can now *see* it, whereas once they couldn't. By the nature of the thing, I can share experiences only from this end of the spectrum; however, I am sharing what it was like *before* my clients could put their experience into that context.

I was quite apprehensive about inviting clients to share their personal stories so candidly. That said, I am grateful I did. Everyone who participated said yes to the opportunity before I could finish the ask. In speaking with their own friends and family, they knew others hadn't heard of fawning, much less found freedom and flexibility from it. They wanted to offer their stories in the hope of helping others. I know even before sharing this book that the way they bared their souls truly helped me, not just as an author, but as a lifelong fawner who continues to wrestle more of herself free.

I married my knowledge and case notes on my clients with additional recorded interviews or written responses to a questionnaire in order to portray the fullest picture possible of the fawn response. In the process, I often heard, "I don't think I've ever told you this before." It seems that mining my client's experiences of fawning brought another layer of insight and healing. In exploring something deeply and intently, for the "reader's sake," they were collectively able to go deeper into their vulnerability. Read that again. Their desire to be helpful gave them the will to go further into their own experience, all in the service of collective wisdom and insight for the reader.

As you'll read in the pages to come, there are costs to fawning, to be sure. However, I'd be remiss not to share that there are strengths simultaneously born of fawning, how it draws out and magnifies some of our best attributes. How it made us safe *enough,* saved our lives, but also shaped superpowers along the way.

All names and identifying characteristics have been altered to protect my clients' identities, but their stories and insights are all true. I'm not the interpreter of their experience as much as the one who is privileged to share it.

Fawning

PART ONE

The Anatomy of Fawning

One

The Fourth F

What Is Fawning?

When I was thirteen years old, I loved sitting outside in the hot tub at night. We lived in Aspen, Colorado, and when the lights from the house were turned off, I could easily identify the constellations in the vast dark sky.

One night my stepdad Randy came to join me. His legs were like tree trunks as he stomped across the deck, commanding my attention. I watched as he stepped into the tub, his shorts puffing up with air before sinking into the darkness. Then I went back to stargazing, wondering which version of him I was getting: the one who seemed to despise me, correcting my every move, or the guy who gave off the appearance of being charming and kind.

Only a year earlier, Randy had gone from being my dad's best friend to my mom's husband, and shortly thereafter he had moved us to this remote mountain town. I was still absorbing the shock, isolated from friends and family in this strange new place. I quickly memorized the local tavern's phone number, as the bartenders often confirmed our parents' whereabouts. This allowed my brother, stepbrother, and me to prepare for the unpredictability that often erupted when they returned home.

The rules of this new household were arbitrary, based on Randy's mood and ever-changing. New standards erupted on the spot. No matter how hard I tried to follow them, it was impossible. And when I didn't, I was grounded—unable to leave the house for months while he gave me the silent treatment.

But now, in the hot tub, he wasn't ignoring or criticizing me. His mood seemed pleasant, and it was a relief. "I bet you wish you could live up there with the stars, huh?" Randy laughed a little, but he wasn't laughing *at* me. It was like he was acknowledging: *I know you wish you weren't here—with me—and that's okay.* Speaking to that truth was disarming. It felt like maybe we could be real with each other. My hard shell softened against the jets, and I gave a little giggle while poking at my braces with my tongue.

"Why don't you come sit on my lap so you don't have to crank your neck?" Randy motioned that I could rest my head against his chest while looking up at the sky. More than anything, after the precarity of the last year, I wanted to feel cared for. I wanted a happy family. I perceived his invitation as an olive branch of stepfatherly love.

I drifted over to his side of the tub, sat in his lap, and leaned back so that my head rested on his upper chest. My toes peeked out of the bubbling water, while his arms anchored me in place. My guard came down even further as I felt tethered, seen, and appreciated.

"I like being this close to you," Randy said as his hands lightly squeezed my hips. "I'm so glad you don't seem to mind."

My body tensed as my thoughts raced. *Why would he say that? What does he mean?* I immediately felt the implication of his words, hovering over the energy of his hands, and knew I probably *should* mind. But I also knew I had to walk a fine line. I didn't want to get in trouble—provoking the version of him that terrified me. So, I responded carefully, keeping my voice thin as the mountain air, "Why would I mind?"

As I waited for Randy's answer in the hot tub, the prickliness of his body hair felt like needles on my skin. The water was creating a suction between us, and I felt trapped. I held my body as still as possible.

"Some girls are uptight," he said. "They might want more personal space from the men in their lives." He paused and then continued: "I'm glad you aren't like them and that we can be this close."

This moment changed everything. At least it changed something in me. It was the first time I felt unsafe with Randy while he was seemingly being kind. All the other times I felt unsafe, he was aggressive and mean. It felt chaotic. But in this moment, his voice was soft and steady. He appeared gentle. Yet I had a conscious sense in my body that he wasn't saying the whole truth. Something was deeply wrong.

If I could slow it down, it's as though my psyche were split in two. On the one hand, I was afraid. I was thirteen, just a child, sensing a threat to my sense of safety. On the other hand, I had to filter my fear through the power dynamics in the hot tub. This was, after all, the adult authority figure in my life. From the minute Randy had moved in with us, my mom's small frame had slipped into his shadow. Her limbs moved only when his did, her words formed only when she'd heard him say them before. I was constantly wondering where my mom was, even when she was standing right in front of me. Randy was in charge, and we all needed to stay on his good side.

So what did I do next? While we typically think of **fight, flight,** or **freeze** as responses to threat, my body instinctively knew that these reflexes were not available.

Fighting wasn't really an option. First of all, Randy wasn't being overtly hostile, so there was nothing to fight against. Rather, he was grooming me—emotionally manipulating me—and it was effective.

I began to second-guess myself, wondering if this was possibly as innocuous as he was portraying. Additionally, Randy was twice my size. Although I'd never witnessed physical violence between him and my mom, I'd seen her bruises. Fighting would have been dangerous.

Fleeing is, of course, also impossible for most children. Where are we meant to run? To whom? We humans are reliant on our caregivers for longer than any other species, needing the adults in our lives to survive. I was far from my friends and family. I had nowhere else safe to go.

Freezing is a common trauma response, but in this situation my body didn't freeze—at least not completely. I had to continue navigating this situation with some presence of mind. I sensed that if I followed his cues, I could likely maintain his affection without making things worse. I didn't *feel* safe, but I had to pretend otherwise. I did not like him, but I needed *him* to like *me*.

So my body found another option. In the hot tub alone with my stepfather, I was terrified, but I acted normal. I played it cool. I appeared agreeable, even ingratiating. My behavior communicated: *nothing to see here.* I lingered just long enough before saying I was ready to get out. Then I peeled myself off his lap and wished I could blink myself into my bedroom as I stepped onto the deck. I wanted to run but forced myself to walk casually, so that every step felt like it was in slow motion. A half-naked, soaking wet, slow-motion parade.

It would be thirty years before I'd understand what happened that evening, and how this event shaped my response to any sign of conflict going forward. It turns out there is a fourth F of trauma responses. It's called **fawning.**

Connection Is Protection

Until recently, when someone used the word *fawning*, what might've come to mind was an employee fawning over a boss for a raise or a girl fawning over a boy she wanted to like her. The definition in Merriam-Webster's dictionary is: "to court favor by a cringing or flattering manner." But that doesn't get to the heart of what fawning is in the context of trauma.

Pete Walker, a psychotherapist and the author of *Complex PTSD: From Surviving to Thriving*, coined the term *fawning* after working with countless survivors of trauma and abuse. He defined fawning as "a response to a threat by becoming more appealing to the threat." Fawners mirror or merge with someone *else's* desires or expectations, to defuse conflict rather than confront it directly. Because it's their best chance to stay safe. At least for now.

When you're being hit on by an aggressive or unwanted suitor and you smile and giggle, that's fawning. If you don't stand up for your values in a toxic work environment to keep your job, that's fawning, too. When you continually dismiss a parent's abusive behavior to maintain the connection, you guessed it. Fawning.

In other words, fawning as a trauma response puts our behaviors in the context of disempowerment or maltreatment. It's not about brownnosing for an A or sucking up to people in power. Fawning isn't conscious manipulation. Rather, it's a way we seek safety in the face of exploitation, shame, neglect, abuse, or other harm.

Interestingly, fawning can be likened to a core principle found in the Japanese martial art of aikido, which means "way of harmonizing." Rather than attack or retreat, the goal in aikido is to move *with* one's opponent, mirroring their energy, their intentions. Connecting with an adversary allows you to sense their next move, to keep both parties safe while orienting toward a peaceful resolution.

This is what happens when we fawn in the face of danger. When we feel unsafe, we sync with our aggressors (or abusers) with the hope of emerging unscathed. We strive to stay connected because we are dependent on the person who is hurting us. If it's a parent (or step-parent), we are dependent on their care. If it is a boss, we are dependent on a paycheck or career advancement. If it's a partner, we are dependent on their income, the ability to see our children, the status that marriage affords.

With fawning, connection means protection.

While fawning is meant to neutralize danger (and it does), it has an invisible downside. Merging with others' desires means surrendering our own. When we fawn, we forgo assertiveness and become overly accommodating. We shapeshift to stay safe. We submit to the very person or people who have harmed us. Essentially, we abandon ourselves when we fawn—our needs, values, and opinions—and this reinforces our vulnerability.

Sometimes referred to as *please and appease,* fawning is often equated with people-pleasing or codependency. However, as I'll explore later, both of those terms imply that we have some agency in our actions. Fawning is not a conscious choice. It is a survival mechanism. In a nanosecond, the reptilian brain selects the response that offers the greatest chance for survival. Afterward, the body remembers what was successful the first time and repeats it in the future. The fawner's intentions then were never to *please* or compulsively *caretake.* We were looking for power in situations where we were powerless.

I'm Fine, You're Fine, Everything's *Fine*

Three years after that evening in the hot tub, as things with Randy continued to get progressively worse, he took me on a secret trip to Las Vegas. My mother was out of town with her dying father, and Randy concocted various lies to steal me away. When we arrived, he made me hold his hand throughout the casinos. He paraded me around as his girlfriend, saying we'd get in trouble if anyone knew I was underage. When we got back, my mom was still gone. It felt as though nothing had technically "happened." He didn't sexually abuse me. Yes, he checked us into a suite with a king-size bed and a mirrored ceiling. Yes, we slept in the same bed, him half naked, me in bulky sweatpants turned away from him clutching my side of the bed. But though my body knew it felt wrong, and I was terrified, what could I truly say happened?

I didn't say anything to anyone in authority until months later, after Randy left a sticky note on my pillow and it felt like I finally had something concrete. Though I no longer remember what the note said, it was enough to signal the dynamic of our relationship. I brought it to school, where I showed it to my school counselor. She looked at me with concern.

"Ingrid, we've got to talk about this." I shuddered as I knew it was time for someone to know the whole story. I told her about Vegas.

This was an example of a healthy fight response. I knew I needed help thwarting Randy's continued advances. I wanted my mother to know the truth, I wanted her to leave Randy, I wanted to be saved from this ongoing nightmare and intuitively knew that I needed someone with more authority to help me. But when my counselor arranged for social services to come to my school for us all to sit down with my mother, rather than being rescued by her, she stayed silent. My mom got a stoic look on her face and demanded that her husband be called to the school, not to "get in trouble," but to manage the narrative. When he burst into the room, it was to call me a liar. He blamed me for all the troubles in our family.

What ultimately hurt me the most was that my mom took his side—pursuing her own version of *nothing to see here*. What Randy did traumatized me, but I truly believed that when my mom heard what he had done, she'd take me in her arms, saying, *I'm sorry, I'm sorry, I'm sorry.* And eventually, *We're leaving.*

Instead, I watched as the one person I thought would save me chose the side of my tormentor.

Many fawners have an experience like this in our backgrounds— something that shows us we can never wholly rely on anyone but ourselves. We've learned that interpersonal safety nets are for *other people,* that unconditional love is either a myth or our job to uphold. Consequently, we often become hyper-independent. Unable to lean into healthy relational support, we have to figure it out for ourselves. So we do. It's common that we don't even tell others when bad stuff happens. We swallow it down, pretend everything is fine, and continue fawning for perpetual safety—an exhausting and lonely endeavor.

Meanwhile, fawners often look perfectly fine, like we're managing well. We frequently are high-functioning, having successful careers or long-term relationships, but it's never the whole story. The truth is that we've accommodated so much for so long, we don't even feel new trespasses. We maintain the status quo through numbing ourselves or depression, aiming to "be better," as the solution to all relational difficulties. We actually believe our incessant self-gaslighting that tells us, *Maybe it's not that bad.*

Additionally, many people have learned to fawn in their families or their larger communities. Touted as simple "respect," fawning is an adaptive response to living in a hierarchal, patriarchal society. Persistent lessons have primed us to be fawners:

- Give your uncle a kiss.
- Say you love the gift when you don't.
- Don't talk about Dad's drinking.
- Don't make others uncomfortable.
- Be the "better" person.
- But she's your *mother.*

- Present more white/affluent/sexy to stay relationally safe.
- Present *less* sexy to stay relationally safe.
- Be a team player.
- How bad do you want it?
- Just go with it.
- Repress it.
- Ignore it.
- Smile.

Countless messages implicitly and explicitly ask that we disconnect from our authentic selves—until we don't know where we end and fawning begins.

This is the most heartbreaking component of fawning. We lose the connection to ourselves. We develop these coping mechanisms that become so ingrained in us we don't even know we are using them. We *are* the fawner and yet we can appear happy, perpetually going along to get along. We might see ourselves as generous, empathic, and compassionate. These are often intrinsic qualities we possess, but we don't know the extent to which they've been hijacked by our trauma response. Oftentimes we don't even know we've experienced trauma at all.

Fawning as a Response to Complex Trauma

Fawning is a common coping mechanism for those dealing with continuing relational trauma. Relational trauma is different from a single traumatic occurrence, such as a car crash or an assault. It's a form of complex trauma, which is a relatively new term in the field of psychology. *Complex trauma* refers to ongoing pervasive threats to our safety, often interpersonal in nature. It isn't a diagnosis, and it isn't an event. Complex trauma results from an enduring painful situation that seemingly has no end. It is the air that we breathe. It can stem from particularly challenging or abusive relationships within our family of origin, like mine did. It can also occur in larger systems of oppression or marginalization, or in any community where we must disavow aspects of ourselves to secure vital membership. Complex trauma can occur in the workplace or in romantic relationships.

The tough part about complex trauma is that we often don't see it as traumatic because we misinterpret it as either the norm or as a personal failing. While I always understood that I had experienced trauma in a colloquial sense, for years I didn't think it was *real trauma*. I thought I needed to have experienced something worse or more obvious. Absent such experiences, my symptoms were mine alone, my problem just *me*.

Part of the problem is how recently society has even begun to acknowledge the existence and importance of trauma. It wasn't until 1980 that a diagnosis of PTSD (post-traumatic stress disorder) was even included in the American Psychiatric Association's *Diagnostic and Statistical Manual of Mental Disorders*, the bible of mental health diagnosis. Criteria for a diagnosis of PTSD included that a person must have experienced "a psychologically distressing event that is *outside the range of usual human experience* [emphasis added]." Trauma was understood to be dramatic, destructive, and rare.

In the decades since, though, our understanding of trauma has expanded. Trauma is in fact extremely common—70 percent of adults in the United States have experienced some type of traumatic event at least once in their lives. And these are just the reported cases. In many families, people have experienced some level of addiction, untreated mental illness, sexual abuse, physical abuse, or rage. In addition, on a societal level, people are experiencing poverty, racism, and a lack of access to proper healthcare.

These things are not generally outside the usual human experience; indeed, they *are* the human experience. And yet they've been seen as situations we are meant to keep secret, manage and tolerate, forgive, or get over—certainly not experiences that are "traumatic" by the old standard by which many people still measure. We now know these pervasive cuts to one's psyche can be as detrimental as wartime experiences or living through a natural disaster. Perhaps *more* so, because they are less obvious to the naked eye, festering in the unseen abyss of "personal problems" one is meant to overcome or outgrow.

During the women's liberation movement of the 1970s, Harvard psychiatry professor Judith Herman, MD, made the distinction between single incident (acute) trauma and repeated traumatic events. She spoke to a parallel between the stories she was hearing from women about sexual and domestic violence and the way we were conceptualizing trauma for veterans. The more women broke their silence, the more Herman became an advocate for them in papers that circulated widely but underground. Attempting to bridge the gaps between men and women, public and private—between legitimate and stigmatized—she coined the term *complex trauma*. She argued that the current definition of PTSD was not sufficient to address the accumulation of everyday trauma that affected a much wider swath of humanity than had been previously understood. She advocated that a new diagnosis be added to the *Diagnostic and Statistical Manual of Mental Disorders* to address this evolving understanding: complex PTSD. That was in 1988; Herman's proposal was denied.

To this day, complex PTSD (and therefore complex trauma in general) is not recognized diagnostically in the United States, a major failure that handicaps both clinicians and the public by limiting funding for research, inclusion in academic instruction, and insurance reimbursement.* Simply put, the medical establishment has not adopted the language necessary to help many of our most vulnerable.

---

* Fortunately, the World Health Organization gave C-PTSD some credibility when they added it to the *International Statistical Classification of Diseases and Related Health Problems (ICD-11)* in 2018.

And the truth is, most of my clients didn't come to my office because they had complex trauma. They came to me with low self-esteem, depression, anxiety, addiction, relational difficulties, and so on. This is how complex trauma manifests itself in our everyday lives. Negative self-talk, substance use, disordered eating, and lack of boundaries are some of the imperfect ways we try to cope amid pervasive ongoing threats to our safety and sense of self. I see it all the time in my practice, across all ages, sexes, and walks of life. If I didn't have some knowledge of these insidious ways complex trauma presents itself, I wouldn't be able to address my clients' real concerns. Our work would have stayed within these other, narrower focuses— often becoming a whack-a-mole game of perpetual symptom management rather than accomplishing any real healing.

When we understand that we come by our symptoms honestly— they are not innately dysfunctional traits—and that healing from trauma requires holistic, body-based solutions, a wonderful thing can happen. We can finally get off the hamster wheel: trying harder, gaining insight, endeavoring to prove our worth, and getting nowhere. We can shift out of survival mode and finally begin healing.

A Glossary of Terms

We use the word *trauma* to mean many different things, so let's break it down:

TRAUMATIC EVENTS: Shocking, scary, or life-threatening experiences such as car crashes, natural disasters, experiencing or witnessing violence, betrayal, abuse, and neglect. These events may or may not lead to trauma for an individual.

TRAUMA: The Greek word for "wound." Trauma is the imprint that is left from traumatic events; it is what happens when these experiences overwhelm the nervous system. Events can remain in the past, but the way they alter where and how we store memories, including our ability to metabolize and consolidate them, is carried into the present. Unresolved trauma lives on as fragmented pieces of a self, as bodily remembrance that feels as though we are trapped in time.

TRAUMA TRIGGER: A felt reminder of a traumatic event. They can be external, such as loud noises, anniversaries, or scenes from a movie. And they can be internal: feelings of powerlessness or loneliness; physical tension.

TRAUMA RESPONSES: The body's spontaneous reaction to threat. These responses are instinctual, not intellectual. Originally thought of as fight, flight, and freeze, they are unconscious attempts to keep us safe. If we add fawning to this list, we can say we don't want to be people pleasers, but our bodies don't ask our opinions when they feel threatened. Trauma responses lead to emotional dysregulation, the inability to regulate our emotions.

COMPLEX TRAUMA: Exposure to repeated interpersonal threats over time and the difficulties that arise from them. Often from childhood, but not necessarily so (long-term domestic violence, for example). *Complex trauma* is often used interchangeably with *relational, developmental, psychological,* and/or *childhood trauma.*

POST-TRAUMATIC STRESS DISORDER (PTSD) AND COMPLEX POST-TRAUMATIC STRESS DISORDER (C-PTSD): Trauma-related diagnoses. Core criteria for both include a long-standing pattern of reexperiencing past traumatic events; avoidance of reminders of traumatic events; difficulties with reactivity, mood, and cognition. C-PTSD extends beyond this to include affect dysregulation, negative self-concept, and disturbed relationships.

Getting Unstuck

My path to healing from chronic fawning started when I got the news that Randy was dying. Like the final hours on my decades-long hope that *he will tell the truth, she will believe me, and then I'll be free,* the sand was running out for us both.

Lord knows I'd tried everything else to overcome my past. After moving out of the house at seventeen, I didn't look back. Determined to break the cycles in my family, I got sober at twenty-one. I received a bachelor's degree in psychology, then a master's, and finally a PhD in clinical psychology. I continued my training after graduate school and started a thriving private practice. I was going to yoga, engaged in spiritual endeavors, and reading *all* the self-help books. It looked on the outside like I'd prevailed over the horrors of my childhood. But on the inside, I was still the same. Still fawning. Still trapped.

Conscious awareness of my family's dysfunction never relieved me of the instincts that allowed me to cope. Well into my thirties, I joked I must be wearing a sandwich board that read: "Users and abusers, please apply here." From bad boyfriends to mooching roommates to exploitative friendships, it's like I was trying to break a spell by drinking the same poison, hoping I'd eventually build up the necessary antibodies.

I talked about my history of unhealthy relationships with many therapists. I was desperate to solve the shame I carried by dating the same person with a different face, over and over. Things always looked so hopeful in the early days of dating, but then I'd find myself in a familiar pattern: financially supporting men whom I tried to get into therapy or with partners who were cheating, emotionally abusive, avoidant, or actively addicted—until they eventually broke up with me.

I tolerated all kinds of mistreatment, thinking I could neutralize or alchemize bad behavior. I avoided conflict like the plague—never even unsubscribing from mailing lists if I thought the sender would find out. I chronically put everyone above myself, helping people heal their wounds as though that would magically heal my own. Exploitation played out in friendships, with family, bosses, and mentors, so I was doing THE WORK, adopting several twelve-step programs while wondering, *How many affirmations must one repeat before raising one's self-esteem?*

All the while, I never knew that my attempts at insight, compassion, and forgiveness were keeping me stuck. Mountains of analysis and being a good girl were simply bypassing my unresolved wounds, colluding with the idea that *I was broken.* I never knew *all* this behavior—the stuff I was proud of, and the stuff I was not—was fueled by a trauma response.

What, Exactly, Is a Trauma Response?

Also referred to as stress responses, trauma responses are the body's immediate and spontaneous reaction to threat. They occur when an event or ongoing events overwhelm our nervous system. A trauma response is an unconscious survival mechanism that protects us from harm.

When we are faced with a threat, the thinking mind disconnects. Imagine animals in the wild. When they sense potential danger, they don't stop to think, *Am I being ridiculous right now?* They just *react.* Humans do this, too.

The most well-known trauma responses are the ones we discussed earlier: **fight** or **flight**. Activated by our sympathetic nervous system, these are both forms of *hyperarousal*, like an on switch that floods the body with hormones. Think elevated heart rate and blood pressure along with rapid breathing—we become mobilized in response to a perceived threat. Fight and flight appear just as they sound: We attack (fight) or attempt to escape from harm (flight).

When fight and flight are not available, the parasympathetic nervous system (rest and digest) triggers the off switch. This is where we see the **freeze** response, moving the body toward *hypoarousal*. Like a deer in headlights, we are panicked but frozen. Freeze is likened to bracing for impact, wanting to move but not being certain if it's safe. Hypoarousal can range from this panicked but immobilized presentation, to going numb, falling limp, and completely shutting down. In hypoarousal, our heart rate decreases and our breathing slows. At the end of the spectrum, we see feigning death, but not as a conscious pretending. The body needs to play dead in order to shut down and protect us from further harm. Playing dead is a last-ditch effort at survival, where the body is said to collapse or submit. As seen in the wild, prey that is caught by a predator goes limp. If the predator drops the prey, the prey might still escape—but not without lingering harm. And indeed, hypoarousal houses the origins of hopelessness, dissociation, and depression.

The **fawn** response is different. Fawning is a *hybrid* response, activating the sympathetic (hyperarousal) and parasympathetic (hypoarousal) branches of the autonomic nervous system at the same time.

- The *hyper*arousal aspect of fawning has us instinctively managing the moods and states of those "in charge." We lean into the very relationships that are causing us harm, appeasing our perpetrators while taking personal responsibility for all relational difficulties. Fawning can be incredibly active.
- But at the same time, we are detaching from ourselves. The *hypo*arousal of fawning numbs our connection to self, our

broader sense of agency, and often our ability to feel the effects of the abuse at all.

We are threading a fine needle when we fawn, neither risking greater harm through fight or flight, nor shutting down completely. This highly adaptive response is moving beyond playing dead to playing LIFE. We are playing pretend, and we don't even know it. We are playing house, playing the game (to survive or escape our situation), playing a part—sometimes as many parts are there are people in our lives.

Shake It Off

When an animal faces threat, their trauma responses take over. When the threat has passed, they literally shake it off, releasing the tension and pent-up survival energy in their bodies.

In our evolution, humans have learned to override this vital instinct. Thus, when trauma happens, our bodies can remain in a constant state of arousal and tension. In particular, when we experience complex trauma, the threat never goes away. We are essentially still living in the war zone. Instead of shaking it off, we swallow it down. It gets embedded inside us. Survivors of complex trauma live in a perpetual state of emotional dysregulation.

The past feels present, our senses are heightened, our reactions are intensified. This is because, as Dr. Bessel van der Kolk, one of the preeminent scholars on trauma and author of the bestselling *The Body Keeps the Score,* explains, the traumatized body does not forget and is stuck in a state of anticipating—sensing potential danger even when no real danger can be found. Unresolved trauma lives on as fragmented pieces of a self, as bodily remembrance that feels as though we are trapped in time, simultaneously wreaking havoc on our present.

Like the arc of a roller coaster, our trauma responses are meant to resolve, moving us through danger to safety on the other side. We are meant to come to a stop, to get off the ride. With complex trauma and chronic trauma responses, we are hovering at the midpoint of the coaster. Living our lives in suspended alarm. Through this lens, we can see how many of us confuse our trauma responses for *personality*. We literally don't know where we end and where unconscious trauma response begins.

Safety over Self

I started writing about fawning before I knew it had a name, desperate to understand why I kept repeating obviously unhealthy patterns. After Randy died, I felt called to go back and examine what happened during my childhood with clearer eyes. I began to write down stories of all the things I remembered, all the times he made me feel uncomfortable. Like that time in the hot tub, the secret trip to Las Vegas, the ways my mom made excuses for him again and again. The memories poured out of me, like a dam had broken, like these stories and all the ways I'd re-created them had just been waiting to be aired, to be given a voice, waiting for my own validation.

As I got closer to finishing what became a book on my experience of complex trauma, I wasn't even focused on having it published traditionally. I just wanted to name my truth beyond the safety of a therapist's walls. It was deeply healing to finally be in control of my own narrative and for it to be visible on the page.

I called my memoir *Believing Me* because so much of my trauma was not just what Randy did, but the way no one did anything about it. The way my own mother didn't believe me. In this naming and *reframing*, I saw that the end of my own story was mine. The final grains of sand belonged to me. It didn't matter that Randy died without validating what happened. I didn't have to keep waiting, appeasing, or pretending. I didn't have to rise above my traumatic experiences or my mother's perception of them. I had to drop into the truth so I could finally process its impact.

I was years into my process of writing and sharing my experiences when someone asked if I'd heard of Pete Walker's work on complex trauma. Walker is the author of *Complex PTSD*, in which he writes about healing from childhood trauma. As I looked him up and discovered his definition of fawning, it set off a cascade of dominoes over my history, liberating one after the other until the entire sequence made sense to me. Fawning made sense to me. *I made sense to me.*

Fawners, or what Walker calls *fawn types,* are "seeking safety by merging with the wishes, needs, and demands of others." Even more, he goes on to say, they learn that the "price of admission to any relationship is the forfeiture of all their needs, rights, preferences, and boundaries."

And there you have it. My life in one sentence. Finally I had a way of understanding my childhood and my past relationships, why I felt so much shame. Armed with this lens and language, I began more excavation, of myself and of my clients' lived experiences. Once I had the terminology, it was like I saw fawning everywhere, in my own life and in theirs. We were having a collective awakening.

Fawning gave me not just the what of my behavior—perpetually playing into harmful hands—but the why. I didn't have a low self-esteem problem. I had a body with hardwired operating instructions, designed to keep me safe. Additionally, I saw why the mental health field had been confused about this reality for so long. When we fawn, there is often a deep incongruence between our feelings about a person or situation and our behavior. In that hot tub, my body and brain wanted to get away. I wanted the confusion and overwhelming fear to stop. My instincts knew that Randy was in the wrong. But they also understood my reality outside of that hot tub. I had to keep him happy to keep myself safe. Fawning happens when we are in a double bind, when there are real consequences for *not* fawning. We can't address every need simultaneously, so the body has to choose. We choose safety over self.

But this forced choice has dire consequences. It clouds our perception; we lose touch with our internal guidance system. We learn to override our gut, our inner wisdom, which means we cannot identify or act on red flags. For fawners, internal safety is always reliant on the condition of external safety, so it remains at arm's length: in someone else's body or ideology, in their perception or story. Merging with distorted views erodes our self-trust and our sense of self altogether.

In addition to causing us to lose connection with our authentic nature, the fawn response leads to deep shame, leaning into danger, disrespect, and behaviors that don't align with our values. We often don't understand why we do what we do—why we appease our abuser, why we butter up our jerk of a boss, why we placate a difficult parent instead of standing up for ourselves—but it feels impossible to stop.

Our conciliation doesn't just give our aggressors cues that nothing is wrong; we often believe it ourselves. Sometimes we know we are not acting in accordance with our values or needs (as in the hot tub with my stepdad). But sometimes the blinders are so complete, we believe wholeheartedly that we're perfectly fine, in love, or in the present moment. In hindsight, I can see so many times, so many relationships, where I was fawning and didn't even know it: self-abandonment personified.

Fawning is . . .

- Apologizing to someone when they've hurt you.
- Befriending your bullies in order to get the job, keep the boyfriend, pay the rent.

- Painting the red flags white—consciously or otherwise.
- Trusting others more than yourself.
- Holding out hope that people will change if you try hard enough to help them.
- Making excuses for people who have hurt you, privileging their pain over your own.
- Not having a voice because speaking up makes things *worse*.

For some people, fawning is about being *more* of who they are—smart, generous, successful, funny, or beautiful—so they will be further adored, accepted, and connected. For others, it's about being *less*: vocal, ethnic, creative, self-assured, or able to set boundaries. Fawning can be visible or invisible; it can take the shape of sex, money, or the perpetual emotional regulation of others. But one thing remains constant: It is about finding safety in an unsafe world, often at our own expense.

Sitting in the hot tub with my stepdad, I'm incredibly grateful my body took over—to help me navigate what was literally out of my control and out of my comprehension. I can't even call this self-abandonment. I call it grace, genius, or higher wisdom bestowed upon me. It was lifesaving, and these impulses helped me navigate four more years in that house.

We are not meant to eradicate our trauma responses. We couldn't if we tried! We need these lifesaving instincts, and I'm grateful for them. But when I drove away, hundreds and then thousands of miles from that dysfunction, I remained the same. I brought these imprints with me, no longer discerning safety on a moment-to-moment basis, but unconsciously accepting life in an unsafe world. We aren't meant to live in survival mode, but these instincts were steering the ship in every relationship—accommodating, shapeshifting, erasing myself until I know longer knew who I was. Fawning was my stunt double, and I had no idea it was acting as me, shielding me—from the bad and from the good. From the good that was inside of me.

Lowering the Bar

One of the things I value most about twelve-step recovery is the access it provides to community and spirituality through our shared struggles. I had been looking for both on my own, but it was like the bar was too high. I knew that the "real me," the one who couldn't stop drinking, could never live up to the expectations that "spiritual" or "regular" people held. So when I found the twelve-step recovery world, it was like that bar was lowered to the ground. In fact, we were often meeting in church basements, not sitting with the congregation above. *This is a place that might accept me,* I thought to myself, clinging to their adage *We will love you until you can love yourself.* In those humble rooms, I found more of myself, and a connection to other people and to spiritual practices that didn't fill me with shame.

That is what I want to do with this book. I am lowering the bar. Taking away the judgment and shame around fawning. Allowing us to connect and be real with one another so we can finally access the tools that are most helpful. So we can finally access ourselves.

For too long, people have talked about the behaviors associated with fawning like something is wrong with us, like we should just get over it, grow up already, stand up for ourselves, set boundaries, and grow our self-esteem. Those phrases have just kept our defenses UP. We must lower the bar to lower our defenses. That's the only hope for real change. Getting to see how we make sense NOW. Understanding why we've done everything we've done, and to be honest, will likely continue to do to some degree.

All of us have defenses. We all have coping mechanisms. Fawning may not be everyone's variety, but we all have one, if not a combination platter. While I want us to have more freedom and flexibility and believe that it's possible, I also don't want to portray unfawning like some fantasyland. I'm afraid I'm often the buzzkill therapist with a very unsexy message: "Get in touch with all your pain, your wounds, the shameful ways you feel like you've coped with them, and then you will get *better*, but you'll never attain the best-case scenario, at least not 100 percent of the time." There is no perfect place of rest and wholeness. As long as we are alive, there is no finish line. As long as we have a body that lives with other people on this planet, we will have coping.

I am a junkie at heart who has tried using a little of this and a little of that to feel as good as possible all the time. In my decades of sobriety, in my personal therapy, and as a therapist, I have tried to find the perfect alchemy. I would not be sharing the contents of this book, holding them up so high, if I hadn't found what I'm advocating here to be the most healing and helpful approach. If I didn't think it was abundantly better than everything I'd tried before. My clients' experiences echo that. No matter what they've had to face, grieve, and process, having more choices—being more of themselves—is absolutely worth it.

The goal in our healing is to come back to the body's natural inclination of flexibility and repair. One grounded in regulation, a whole and true self. We cannot eliminate all threat, but we can move out of binary responses to it: healed or broken, safe or unsafe. I believe there is more room for us to learn how to tolerate discomfort and to enlarge our capacity to *be* ourselves.

Healing requires only that we shed what doesn't serve us. We retain the inherent gifts and skill sets that we honed along the way while reclaiming many of our goals, values, skills—the parts of ourselves that were left behind. Unfawning is a journey of self-reclamation. A journey of finding our voices, stepping into our authority, and finally living life on more of our own terms.

The Fawning Family Tree

• • •

While *fawning* is a relatively new term, others have been placeholders for some time, namely *codependency* and *people-pleasing*. These terms point to some of the easily recognizable symptoms of fawning, but they have missed the WHY behind those actions. When we focus on problematic behaviors rather than understanding their roots, we perpetuate the idea that we are *broken* or a problem that needs fixing. Unpacking the nuances of fawning brings self-compassion and self-awareness and offers a path to what we've been seeking all along, a right relationship with ourselves and others.

I am a fawner, so I want to preface this section by saying, *Please don't be mad at me.* I know that people have found solace in the framework of codependency and people-pleasing. Having terminology, community, and a reflection of your lived experience is a gift. I'm not here to take that away.

What's also true is that after I read all the books, went to the programs, and took the questionnaires, these terms didn't entirely resonate with me. They left me, many of my friends, colleagues and clients feeling unseen and, well, shamed.

Codependency: Codependency was originally defined in the context of chemical dependency, as a counterpoint to addiction—that is to say, the codependent enabled the addicted one. It provided language and support for friends and family members of alcoholics. But some fawners don't identify with the term *codependent*, particularly if their fawning didn't look like eradicating problems for their alcoholic parent or partner or rescuing others from the consequences of their own actions.

To distill the various definitions of codependency in the 1980s, Melody Beattie did what I am trying to do now with fawning. She wrote a now-classic tome called *Codependent No More: How to Stop Controlling Others and Start Caring for Yourself.* In it, she provides this definition: "A codependent person is one who has let another person's behavior affect him or her, and who is obsessed with controlling that person's behavior."

Um, do you see why I might have a little trouble with the codependency literature? Right there in the definition, from the very woman who popularized the term, is a tone that feels a bit, well, judgy. I mean, a person "who is obsessed with controlling"? *Sign me up!*

Fawning as a trauma response originated as instinctual reactions to threat. This preoccupation did not develop with the intent to control. It developed to find personal safety. I also struggle with the idea that a codependent person lets another person affect them. This implies both conscious choice and immunity from *relating,* as though we aren't literally hardwired for relationship. We co-regulate and co-habitate. We impact one another!

We need to take back the realities of *healthy* dependency and caregiving. Caregivers in particular have been shamed for anticipating the needs of others, when that is the job of raising human beings who can't anticipate or name their own needs. Fawners have been socialized to cultivate these very behaviors for the greater good of family and society and then targeted as a problem for carrying them out.

People-pleasing: My name is Ingrid, and I am a recovering people pleaser. As the term has grown in popularity over the last five years, especially in online therapeutic discourse, I've been nodding my head as enthusiastically as everyone else. People-pleasing equates to an inability to say no. If there's a need, a people pleaser can fill it. Everyone and everything else come first in our lives. Relationships can feel one-sided because it's hard for people pleasers to stand up for themselves. Conflict is terrifying, and therefore boundaries (that might instigate conflict) feel overwhelming at best, impossible at worst.

Where the term falls short for most fawners is that our behaviors might *appear* to be people-pleasing, but they aren't about pleasing at all. The chronic fawner just wants to exist, as safely as possible, often while experiencing a host of complicated feelings such as fear, disgust, or resentment. This cacophony of emotion is hard to reconcile with a label such as *people pleaser,* so the catchall phrase has disenfranchised many. Additionally, it evokes a goody-two-shoes type of person: excessively virtuous, overly generous, and kind. While some might see themselves reflected in these depictions, others find that the label isn't a great fit. Lastly, people-pleasing connotes satisfaction on the other end, and as my friend Alyson says, "Ingrid, people were *not* pleased!"

Like branches of the overall fawning tree, *codependency* and *people-pleasing* were our best attempts to name something important with the information we had at the time. They were conceived of and grew up alongside our understanding of relational trauma. But until now they weren't in *conversation*. Consequently, they weren't trauma informed.

My problem with the discourse around these terms is that they've been framed as personal problems, originating out of thin air. Ones that require strictly personal solutions. But codependency and people-pleasing develop in systems that *create* these dynamics: cultural, structural, familial, societal.

Codependency and people-pleasing are *adaptive* coping mechanisms in *dysfunctional* environments. These patterns are not a reflection of our character, values, or self-esteem. Somewhere along the way, Western psychology extracted these patterns of behavior from their context and viewed them through a lens of "optimal" environments and relationships. Of course, this made these behaviors appear problematic. And then WE appear dysfunctional.

Codependency is often described as selfishness, a pathological need to be needed. But what is truer is that it's a need to be safe, to belong, in a situation where healthy reciprocal relationships did not exist.

Many fawners feel unseen reading about the "disease" of codependency. We are not sick—we have been stuck. So we bristle at phrases like "Don't be a doormat" and "Put yourself first!" Because how do children put themselves first? How do marginalized people prioritize themselves over systemic oppression? Many fawners don't *feel* like doormats. We know we deserve better, it's just that better wasn't available at critical points in our life.

I wasn't enabling my parents' drinking; I was mad as hell about it. I wasn't losing my center because I didn't love myself . . . I was losing it because I do. I was trying to protect myself using the only tools I had at my disposal at the time.

Fawning wasn't a problem that needed fixing. It was in fact the solution. Fawning was *working*—taming monsters, moving mountains, maintaining vital structures of my life—and it was happening without my expressed consent. So being judged for fawning, without respecting its intelligence, appreciating and having compassion for it, was, dare I say, a mindfuck.

Once I had the bigger picture (the one that included both my nervous system and the environment), I could see codependency and people-pleasing as external manifestations of fawning. And in that light, I could agree—those behaviors *can* be problematic, for ourselves and for others. But we'd labeled the entire constellation of behavior as problematic, or those of us who exhibited it as having a self-esteem problem, when these terms could never tell the whole story. For many, it's only after recognizing that fawning was our body's best defense, offering needed protection, that we could begin to see how chronic patterns of fawning might have overstayed their welcome.

———

In cases of childhood trauma, we often can't tolerate the fact that our caregivers are deficient. We instinctively place the blame on ourselves to avoid feeling the terror of being that alone. This is how the body seeks power in powerless situations. *If I broke it, I can fix it.* This also sets up the rescuer dynamic as a proxy for secure attachment. We learn that safety and connection happen only when we prioritize someone else's needs.

In my relationship with my mom, I was responding to her lack of action. Her *absence*. So my fawning leaned in the direction of caretaking and codependency. Fawning gave me blinders to mask her neglect, so I could withstand it while I waited for her to get better.

I didn't even see my mom's bad behavior because I was living for the day she'd become free. *When my mom gets sober* or *when she leaves Randy* became the conditions for her freedom and ultimately for her ability to show up. In the meantime, her collusion with Randy and her absence as a motherly figure got a free pass.

Fawners are masters at seeing the solutions to others' problems, then helping/waiting for/hoping for them to be realized. In the meantime, the fawn response dulls our ability to fully admit to—or feel the impact of—such neglect. My mother's emotional absence meant I had to abandon my own center and lean *all the way* over to her just to have contact. I saw her as powerless, so I needed to pick up the pieces, to absorb the entire shock, to feel so much empathy for her that it overrode the fact that my needs weren't being met. I had to compensate for her invisibility, as though I could lend her parts of myself, endowing her with resources I believed she possessed—but this was based primarily on my wish for it to be true.

With Randy, I was reacting to his predatory and volatile actions. He was coming for me, closing the distance, and I needed to maintain at least a shred of self. But he still held all the power, and I needed to be taken care of. This is what taught me to flatter and flirt, to seek to be perfect in the hope that I could maintain what little distance remained between us. I was performing for protection while hoping to keep him at arm's length. Hoping to please him *just enough* so I could still be, even just a little bit, me.

In both codependency and people-pleasing, we are pulled from our own center and must recalibrate to a center that includes someone else. The goal is to keep everyone upright by helping others to stand or ensuring that we ourselves don't fall. When we fail, not only do we topple over, but everything falls apart.

Conversely, if we ARE managing it, I mean . . . this is the genius of fawning. When it's working, it feels powerful. We can feel capable, smart, flexible, generous, empathic, kind, and on and on. No wonder fawners don't always resonate with language that can feel steeped in shame and weakness. We are freaking acrobats!

So the term *fawning* isn't just about swapping out the old words for a new one. It's about honoring the roots of fawning rather than seeing it strictly as a malady.

Healing (from anything) rarely happens from directly exposing our wounds or feeling shame about the ways we've guarded against them. Healing happens when we honor the ways we learned to protect ourselves. When we stop focusing on the imperfections of our coping mechanisms and can validate their valiant and necessary efforts. Then, and only then, will those old protectors step aside, allowing space for another way.

Anthony

Anthony was referred to me when his twenty-year-old son went to rehab. On paper, Anthony was impressive: Harvard grad, law school, partner in a global powerhouse firm—details that could've intimidated me. But I've never felt intimidated by Anthony. In part, because he is a genuinely nice guy. He is one of the most loving and loyal fathers I've ever encountered as a therapist or otherwise. But also Anthony is a fawner, and fawners want to be liked. With his black T-shirt (always a black T-shirt) and salt-and-pepper beard, he logs onto every Zoom session with a cheerful smile that evokes one of my own.

Early in our sessions, Anthony remarked, "I think I'm trying to win therapy." We both laughed before he continued, "It's like I'm implementing insights from our work so you can tell me all the progress I'm making. It's all about the pat on the head."

Having spent his life doing the *right* thing, Anthony was beginning to question if it was always the *best* thing. Although he didn't have the language of fawning, he'd reached a point in his life where it had stopped working. Driving his son to rehab, where he'd stay for five months, incited Anthony's own crisis. He told me he was consumed by the thoughts: *How am I going to fake this at work, fake this with family? Be the person I've painted myself into a corner to be?*

He couldn't keep seeking external validation at any cost, but he didn't know anything different. It felt terrifying.

Going back to his joke about "winning" therapy, I asked him to slow things down.

"I wonder how it feels to orient to you, rather than my opinion of you?" I asked.

"It's a relief," Anthony said with an exhale, seemingly dropping into his body for the first time.

While Anthony poured himself into his work, thinking he was happy and a good employee, his work ethic was predominantly defined by an inability to set boundaries. The longer we explored these themes, the more it became apparent how much he hated the pretentious environment he worked in, which promoted urgency over things he didn't really care about.

A law firm is the perfect environment for a compulsive fawner. Administrative assistants fawn to lawyers. Associates fawn to partners. Partners fawn over clients. It's a very clear hierarchy, and self-abandonment is expected. The more hours you bill, the more the firm makes. Anthony was living a life in six-minute increments, plugging himself in like a machine.

For some fawners, it can be hard to identify their fawning because they're just "meeting expectations" . . . and in that context, fawning looks an awful lot like success. We pursue these paths in part because success is *safety*. It's a shield. It brings us titles and money and all the *things*. At least that's what we are told and sold. While Anthony was at the top of his game, he was also just like the rest of us, at the mercy of the culture he was in—avoiding conflict to gain financial security and access to a life.

Although there's no denying the relief of not having to worry about necessities, success doesn't make us relationally safe, particularly when it demands self-erasure. Success doesn't heal trauma. It doesn't mean we are authentic and alive, connected to purpose. Success doesn't mean we know who we are. In this way, it can be like a prison—keeping us from greater self-awareness because, after all, "What do we have to complain about?" Anthony just had to smile and appear balanced. But in reality that smile was camouflage.

Anthony didn't feel powerful staying up all night fixing typos for a client. He wasn't even intellectually stimulated by the work he was doing. But when he noticed these things, instead of making a change, he simply buckled down and kept going. He knew this wasn't him, but he came to see that it resembled a pattern he'd been re-creating his whole life.

While Anthony's parents never told him to go to an Ivy League school or to become a lawyer, he always felt he needed to do those things. In a way, it was their *lack* of interest—he never got approval for anything—that led to his endless quest for validation. As the stakes of achievement kept getting higher, he thought, *How can my parents deny me approval now?* And yet they did.

The traumatic events of his upbringing weren't obvious. His trauma (a word he bristled at for years) was growing up in a household of pervasive invalidation. Even when I shared that the definition of trauma is more related to how the nervous system responds to events than it is about the events themselves—in other words, how his body reacted to the lack of acceptance from his parents—he was focused on his shortcomings and not on the implications of his parents' actions.

Anytime I brought up his parents, he would defend them. Anytime he started to speak about how they hurt him, he would backpedal. "I can't speak badly about my parents. I'm making them sound like monsters." He stuck with the party line he had learned over the years: "We are a close and happy family."

As we'll see throughout this book, fawners are very good story-tellers. We cling to narratives we want to be true, blocking out any information that might contradict them. But when Anthony spoke about his childhood, I could see what he initially couldn't. He was trapped in the life he was in now because he was still so desperate for his parents' approval.

When Anthony tried to express himself during his childhood, he was called obnoxious or a know-it-all. His parents loved to point out when he didn't know something and laughed at their recurring joke: "You're pretty dumb for a smart person."

Anthony was sensitive. He remembers trying hard to hold in his tears, and when he couldn't, he heard, "Don't be a crybaby."

Sexist and gendered ideas were the norm in the small town on the East Coast where Anthony lived. Using the language of "we," Anthony's mom appeared deferential to his dad, but in reality she ran the show. Everyone knew not to challenge her.

Together for over fifty-five years, his parents never did anything apart. To this day, Anthony never speaks with his dad alone. Anthony's mom can't tolerate feeling left out. In the rare instance a conversation happens without her, she launches into weeks-long campaigns digging for information. She recognizes no boundaries. She wants the information, and she wants to control it: who knows what, how they know it, and what they are going to do with it.

When Anthony did well as a child, it was a reflection of her. And when he didn't, he needed to get back in line. He was a classical musician in high school, quite advanced in clarinet, but his mom was also musical, playing piano for all the community events. He recalls recitals where he'd taken on difficult pieces, but the performances were all about *her*. It didn't matter how well he did or if he was nervous. She engaged with the audience as though it was *her* big night. She seemed resentful when Anthony got any attention. He never heard from his mother, "Can you believe my son's talent?" Only "My son got his talent from ME!"

"That makes me so sad," I said honestly as he relayed a story to me one day. Because it did. Anthony immediately became uncomfortable. "Maybe I'm blowing things out of proportion," he said, trying to brush the story aside. Like so many of us who grew up with emotional abuse and neglect, he learned to self-gaslight—taking all the blame. *I'm too sensitive, too dramatic. What do I have to be upset about?*

But then, a couple of years into our work together, Anthony received a voice mail that altered his life.

He was in a period of real transformation, beginning to advocate for himself in personal and professional relationships, setting boundaries, and leaning into new interests. He was trying to communicate differently with his parents, expressing apprehension about an upcoming family wedding. It would be the first time his son would be exposed to both extended family and that much drinking since his time in rehab, plus Anthony had an ongoing conflict with his sister-in-law. So he made himself vulnerable, telling his parents his concerns about his son and their possible reactions to this potentially stressful event.

His parents' reaction to his son's recovery from addiction had always been, *He's all better by now, right?* They had never wanted to hear about their grandson's struggles with addiction, and they really didn't want to talk about anything that might throw a monkey wrench into what was shaping up to be a "perfect family event." Their avoidance made Anthony's skin crawl. But he dug in, trying to be in *real* relationship, giving them the benefit of the doubt. "I know you guys are really excited about the wedding, and I am, too, for a lot of reasons, but I'm also nervous . . ."

It soon became clear that they didn't want to talk about his genuine concerns, so Anthony just got off the phone.

Two hours later, he saw his mom calling back and he let it go to voice mail. When he listened to the message, his stomach dropped. *Holy shit.*

It was a butt dial. His parents had accidentally recorded a vicious two-minute snippet of their private conversation about Anthony and left it as a message on his phone.

"Does he think he has to protect his son *forever*? He just needs to suck it up and get in line for this wedding! And how do we even believe him with this fight with his sister-in-law, when he's always exaggerated everything?"

As Anthony shared some of the content of the voice mail in our session, I saw his devastation. Decades of truth that he'd always known but never wanted to see was washing over him. Anthony never felt loved, but he'd felt the need to show his parents' friends what a loving family they were. He was the scapegoat, always to blame for any discomfort or upset he exhibited. Suddenly, admitting the truth about his family no longer felt like a betrayal.

"Deep down I knew all of this was true," he said to me. "But maybe I needed to hear it. Now I know I wasn't making it all up."

After that day, Anthony made a conscious choice to stop living for his parents' approval. He saw that he couldn't fawn enough to ever get it. This was all deeply painful but ultimately freeing. Grief unlocked necessary anger about how long he'd lived his life with a diminished sense of self. And that anger led to change. I call that behavior change *unfawning*—and it's a powerful healing step in our recovery journey.

When we learn to unfawn, we learn to detach from our old ways of people-pleasing and tune in to the self we had to abandon long ago. Anthony's parents didn't change. Knowing they'd never take personal responsibility for their cutting remarks, he never confronted them. The culture at his firm didn't change, and he didn't have to retire early or find a new career.

His son was living his own life, in a new relationship, starting to find his own way. Anthony was doing the same, changing the way he showed up in every area of his life.

Here's one way he took back his power: He started to lean into the weird stuff his family had made fun of, but that he had always been drawn to. Battling a lifetime of messaging along the lines of *This is not what a man does,* he spent a week at a men's wellness retreat. While some guys swapped the more vulnerable activities for golf and networking, Anthony immersed himself in all the taboos he'd avoided out of ridicule for fifty years. He enjoyed an incredible facial and yoga and Pilates classes. Then he went to meet with a shaman.

After walking along a trail of manicured bamboo, he made his way to what looked like a traditional Japanese teahouse. The shaman invited him to lie down, close his eyes, and journey toward a safe and happy place he could always rely on. For no reason that made sense to him, an image came of Anthony and several bear cubs.

He was surprised by their appearance. He had no prior connection to bears, but he felt both an absence of fear and embodied joy as he engaged with the imagery. They were playful, childlike, vulnerable, but safe. He felt like they were trying to tell him something. *Be yourself. Drop the mask. You can be soft. Expose your underbelly. That* is *the safe place.*

As the session wrapped up, the shaman asked if he wanted to take a reminder of their experience, a coin or feather infused with the imagery of the vision, but Anthony didn't fawn. He knew the idea didn't resonate. But he also thought, *Maybe I'll just tattoo a bear cub on my arm.* And that's what he did. And the day after he got the tattoo, there was a live bear sitting in his front yard.

He'd never seen one in his neighborhood, but there it was, a young bear. He wasn't tearing things up or raising a ruckus; he was contemplative, hunched, looking out into the night. And there have been many magical moments with bears ever since.

He has seen cubs with their mom in his backyard. He watched them from a safe distance as they lingered all day, the mom being so attentive it was almost hard to watch. Her whole job was to get her cubs to be successful bears out in the world, to prepare them to go off on their own. She had no intention of keeping the young bears around for her own pleasure or comfort. And Anthony felt another layer of grief, seeing such matter-of-fact nurturance and protection.

One of the cubs lives in his neighborhood now. She often visits his yard, coming to his tree, where she naps for hours with her bear belly exposed.

Anthony's life is a testament to what happens when we stop fawning. Something finally turned. He went from making *nothing* in his own life about him to truly reveling in the life he has. He dropped the script he'd been reading from forever, and in letting it go, he found a life that feels unique, creative, and expansive. Unfawning is a growing up. We who have relied on this safety strategy since childhood inadvertently stayed small and childlike and didn't know it. We were stuck in time. Unfawning means getting reacquainted with the self we tucked away. Discovering who we truly are.

I love so much about Anthony's story, but especially that he didn't need to have an obvious (to him) childhood of horror. The threshold for accessing this healing was that he identified with the symptoms. Being fifty and feeling like you've never done anything that reflects your true self is a pretty big sign.

Today, after getting his first tattoo at fifty, Anthony has many. After having no hobbies and hating spending money on himself, he started collecting art. He became drawn to fantastical, whimsical otherworldly creatures, all with big eyes.

He used to be bored and depressed on weekends, at a loss for what to do. It wasn't natural for him to even be curious about what he might like to do. Now his home and life are full of activity and color. He wishes he had more free time.

Anthony's son is doing really well. Anthony shared, "I'm here to support him when he needs it, but I'm not a monitor anymore." They both get to be *themselves*.

And now Anthony's son and his girlfriend are expecting a baby. It's a boy, and Anthony is overjoyed, painting a giant underwater scene for his grandson. He told me, "I know my grandson is going to know the real me, not the role I think a grandfather should play."

Knowing who he is and what he values brings him tremendous calm and confidence. While Anthony never intended to pass down his need to perform, he is consciously sharing his healing from it now. And he knows that all three generations are going to be just fine.

· Two ·

It's Not Your Fault

Why Fawning Flourishes

So we see the problem with fawning. Then why is it so hard to stop? As you'll see, there are power structures everywhere we turn that reinforce, reward, even *require* fawning.

We can't just say, *Stop doing that!* when we continue to live in contexts that encourage, and actually necessitate fawning.

I was listening recently to an episode of the podcast *Armchair Expert* with Dax Shepard. His guest was Anna Kendrick, who had just released her directorial debut, *Woman of the Hour*.

I watched the movie soon after it released on Netflix. At first glance, it appears to be based on the true story of a serial killer from the seventies. How he'd raped, beaten, and murdered what is likely as many as a hundred women. But after sitting with it for some time, I realized the movie wasn't focused on his madness, his trauma, or why he did what he did.

It was about the *women*. How we are abandoned at our most vulnerable, ridiculed when we ask for help, shamed when we take care of ourselves. How standing up for ourselves often means losing partners, jobs, and friendships along the way. How we are told to smile, be sexy and play along, don't be too smart, elevate the men in our lives.

It's a story about the subtext that women live with every day. I almost couldn't see it at first because it felt so normal. But that was the point. Every single woman in that movie, no matter their personality type, age, or intellect, experienced a moment or a lifetime of fawning.

At the end of the film, the protagonist has raped a runaway girl, who is at most fifteen years old. She turns from where she is lying to see her attacker crying. Tied up and brutally beaten, she cannot run. She can't fight back. So she asks if he is okay. Catching his eye, she smiles before saying, "Please don't tell anyone about this. I would be so embarrassed."

This is how she escaped. By fawning. Cozying up to the man who tried to kill her, calling him Baby, getting back in his car.

In the podcast episode, Anna, Dax, and his cohost Monica Padman began to talk about fawning as a trauma response.

Anna asked whether Dax's go-to response in his childhood was always to fight. And he said no.

He told a story about when he was twelve years old and a grown man got out of his muscle car and approached Dax and a friend. Dax said something that angered this man, and he grabbed Dax and slammed his head against a telephone pole.

Anna reacted. "Was the strategy then, just flee?"

Dax replied. "In an ideal world, it's flattery," he said. "'No, dude, I'd never fuck with you, you're a fucking badass.'"

He went on to say, "I don't think anyone is excluded from [fawning]. And it's very, very visceral and familiar . . . If it's a stepdad, there is a game we play where we downplay what happened and we blame it on another thing, and we really hunker down on that other plausible explanation to get him out of the shame, because if shame takes off, then we are really in trouble."

Dax knew what it felt like to fawn. But he said, "I got to an age and a size where any dude that rolls up to put my head into a telephone pole, they are gonna have their hands full. I got to escape it to some degree."

This stopped me in my tracks. Dax was saying that because he grew up to be a six-foot-two man, he literally grew out of the need to fawn. He recognizes this privilege: "If you're five feet tall and 112 pounds, that option is not going to be on the table for you."

The moment his fight response felt like an option to him, it became the only one.

He goes on to say: "If I couldn't have outgrown that [fawning], that would have been so paralyzing to me. Because I hated that. . . . it killed me. In my self-flagellation of not being able to stand up to those people or find my voice or say the truth, that hurt way more than any of the interactions did."

The feeling of shame after fawning to stay safe hurt more than the violence. This is true for many fawners. We berate ourselves for appeasing, for flirting, for pleasing, instead of standing up for ourselves or fighting. But the truth is, for many of us, fawning is SAFER.

Many of us can't escape the contexts of our powerlessness. I couldn't help but think of the other people in the room with Dax as the podcast was recorded—Monica and Anna, who are both women, both petite, Monica a woman of color. Of all the women who will never be able to successfully fight their aggressors. We never reach a point when we don't have to fawn.

So it is important that we see the structures that necessitate and reinforce our fawning so we can remove the shame. While separate books could be written on each of the following topics, these are some of the environments, structures, and contexts that reward, support, even demand fawning.

It's a Man's, Man's, Man's World: *Patriarchy*

Let's be honest, the traits of a fawner have historically been labeled as *feminine*: to defer, acquiesce, caretake, speak softly and sweetly, appease, and please. Handy synonyms for a system in which men hold all the power, aka the **patriarchy**.

Like greeters at the Gap, women are meant to welcome everyone to the sidewalk we happen to be sharing, to look attractive through our countenance and dress, appealing to a gaze other than our own. Men often find it their business to comment when a woman isn't smiling.

While fawning is not gender-based (like all trauma responses, it's an equal opportunity defender), every woman I know can identify a need for fawning in their lifetime. Many of us were raised and socialized to *be* fawners, our bodies necessary support staff for our families and society at large. We've carried the emotional burdens, done the primary caretaking, and had to find a sense of self and safety through the pecking order of our lives:

- How can I please, help, or elevate you?
- What can I take off your plate?
- How can I dull my drive, soften my tone, so I'm not seen as a bitch?

Fawning has always been a necessary part of the gendered systems we are living in. But instead of fawning, it's been called being a team player, going along to get along, taking initiative, being *nice*—things that are not just socially accepted, but expected.

But it's not just women who are affected. Men also have to fawn due to patriarchy. As feminist scholar bell hooks writes in *The Will to Change*, "Learning to wear a mask (that word already embedded in the term 'masculinity') is the first lesson in patriarchal masculinity that a boy learns. He learns that his core feelings cannot be expressed if they do not conform to the acceptable behaviors sexism defines as male. Asked to give up the true self in order to realize the patriarchal ideal, boys learn self-betrayal early and are rewarded for these acts of soul murder."

Respect Your Elders: *Cultural Norms*

As the keepers of tradition and wisdom, elders have long held positions of power. In an ideal world, they bridge lessons of the past with a reverence for future generations, maintaining hierarchal structures based on *mutual* respect.

But for many, the phrase *Respect your elders* carries a different connotation. It inspires the feeling that one must always obey or never ask questions. It means endowing people who are older or who hold higher status with our allegiance *no matter what*. It means being ruled by fear, put in our place—often with a "do as I say, not as I do" attitude.

Rules, order, and the upholding of **cultural norms** are functions of a healthy ecosystem. But privileging compliance over fostering self-reliance can equate to an abuse of power. I can't help but think of USA Gymnastics. The culture of gymnastics encouraged athletes to push past their pain for decades, often to the point of incurring major injury. Gymnasts were meant to trust their coaches more than their own finely tuned bodies. Then they were placed in the hands of a team doctor, a serial pedophile, without any supervision or oversight.

Our hierarchical society requires that we understand the pecking order and follow accordingly. Pushing back against these norms can often be incredibly risky.

Anywhere hierarchies are present we see the necessity of fawning. Consider the following structures in our society:

- Corporate culture
- Academia
- Religious organizations
- Politics

We privilege those who are neurotypical, able-bodied, cisgender, and heterosexual, not to mention our systems of class. Everywhere we look, there are structures of power and unwritten rules to keep them in place.

No One Loves You Like Family:
Family Systems

There is a long-held saying about family, that no matter their composition or disposition, they are your ultimate support system: "No one loves you like family." As a trauma therapist, I'm saddened to report how often this simply isn't true. Our **family systems** are often terribly dysfunctional; yet that doesn't erase the platitude. Instead, children still believe family is *love,* forever equating that word with whatever they experienced at home.

We are hardwired for relationships. As a species, human beings are more dependent on our caregivers than probably any other, certainly for a longer period. And within that extended time frame of childhood, if your nervous system was oriented to safety in a context of abuse and neglect, you likely felt like you couldn't survive unless you devoted significant emotional resources to appeasing your parents and other family/caregivers. Like a fish who can't conceive of life outside its bowl, fawning becomes a condition of living in a toxic system.

This often means living with people who said "I love you" but didn't seem to care. Where forgiveness (or blindness) was necessary. Where even saying "Good morning" became an aspect of fawning, because it implied that things were good . . . when nothing felt good at all.

Additionally, many parents with dysregulated nervous systems can't tolerate their child's full range of emotion. Under the guise of good parenting and fostering respect, parents have introduced their children to a life of survival mode, disconnected from themselves to be more palatable to others.

The fact is, children can't learn to regulate emotions they aren't allowed to have. It is our job as parents to learn to regulate ourselves so we can tolerate our own feelings, teaching our children to do the same.

But many of our caregivers were experiencing their own legacy of trauma, handing it down perhaps with some awareness, but often unknowingly. Alcoholic and narcissistic family systems. Parentified children, where the roles were always reversed, kids feeling responsible for a parent's pain and problems rather than the other way around. Children "raising" their parents, hearing them complain about each other or giving them advice. Children learning to pretend nothing is wrong, because they see everyone else in the family doing the same. Learning to shake their heads yes, when their body is screaming no.

Assimilation Nation: *Racism*

Fawning has been an essential aspect of coping with **racism,** as well as a gateway to internalized racism. This doubles down on the overwhelm one is holding, perpetuating traumatic cycles, and once again has people mistaking their *response* to trauma as the problem, rather than the traumatic contexts they are living in.

My client Davis is a Black man in his early forties. We've been working together for many years, and when we discussed his relationship to fawning, he said it feels the same as code-switching—

adjusting how he presents himself depending on the situation or environment. Code-switching is not just about language; it's about adjusting one's entire presentation to make others feel comfortable, often at the expense of one's own comfort.

Davis has a great sense of humor, and yet his facial hair frames what is often a serious face. He looks contemplative, like there is a lot going on within him that he isn't necessarily going to grant you access to. As we've been working with his experience of complex trauma, stemming largely from childhood, he's been trying to "bring his more childlike parts online." Reconnecting with vulnerability, softness, and playfulness.

One day he shared, "I know I am full of smiles, but I don't give them to people." He's told himself that he shouldn't. In the neighborhoods where he has lived, there is an expectation that maturity and masculinity call for one to be hardened, not curious, intensely minding one's own business.

Davis's socialization had always been *Don't smile*. He needs to perform a lack of interest, toughness. Davis said he thinks this is common in Black neighborhoods. You don't want to come off as weird. "Smiley is weird," he explains.

Fawning in Davis's case means playing it cool, *not* being open, *not* being overly friendly to those around him. But he's been experimenting with doing things differently. At least he wanted to try. At his daughter's basketball game, he found himself doing the cool speak again. It didn't feel appropriate to be smiling or joyful with the other Black parents, mostly strangers to him. He was sitting on the sidelines, thinking, *I said I wasn't going to do this anymore,* but the compulsion to play it cool in this situation was too strong to override.

It's not like he allows the smiles in the company of white people, either. In that environment, he closes off. He shared that he doesn't feel that "happy and carefree, elbowing each other" vibe that white people often display. Davis finds the small talk strange, but he fawns with them, too. Matching his speed and tone to theirs, getting on their small-talk frequency, when he doesn't really care. But he doesn't feel comfortable enough *not* to care. He doesn't want to be rude. But underneath all of it, he feels anxiety. He knows he's playing a game and can't wait until he gets to go home and take off the mask.

The New York Times Magazine published an article about an unreleased documentary on Prince. It shared Questlove's reaction to the film, in which he used the exact same language and sentiments as Davis, how they'd both been living with perpetual masks of "cool."

> Watching the film forced [Questlove] to confront the consequences of putting on a mask of invincibility—a burden that he feels has been imposed on Black people for generations. "A certain level of shield—we could call it masculinity, or coolness: the idea of cool . . . was invented by Black people to protect themselves in this country," he said . . .
>
> But Questlove feels the film performs a cultural service: a cracking, particularly for Black men, of a facade of invincibility.

While the documentary on Prince may or may not ultimately be released perhaps due to this very reason—it shows Prince as a full person, not a caricature—it seems to portray what Prince and people of color have contended with forever.

This is not just required of Black people but any person of color living in a society where "white body supremacy and our adaptations to it is in our blood," as Resmaa Menaken, author of *My Grandmother's Hands*, so powerfully describes.

It's Not You: *Narcissism and Emotional Immaturity*

Even as a clinical psychologist, I never realized I came from a narcissistic family system until I wrote my memoir. As a child, I just thought Randy was an asshole. While I could recognize my stepdad in traits such as grandiosity, lack of empathy, and high reactivity, as is often the case, the clinical criteria of **narcissism** fall flat compared to one's lived experience.

Dr. Ramani Durvasula is a clinical psychologist and the author of the bestselling book *It's Not You*. I came across her on social media years before her book came out and appreciated how she turned the focus from the traits of a narcissistic person to those living with the fallout from such people. It was deeply validating to see someone with her credentials and expertise bringing survivors into the spotlight. In her book, she writes, "Identifying a narcissistic person is far less important than understanding what qualifies as unacceptable behavior and what it does to you."

She talks about how living with a narcissistic person, whose problematic behaviors become normalized, equates to abuse: "Narcissistic abuse can be defined as the interpersonally harmful, deceitful, and invalidating patterns, behaviors, and alternation between disruptions of safety and trust and periods of normalcy and even enjoyment observed in any relationship with a person who has a personality style characterized by narcissism or antagonism."

When I first reached out to Ramani in an email as a survivor and a colleague, her response was so thoughtful and compassionate, it launched a deeply meaningful friendship and mentorship that continues to this day. Thanks to Ramani's commitment to survivors, I finally understood that complex trauma was what happened to me, and narcissistic abuse was foundational to *why*. In fact, Pete Walker states that fawners "are usually the children of at least one narcissistic parent who uses contempt to press them into service, scaring and shaming them out of developing a healthy sense of self."

You don't have to be a chronic fawner to experience narcissistic abuse, nor do you bear any blame when you are emotionally abused and manipulated. And yet, once you are ensnared, fawning might be your best chance at making it through the gauntlet. That was certainly the case for me.

Additionally, a chronic fawn response can make us more vulnerable to narcissistic abuse. After I left home, my fawn response created a feeling where I knew safety only in the context of exploitative, abusive relationships. It's where my skills were honed, where my patterns of relating were initially developed. So I found myself in repeated dynamics where my fawning could "save" me once again.

Many of my clients share similar patterns, highlighting the storied partnership between beauty and beast, empath and narcissist. This goes beyond the family system to any relationship in which these dynamics are present.

In addition to narcissistic systems, fawning can develop in relation to **emotional immaturity**. Emotionally immature parents overshare with their children. They require sympathy, self-esteem, and soothing from them, as though their child is the caretaker. Consequently, children of emotionally immature parents often feel guilty, like they must meet their parents' needs, feel sorry for what their parents have been through or bad about showing up for their own lives. Never having had their instincts validated, they have difficulty trusting themselves. And when these children try to share their feelings or their life, the emotionally immature parent offers the bare minimum and doesn't engage or bond over their child's interests.

Of course, many of these very traits originate from a parent's own unresolved trauma. People who are stuck in chronic trauma reenactment and responses *are in fact* emotionally immature, never having had access to their own feelings or the ability to process them. In this way, we can see how generational trauma is the seed of so much hurt and pain, and why the need to break these cycles is stronger than ever before.

Good Vibes Only: *Toxic Positivity*

Every client of mine has heard a version of "You just need to forgive and let it go." If that *worked,* we'd be the first to sign on the dotted line. In fact, fawners *have been* quick to forgive, let go, merge with another's point of view to defuse conflict. We practically invented forgiving at any cost. Particularly when we've heard things like "Everybody makes mistakes" or "The past is in the past," we've run to forgiveness as a finish line, hoping to stop the shame from seeping in.

And frankly, it didn't work. Trying harder isn't going to move that needle. When it comes to complex trauma, the message of forgiveness and rising above it is really more manipulation. It's wrapping avoidance up in a big fuzzy blanket of faux superiority and **toxic positivity.** Particularly when trauma survivors are told something like "But forgiveness is for *youuuuu.*" Is it, really?

Resilience can also be weaponized in a toxically positive way. We hear it in platitudes like "You're so strong—you've been through so much" or "You'll bounce back; you always do." While resilience can indeed be a strength, when it's wielded as a mandate or an expectation, it becomes yet another tool of dismissal.

For fawners, the narrative of resilience often reinforces a damaging cycle. It says: *Keep giving. Keep surviving. Keep pushing through.* But true resilience doesn't mean ignoring our pain or soldiering on at any cost. It means creating the space to feel, process, and integrate what we've experienced, something fawners are often conditioned to avoid.

On the surface, who doesn't want to release negativity? For fawners specifically, the idea that we could release negativity sounds super compelling. NO CONFLICT, EVER! But if we don't allow our-selves to feel our anger, discomfort, and frustration, we can't see our truth. We can't feel the reality of our circumstances. We can't advo-cate, learn new coping, or find our voices. We remain stuck in dis-connection, from ourselves and others.

Reading *The Secret* by Rhonda Byrne, repeating positive affirma-tions, and making vision boards did not heal my trauma. "Letting go" of everything that hurt me only kept me stuck. And honestly, I'm angry I was ever encouraged to do so. There is a difference between processing negative experiences and *then* choosing to authentically forgive and feeling like our internal safety lies in jumping to artificial forgiveness. The latter isn't forgiveness at all; it's denial.

No Shortcuts: *Spiritual Bypassing*

A sister of toxic positivity is **spiritual bypassing,** defined by clinical psychologist and Buddhist teacher Dr. John Welwood as the act of using "spiritual ideas and practices to sidestep personal, emotional 'unfinished business,' to shore up a shaky sense of self, or to belittle basic needs, feelings, and developmental tasks." Spiritual bypassing is a defense mechanism, and although it looks holier than others, it serves the same defensive purpose: shielding us from the truth. It is more about checking *out* than checking *in*—believing if we pray hard enough or meditate long enough, we will transcend the messy human experience of *feeling*. It is spiritual practice in the service of repression, usually because we can't tolerate what we are feeling or think that we shouldn't be experiencing what we are feeling.

Sentences like "Just turn it over to God," "It's God's will," or "The universe has your back" aren't inherently wrong, but they can be destructive for the fawner when they encourage us to orient away from our feelings.

If you have found a way to transcend the human condition, my hat is off to you. Truly. But for the rest of us who continue to wrestle with emotional growing pains, I'm here to remind you that we are not supposed to rise above it all. We can't outrun our own feet. We can't outthink our own brains. We can't override this human operating system that we live and breathe in every hour of every day, freeing ourselves of pain and problems. Not perpetually, anyway.

Spiritual bypassing can be a bolster for fawners, supporting self-abandonment for supposed altruistic and spiritual aims. Additionally, these can be weaponized by others: "If only you were more spiritual and could let it go."

Light It Up: *Gaslighting and Self-Gaslighting*

Gaslighting is a form of emotional abuse that uses manipulation and minimization to make someone question their reality. It can sound like:

- "You're overreacting."
- "Stop being so selfish."
- "You know I would never do anything like that." (*That* being something the person is absolutely doing.)

The deeply troubling thing about gaslighting is that it works. It's effective in robbing someone of their truth and their ability to trust themselves.

When it comes to fawning, gaslighting actively encourages someone to see harmful situations as harmless. It tricks them into soaking up all the shame. Gaslighting solidifies a fawner's avoidance. It endorses self-abandonment and appeasement, propping these coping strategies up. Gaslighting deepens the split in the victim's psyche between the one who knows the truth and the one who has to take responsibility to survive it.

Self-gaslighting is when we internalize these manipulations (or lack of protection from them) and begin to gaslight ourselves. For me, it sounded like:

- "Maybe it wasn't that bad."
- "I didn't experience 'real' trauma."
- "He didn't mean what I thought he meant."
- "I should be over this by now."

I've been gaslighting myself for most of my life. It ran so deep that I became a psychologist who specialized in trauma but *still* couldn't believe or reconcile my own traumatic past. It was like a ghost that haunted me, as I kept thinking, *I'm being too sensitive, I'm probably overreacting.*

The first social worker I spoke to in my childhood, long before my self-directed intervention, said, "Emotional abuse isn't a reportable situation." In my developing brain, I learned that the problem wasn't going to be resolved *out there*, so it must reside *in me*. This resulted in a storm of emotions, including anxiety, depression, confusion, and shame. But even my symptoms felt like impostors, because they weren't related to anything "real." So I kept telling myself I shouldn't be feeling them at all.

And here is where the fragmentation of complex trauma can happen. As though I were two different people sandwiched together: the one who knew what happened—who knew it was wrong and that I wasn't to blame—and the one who had to take responsibility just to survive it.

One of the insidious things about gaslighting and self-gaslighting is their invisible nature. It makes them hard to identify. I remember wishing I had bruises as a child. I thought, *Maybe the social worker would have listened then.*

It's easy to question invisible wounds, and once I started questioning the big things that happened, it generalized to everything. *Am I deserving of care, good things, or my accomplishments?* I started to feel like I couldn't trust myself at all. *Am I stupid?* I was constantly searching for an irrefutable truth, but everything looked more like a spectrum of possibilities. The constantly moving gyroscope was operated by an unrelenting critic, always pointing her finger directly at me.

Today, if someone said to me, "I don't believe you. You are a liar. You made the whole thing up," I would be appalled, and rightfully so. I can't imagine any scenario where I'd say that to another human being, and I will not keep saying it to myself. Self-gaslighting solves our cognitive dissonance, but it leaves us holding the bag. And this is the real kicker. We lie to ourselves. We believe we can't be trusted. I lived in this lie for decades, and I've seen so many of my clients come out of the same fog: *I must be crazy. I am the problem.* There is a reason I called my memoir *Believing Me.* Because today, I do.

I hope this book helps you believe *you*, too.

Fawning is taught, encouraged, and expected in so many contexts, which is why we can miss it as a trauma response and why we can think it is just our personality. Fawning flourishes and is perpetuated because it's bigger than one person's body or coping mechanism. It is ignited in us, then, through a feedback loop, becomes amplified and rewarded in the world. Our sense of self becomes distorted not just through personal adaptation, but because systems of oppression accelerate this process of change, moving us further away from our inherent state. This is why so many fawners might need to "turn off the comments," so to speak. To stop or step out of the feedback loops that prefer our deference and encourage self-doubt and self-censorship. So we can discern, and truly hear, our own voice.

The Double Bind

· · ·

The fawner's dilemma is that we can't satisfy two contradictory requirements at the same time. Will we be our true selves? Or establish safety? We often can't have both.

People say, "Don't be such a people pleaser!" But then they peg you as rude, selfish, dramatic, aggressive.

People say, "Learn to set boundaries!" But when said boundaries are crossed and you speak up, you are admonished to let things go, told it's no big deal or to be more flexible.

People say, "Stop being so controlling!" But they also expect you to do the emotional labor for partners, family, friends, and coworkers.

People say, "Just be yourself! Don't worry about what others think!" But then you lose jobs, opportunities, and raises because people think you're too opinionated or not a team player.

Basically, fawners are damned if they do, damned if they don't. This is the essence of the double bind.

There is always a sacrifice when we're in a double bind, and fawners have instinctively sacrificed themselves. Not in a "prioritizing a higher good" kind of way, but out of necessity. It wasn't possible to put ourselves first. We couldn't even find equal footing.

But when we start to become aware of our fawning, we can start to see some gray areas where we previously saw only black and white.

Years ago, I was visiting my cousin's flower farm in Colorado with my husband, Yancey, and our son, Henry, nine months old at the time, when my mom asked if she could speak with us in private.

"I'm not supposed to tell anyone, so you can't say anything," my mom said, sobbing, "but I can't keep it a secret anymore. Randy has cancer. He is dying and doesn't want anyone to know."

I sat there, stunned. Shocked. Realizing he wasn't there that weekend because he was too sick to travel.

My mom started speaking fast, as though she had to get the words out within a certain amount of time. "I'm terrified of being alone with him in that house, and that he'll take a long time to die. I just can't do it by myself. I don't know what I'll do if he hangs on for months and months. I just can't do that."

I couldn't believe what I was hearing. Not just that Randy was dying, something I'd fantasized about more times than I could count, but that my mom was admitting some of the terror she felt with him. She'd always kept her allegiance, but in her grief and fear, she had let it slip.

I didn't blame her. She and Randy lived alone in the mountains, down long dirt roads she couldn't drive in the winter. Even though they'd been married for decades, they kept to themselves. With this illness, she would have to take over as his nurse, and we all knew that his moods were aggressive and erratic even when he was physically well.

I knew underneath her words was a request. She wanted my help.

I tried to comfort her. Although we lived far apart, I assured her I was there for her emotionally and that we'd keep her secret.

As the months passed, we spoke almost daily. I promised I would show up for her. "Don't worry," I said. "Henry and I will come visit and you won't be alone."

I meant that we would go *after* Randy died and thought this was clear. I had no intention of speaking with or seeing him. While I had a small hope that the fact he was on his deathbed might mean he'd finally right his wrongs, no phone call came. We hadn't spoken at all since he was diagnosed. If he couldn't make amends for his past behavior, I couldn't keep pretending none of it happened.

When the hospice nurse told my mom she was certain Randy would pass away in the next day or two, I made travel plans for the following week. But then he had an energetic rally, as people often do at the end of their lives.

On one of our calls, I heard Randy in the background for the first time. His voice was gravelly and weak, but it was the same one that had haunted me since I was a kid. I could hear his words through the receiver: "Tell her I'm so happy they are coming."

Panic filled my veins, and I felt sick to my stomach. *He thinks I'm rushing to his bedside to pay my respects and introduce him to my son? NO!*

My mom started crying as though this was a sweet moment for us all. "Did you hear him, Ingrid? He's so happy you guys are coming," she said.

I was angry Randy knew we were coming, but even angrier my mom imagined this was a heartwarming situation. Fury rose within me.

"Yes, I heard him," I said, trying to keep my voice neutral. "I have to run now, Mom. I'll call you later, okay?"

"What the FUCK?!" I cried out as soon as I hung up the phone. *How could she expect me to come when he was still alive? Did she remember nothing?*

But even as I knew I had to hold my boundary, I felt so ashamed. *Don't good daughters support their mothers when a partner is dying?* Going to be with her seemed like the right thing to do. But I couldn't minimize my feelings this time. The idea that Randy would be perceived as my son's grandfather made me physically shake.

I called my friend Bill, whom I often turn to for guidance. "How can I be such a coldhearted daughter and not help my mom? What are people going to think? If I change plane tickets to avoid him, it seems so cruel!" I sobbed. "But I can't watch as he leaves this earth with all his secrets and lies!"

Bill then asked me a simple question: "What would you do if you were putting yourself first in your own life?"

I let his words sit in the silence between us. My answer was obvious. If I were putting myself first, I would never see that man again. The choice seemed clear, but I was still wavering. The stakes felt so high. The last time I took a real stand against my mom and Randy, I got burned. My entire body recoiled at the thought of standing up for myself again. Besides, my mom was in *distress*! Was now really the time to take care of *myself*?

I'd been in this bind so many times before.

Staying in relationship with my mom meant keeping my abuser in my life. Having my mother at my wedding meant inviting him, too. Hearing him grab the microphone after my friends gave a toast, saying, "Yay for high school friends!" and then in a more sinister tone, "I've always loved high school girls, ha-ha-ha."

When Randy was dying, I was a forty-one-year-old woman. A mother. Someone deeply committed to healing after all the ways I'd lost myself. I couldn't do it anymore. I had to choose ME.

I would have honored that decision at any cost, but only two days later, my cousin texted: "He's gone."

Choosing myself over helping my mom navigate her own life wasn't a finish line as much as it was a necessary pivot point. And I'd be lying if I said it didn't have emotional consequences. Our relationship continued to unravel from there. But part of my lifelong sacrifice had always been in the hope that she might choose me back. She might see my worth. But when I finally saw my own worth, it changed something vital within. I could choose myself over my need for her to choose me.

Choosing ourselves in the bind isn't a one-and-done deal. But I encourage you to look for your own pivot points. Start small. Be curious. See where it might be possible to choose differently, to orient toward yourself. Will there be consequences? Yes. But we can't grow without growing pains.

Francis

Francis could feel the heat of her boyfriend's anger rising through the floor as she was cooking dinner upstairs.

Always respectful of Colin's deadlines, attempting to accommodate his needs, she had checked to make sure the timing of this dinner was okay. Having a new friend over to their place meant a lot to Francis.

On her way home from work that night, she got a text from Colin that said, "Can you pick up a tea from Starbucks?" She was running late, but Francis knew he was in a mood and didn't want to make things worse. She also loved acts of service, both giving and receiving them, so she made the stop happily.

Arriving home, it was quiet. Their dog didn't even greet her, so she imagined they'd gone for a walk. Chopping veggies, she glanced at her phone. She had a text from Colin:

"What is going on?! Where is my tea?!"

Leaving the pasta boiling on the stove, Francis went down to Colin's studio, "Babe, I didn't even know you were here. Here's your tea. I've just been prepping dinner for the last twenty minutes."

"You've been home for TWENTY MINUTES and you're just bringing this down now?!"

Profusely sweating, Colin exploded, "I JUST NEED HELP!"

Torn between two potential fires, Francis reflexively knew she had to put this one out first. Outwardly calm she offered, "How can I help? What do you need?"

Canvas and wood were strewn all over the basement studio. Wires, paints, and thinners were piled so high she could barely move. She began to forge a path before saying, "I really need to go upstairs and finish cooking before my friend gets here."

"Fine, but don't bring her down here. I don't want to meet anybody."

Returning to the kitchen, Francis heard him throwing things downstairs—sounds her friend would hear in about ten minutes. All she could think was, *This is going to be bad.*

Her friend arrived and Francis hoped that inviting new energy into the house might let all the tension out. She felt awkward but was pretending that everything was normal.

"Come on in! It's so good to see you!"

Sitting down to catch up, Francis opened her belated birthday gift before glancing back at her phone.

I NEED HELP

I NEED HELP

I NEED HELP

Her stomach dropped as she turned to her friend with a smile. "I'm so sorry, my boyfriend has been texting and I didn't see it. Do you mind if I go downstairs for a minute?"

As she reached the foot of the stairs, Colin yelled, "I've been texting for thirty minutes, what the fuck?!"

"I'm really sorry, I wasn't by my phone, I was cooking and then we sat down to eat."

"You're telling me you didn't even look at your phone *once*?!"

"That's correct. I wasn't ignoring you."

Colin was on the floor. Fueled by Adderall, he hadn't slept in days and rather than cleaning up, he was ripping the studio apart. "I need your help for just a *second*, I'm doing this all by MYSELF."

He handed Francis an old coffee can, and she got down on her hands and knees. Placing brush after brush in the can—humiliated—crushed—she began to cry.

She had checked and double-checked, like a child wanting a play date with her friend, and yet here she was in her thirties, feeling like she was in trouble for doing something wrong. In a tone of voice shaped by fawning—detached but connected, firm but soft, defusing an explosion by swallowing it down—Francis said, "Colin, my friend is still here. I need to go back upstairs."

And with Colin's "Fine!" that's what she did.

As she sat back down at the table, her friend could tell Francis had been crying and she put a hand on her arm. "Are you okay?"

Still trying to neutralize the situation, Francis didn't want her friend to think badly of Colin. "My boyfriend is just having a really hard day. He has a big art show coming up and is pretty stressed about it."

Attempting to hold it all together, she half dissociated and could barely eat. Her friend was attempting meaningful conversation, but all Francis could hear was the angry hammering downstairs.

"What is happening down there? Is everything okay?" her friend asked.

Francis's heart sank. Beyond embarrassed, she replied, "I'm so sorry, but I think I'm going to have to ask you to go."

Her friend had been there for maybe thirty minutes and drove from the other side of town. Francis couldn't believe she was asking her to leave.

Apologizing over and over, Francis walked her friend to the car.

"What can I do?" her friend asked as they stood in the driveway.

"Please don't worry about me. I completely understand. But if you need to come over later, please come to my house." Francis nodded, her eyes full of tears, and she hugged her friend before she pulled away.

When she returned to the studio, Colin was in the same tantrum, saying he couldn't figure anything out but that she should just go back to her friend.

"I asked her to leave," Francis replied.

"Why would you do that?!" Colin appeared confused, as if he hadn't just made her dinner impossible. Francis began to clean up his mess, tiptoeing around him, reminding herself that when things were good, they were amazing. She'd never felt so cared for as when Colin was his best self. Sometimes he devolved into a stress case, like now, when he was preparing for a show. Francis learned to tolerate these turbulent times by anticipating the good ones she knew were around the corner.

When I first started working with Francis, I did not hear stories like this one, only that Colin was "the love of her life." He adored her. She'd never felt so seen. Of course she wanted him to go to therapy and take better care of himself. But her desired solutions to his problems seemed almost a proxy for them. Then she dug her heels into the fact that things were bad because she had "fucked things up."

I heard how Francis thought she was selfish and manipulative, how she'd engaged in an emotional affair and needed to make things right. She wanted me to really see how bad she was. So I could help to "fix her."

Francis had been sober for years. While vital to her well-being, her twelve-step program encouraged her to take responsibility for her "wrongs," "shortcomings," and "defects of character." It suggested being of service to others as a way to mitigate her "selfish, self-seeking, and dishonest" nature. Although it's hard to argue with altruism, the self-blaming language and constant messages to "get out of yourself and be of service" inherent in twelve-step messaging can reinforce our fawning: disconnecting from our feelings, taking all the blame, compulsively caretaking, and never asking anyone else to take responsibility, too.

All the overintellectualizing and shame never pulled Francis out of complex trauma or her responses to it. In fact, these so-called solutions were overriding her deeper wounds. All those interventions missed her physiology. They missed the context of her toxic relationships. When she was triggered, her body felt only I NEED SAFETY AND I NEED IT NOW. Seeing our part in something is compelling, but it is not a panacea, and it does not heal trauma.

When Francis finally opened up about Colin, I could see that she was in an abusive relationship. But I knew she didn't see it that way at all. She kept reminding me that this was her *person*. There was no option but to be with him. And this is what I had to confront, shifting the conversation from her perceived badness to a relationship that was making her believe it was true. Francis was in a trauma bond.

When we are faced with abuse and neglect in relationships, we are chemically wired to focus on getting to the other side. When the abuser is the person who brings us relief, the brain associates *them* with safety. The brain latches on to the positive experience of relief rather than the negative impact of the abuser. This creates the feeling that we *need* the abuser to survive and is often mistaken for love. The highs and lows of these relationships can elevate "love" to great heights, magical even. We don't realize it feels that way only because of the inconsistency, because the highs are such a contrast to the lows.

Trauma bonding is a hormonal attachment created by repeated abuse or neglect, alternated with being "saved" by the person harming us. We'll talk about this more in chapter 4, where we discuss the kind of cycles fawning can keep you trapped in. Picture a slot machine, which keeps you hooked with varying payouts, promising an even bigger one if you hand over your hard-earned savings. This is called *intermittent reinforcement*, and it serves as a powerful hook, sowing the seeds of obsession. It's the foundation of trauma bonding, where the excitement and elation come from the unpredictability, the never knowing if you'll be cherished again or when it might happen. The relief when it happens feels like a jackpot. Like heaven.

For Francis, these cycles of invalidation and praise started in her childhood. Her mother had untreated borderline personality disorder as well as active alcoholism. She was chaotic, unpredictable, and physically abusive. Francis's father was a successful lawyer who expected perfection and success. Francis was the golden child. Her mom told her she was prettier than her two sisters. Her dad called her the "total package," reflecting her beauty and intellect. "Look at that face," he would say, "If I were a teenage boy . . ."

Francis is beautiful and has a sensuality that is undeniable. And yet her father's comments led her to believe that her currency in this world was how she looked. How she could appeal to boys. How she could become smaller or prettier, to gain acceptance. As Francis talked about her relationship with her mother, it was clear how she'd learned to drag her mother out of her depressed state by achieving academically or by being thin or pretty. As we discussed fawning specifically, Francis sighed, her face resigned. "Every time my mother beat me, she would return with a dramatic apology accompanied with a childish 'sad face,' and I would then be the one who had to comfort *her*. She felt so much shame over what she had done that I didn't have any space for how bad it felt to be her punching bag. The pity I felt for my mother always trumped the distress I felt at her hands."

Every time the tide would turn, her mother calling her a "bitch" or a "little shit," Francis fawned her way back into her mother's good graces. And then she was rewarded with hugs, kisses, gifts, and the ability to take a deep breath because her mom wasn't mad at her anymore. Francis was a "good girl" because she didn't show her sadness or anger. Because she loved her mother unconditionally. Because she fawned. She was a good girl who felt rotten inside.

The more Francis discussed her childhood, the more I understood why she was staying with Colin, blind to his abusive behavior. She found safety in the cycles of abuse long ago. That is what the fawn response does, making it safe(er) in chaotic situations. Francis's internal alarm system no longer signaled "Get out!" as much as it argued for her to keep fawning.

To bring her alarm system back online, we had to talk about trauma. How it changes the brain, how she had deep muscle memory that was reacting as it always had, to keep her alive. I had to start naming all the things she'd tolerated as abusive. Her best friend had previously tried, but Francis said calling it abuse felt "over the top."

Then we had to *stop* talking about these things and *start* working with them, using trauma therapies like EMDR and Internal Family Systems (which I'll cover more fully in the unfawning section of this book). We worked with her nervous system, learning how to tell the difference between being dysregulated and regulated and how to bring more regulation online. I shared my personal experiences as a trauma survivor, being in real relationship with Francis, normalizing how we both normalized what is actually terrifying, so she knew she wasn't alone.

During this time, I scheduled a call with Francis's couples therapist. Often, couples therapy is in the service of mending fences, offering the fawner more opportunities to do all the work. The charm of many abusers (who can say all the right things in session) can cloak the underlying relationship dynamics *outside* the therapist's office, and I worried that Colin was minimizing his emotional abuse and painting himself as the victim. I told their couples therapist point-blank: "I have no qualms saying this relationship is abusive;

they are in a trauma bond. Please don't mistake Francis's fawning for a healthy and loving connection."

The truth is that breaking trauma bonds that formed in childhood is a brutal business. But Francis and I both saw the subtle shifts, as though she was coming to on my couch. Week by week, she seemed to be more and more herself as she let go of the narrative about her and Colin she was trying to uphold. She could see the truth. She could feel the incongruity, knowing something in my office that seemed to disappear once she left.

Months later, Colin was asking for her help again. He was kind but hoped she might stop what she was doing to come to his aid. After all her therapy, the work she and Colin had been doing to establish better boundaries and communication, she took a risk, saying, "You know, I'm so sorry, but that doesn't feel good for me today."

And Colin lost his shit. He started berating her. "Of course you'd say that. I'm asking for such a small thing, and I do so much for you . . ."

She was sitting on her couch at home, listening to him, knowing there was nothing wrong with what she'd said. Colin's response should have been something like "Oh, bummer, I'm really disappointed, but I understand you're busy."

Francis tried to make a little space for herself, and it spun him into a rage. She became speechless, but a part of her was really seeing it for the first time. She could see the pattern. *This is disproportionate, this is mean, this is anger-fueled, this is not about me doing something wrong.*

The veil lifted. Sitting on her couch, at home with Colin, she connected to the part of her who'd been sitting on mine. The two were becoming one; she was becoming integrated, seeing the bigger picture. *This is emotional abuse.* She saw it objectively. And she knew there was nothing she could do or not do to change it. Except she was NOT going to abandon herself one more time.

This was not a cognitive strategy, it was a bottom-up awareness, one she embodied. One she'd *become*. Once she saw the truth, she couldn't unsee it. And her body wouldn't allow her to backpedal, to ask for forgiveness or try to make it better.

Francis decided to go to a friend's house that night, and Colin started following her around the house, trying to get a rise out of her. She wouldn't fight back, she just kept saying, "I did nothing wrong. I did nothing wrong."

"Of course, you NEVER do anything wrong!" he yelled.

And she kept repeating this mantra softly: "I did nothing wrong."

The second all this awareness dropped into her body, it shattered the hope she'd been carrying for years, that change was coming. Shattered her determination to stick around for that day. And she felt immediate grief.

Walking out, she knew it was over, and she was devastated. It was like all the young parts of her, with gaping wounds, who'd been waiting for help from someone else for decades, were all just told, NOBODY IS COMING. There was no rescue mission. Now sobbing uncontrollably in her car, she was hysterical when she called her sister. "I need to come over right now."

Previous iterations of Francis would have reached out to make peace. Would have sent Colin a text: "I'm really sorry I didn't want to go downtown. I should have said, 'Can we just go for an hour and then I can get some work done?'" If she offered a solution that seemed normal, maybe the whole thing was. But she had no intention of playing nice this time.

There is no sugarcoating what happened next. Crying harder than she ever had, rocking back and forth, shaking, sick to her stomach, she later explained how she felt.

I felt like I was never going to be okay, ever again. Part of me wished I could die. I was not safe in my body or in the world. The LOVE OF

MY LIFE let me leave with no acknowledgment, no apology, no awareness of his behavior, completely villainizing me. The lack of empathy or understanding after five YEARS of doing everything I could for this person, who TOLD ME he loved me more than anyone he'd ever loved, made me realize our "love story" was a mirage, and now it was gone.

Somewhere in there was a realization that she was going to have to rebuild every part of herself and her life. It had never been so clear. None of it was working. Her relationship, job, recovery, relationship to her body . . . she could see how dark and awful her life had become. The only thing that had tethered her for so long was him. Now she was truly alone.

In Francis's unraveling was her unfawning. It was the new beginning. In it, she needed a lot of support to rebuild.

She began having debilitating panic attacks that lasted from several hours to several days. As we processed her experiences, it seemed her body felt safe enough outside of her relationship to begin processing the trauma of it. But she was still in the world where threat felt ever-present. The combination was crippling.

Francis was conscious of all her previous fawning and endeavoring to do things differently, but the enormity was too much to hold. Coming out of a chronic trauma response can feel like you don't have any skin, where every nerve ending is exposed. Francis had to stop working to pursue more intensive forms of healing, including ketamine-assisted psychotherapy to quell the constant activation in her nervous system while she recalibrated.

Her panic was so destabilizing, she went on disability. She couldn't leave the house, couldn't eat. She lost twenty-five pounds in a few months. In a lot of ways, things felt worse than they ever had. Because she was feeling a lifetime of unmetabolized pain.

It was like a dam had broken, but she kept showing up and asking for support. She held on to herself. And in the months ahead, she became clearer. *She* wasn't broken. And she wouldn't go back to her previous life.

She decided to go back to school instead, to live in accordance with her actual priorities. Not because she was fawning for her parents by getting another degree or making herself more palatable for anyone else, but because she finally *wasn't*.

As she and I later talked about what happened and *how* it happened, she shared that being in therapy with someone who was talking about their own experience with similar issues, putting it in the context of the nervous system, set in motion a complete rewiring of her insides. She never understood these things before. Could never make sense of the literal pain in her body. But she was finally accessing emotional processes that were trapped.

She began to cry with sadness toward herself and also gratitude for our process. "I'm so grateful, because I never would have left."

It took a couple of years of hearing "His behavior is not okay" until she could truly register it, then see it, and finally feel it herself. And then, what felt like all of a sudden, there was space for her to really see what was happening. To FEEL the truth of it in her body. To know that safety IS NOT out there. This is unacceptable.

Doing trauma work moved her into PRESENT TENSE. The stories, fantasies, hope, and anxiety weren't running the show. There was a new connection to herself, so she could hear his words, experience his behavior, and feel her own hurt and sadness. Rather than her old version who believed, "I just have to get him to love me!" she'd become the 2.0 version of herself: "This isn't right. This is not okay. And it's not my fault."

Francis continues to step into her power. She is training to become a couples therapist. When she shows up in session, I feel her settling not just into her body, but into the essence of who she is. She remains stylish, with a nose ring and a Brooklyn fashionista vibe, but she knows her value isn't inherently tied to her outward appearance. She knows how much she brings to the table with her life experience, her wisdom, and her growth.

Three

Who, Me?

The Signs of Fawning

Fawners don't often realize when they're fawning. It is an involuntary and automatic response, so it can be hard to see. This is particularly true when fawning stems from childhood trauma, where we weren't consciously responding to threat as much as we were orienting *toward* safety, connection, and security. Our focus was on what we were gaining, and these attachment needs reinforce all our fawning behaviors.

And yet despite the worthy objectives, chronic fawning has consequences. The most prevalent of those is self-abandonment, and it manifests itself in a variety of ways. From minimizing our feelings to conflict avoidance, shapeshifting, and anxiety, this chapter will cover the most common signs of fawning, so you might see them (and yourself) more clearly.

In teasing the signs of fawning out of the bigger picture, remember that all these signs are interrelated. They overlap and are bidirectional: Sometimes one leads to another, sometimes it's the other way around. In other words, there is no road map for fawning, but these are some of the signposts my clients and I have discovered along the way.

Honey, I Shrunk Myself: *Self-Minimization*

Before Mark and I were married, he moved in with me. Although I was thirty-two, I had this funny feeling, like we were playing house. Not in a *This is new and exciting* kind of way but in a *I am pretending this is real* kind of way. Particularly when he stopped contributing to our bills and I had to make up the difference with my student loans. I didn't mind if he wanted to be an actor, but I wanted him to get a job to support that dream, not depend on me to finance it.

A few months into our cohabitation, we opened a joint savings account for a future vacation to Italy, but one day I discovered he'd been withdrawing funds as fast as I deposited them. It took a lot for me to feel my anger was justified, but this seemed like an obvious trespass. Reviewing each transaction a hundred times, building my case before presenting it to him, I was sitting at my desk when he got home. My tone was more inquisitive than angry when I finally said, "Hey, can you tell me about these withdrawals? I thought we agreed not to spend this money."

He claimed he'd done nothing wrong and was angry at *me* for bringing it up. Disoriented by his response, I immediately adopted his viewpoint. *Of course, paying his union dues takes priority over Italy. Why am I so upset?* I **minimized** my feelings until this was no longer a big deal. Problem solved. We could be a "happy couple" again, the thing I wanted more than anything.

This happened so quickly and seamlessly, I almost didn't know I was doing it. And yet minimizing my upset meant minimizing my ability to see the truth of Mark's lies and financial exploitation.

Getting smaller through fawning is basically solving a math problem. It's proportional. The relationship is a cup, and if someone else is taking up 80 percent, we need to figure out how to live in the 20 percent that's left.

Our life becomes a series of strategies to help us maintain those ratios:

· We hope that the situation is temporary and practice patience.
· We don't know anything but keeping ourselves small.
· We believe that their taking up so much space is best for us both (and it might be, particularly with financial or physical security).
· We are mad, but our anger doesn't get us anywhere, so we stuff it and move on.
· We have magical thinking/toxic hope: "If *this*, then *that*." For example, "If he would get a job, then our relationship would be fine."
· We justify their behavior: "I know they do that because _____."
· We stay focused on what's working: "When it's good, it's *so* good."
· We lower our expectations in the name of being "realistic."

All these justifications are the fawner's way of minimizing themselves. We have to; the relationship cup isn't getting any bigger. And the fawner's body has learned through long-term complex situations that *Mom's anger is huge, I must get small.* And this has become the safety map. It's not conscious, it's involuntary accommodation.

When we minimize ourselves and our needs for weeks, for months, for years, we ultimately don't recognize that we're operating at a portion of our capacity. It becomes normal, who we *are*. It's amazing what we learn to live with. I remember once when I was house-sitting, and my friend's closet was as big as my living room. I thought, *I'd never get used to this much space!* Five minutes later, I'd adjusted just fine, thank you. We adapt!

Fawning

In fawning, our adaptation is often to minimize what we need, how we feel, what our bodies are telling us. And in the process, we minimize our worth. Sometimes we use a younger or softer voice. We appear physically submissive, perhaps even crouching down, taking up less physical space. And in our smallness, the other—whether that's a person, a community, a corporation, etc.—gets BIG. Their needs matter more.

Minimization is protective. When you see an animal crouching down, you don't think, *Gee, that squirrel has a self-esteem problem.* You think, *That animal trusts their instincts. I wonder what they are sensing.*

I first met my client Sadie when she was twenty years old. She was a lesbian who wore baseball hats and boxy T-shirts that revealed her tattooed arms. Because she was a student who couldn't afford my fee, her aunt was paying for therapy. While she wanted help with an active eating disorder, much of our early work centered on her volatile romantic relationship and what she later came to understand as her fawn response attempting to keep her safe from physical violence.

Sadie and her girlfriend, Margaret, were in the bedroom one afternoon when Margaret started screaming at her. Sadie was terrified and, initially mobilized by her flight response, attempted to run for the door. Margaret grabbed Sadie so hard she ripped her shirt. Then, looking at the garment in her hand, Margaret started laughing.

There was nothing funny about this moment, but Sadie started laughing, too. This was not a choice. She involuntarily matched her girlfriend's energy. Eventually they were talking about how crazy Sadie was, how dramatic, trying to leave, and it all led to *this*. Before she knew it, she'd switched tactics—from flight to fawning—to defuse the tension and stay safe.

Nobody wants to make themselves small, minimize their feelings, or tolerate abuse. We do it out of necessity, to preserve our relationships or survive our environments. We will see this necessity echoed throughout this book, but it's important to know that most fawners aren't inherently submissive. Shrinking was never our goal.

When we think about a fawner's relationship to proportion and proximity, we can see why we can feel different in different situations, almost becoming different people in different contexts. I've seen many clients almost come to or come *into* themselves in therapy. They become rightsized with me, where they feel safe, but find that they are still fawning out in the world.

This incongruence can feel frustrating, but fawning is a *relational* trauma response—dependent on the relationship we are in at the time. Sometimes we can turn down the volume on our fawning—practice becoming more assertive—but other times we are heading back into the lion's den. On a scale of "de-escalate abuse" to "raise your self-esteem" . . . de-escalation wins every time.

While this appears less active than fighting or running, we are still showing up! We mustn't confuse the hybrid of fawning for a maladaptive response. Yes, we are minimizing ourselves, but it's in service of not disappearing altogether. It's because we are choosing to exist, no matter how small.

The Art of Walking on Eggshells: *Hypervigilance and Anxiety*

Sadie remembers holding her breath in childhood. An inhale might distract her from her heightened sense of perception. An exhale might trip a wire. Only when she left the house did she realize she'd been barely breathing.

She held it the most after disagreements with her mother. Maybe she'd stayed out too late the night before or hadn't put the dishes away. The arguments resembled those between most teenagers and parents. But Sadie knew that something else was coming. Thus, in the moments, hours, or days to come, she'd be constantly on edge.

Hypervigilant and highly attuned to the slightest shifts in her mother's behavior, Sadie was anticipating a deeper punishment—physical violence, shame, or deprivation. And then sometimes her mom would become silly instead, signaling that Sadie could let her guard down. That was such a relief . . . until it wasn't.

One day in her mother's bedroom, they were arguing about the laundry when Sadie's mom threw a sock at her. The velocity with which she threw it, coupled with its impotence, had them both laughing. With a giant exhale, relieved to feel connected after their spat, Sadie left the room. When she came back to grab more clothes, her mother slapped her hard across the face.

The truth was, in that relationship Sadie could *never* let her guard down, and this led to constant **anxiety**. By age seventeen she started smoking weed 24-7 just to cope. Her experience shows that when it comes to anxiety and relational trauma, the cure is rarely about cultivating more calm through breath work or mindfulness; it's about needing relational safety.

Survivors of complex trauma are constantly assessing people's moods, scanning our surroundings for potential threats. We notice subtle cues and facial expressions. We see things coming from a mile away. Our hypervigilance has us walking on eggshells, being preoccupied with the worst-case scenario, not sleeping well, startling easily, overanalyzing, and waiting for the other shoe to drop.

I've been a detective as long as I can remember. During my childhood, I left no stone unturned. I would track my parents' comings and goings. I scoured the house when they were gone to discover where they hid their drugs. I was always looking for evidence that would help me understand what was going on in our household. This sort of hypervigilant behavior leads some fawners to be labeled *controlling*. Man, I hate that term. While it's true—we try to control because we *feel* so out of control—that doesn't mean we are controlling. It means we're afraid. We're off-balance. We're experiencing the effects of being disempowered.

As the fawn response attempts to protect us from further harm, many of us ultimately don't know we're anxious. Our fawning is masking our anxiety, managing it through caretaking, appeasing, or blending in. Saying "I'm anxious" implies bodily autonomy most fawners don't feel. We tend to be concerned with what other people are thinking or feeling. Our anxious thoughts might sound like:

- *Are they mad at me?*
- *Did I do enough?*
- *What will they think if . . . ?*
- *I don't want them to think that I'm unkind, selfish, overreacting, etc.*

Because of these fears, fawners have trouble asserting ourselves, asking for help, or expressing opinions. We have difficulty setting fees or asking for money we're owed. We're afraid of taking up too much space in the overhead bin. We don't want to disappoint people or "get in trouble." Most people want to be liked, but fawners need it like Linus needs his security blanket.

Many fawners are managing equity in our relationships. We feel anxiety when we perceive that someone holds more power—even through their generosity. Any imbalance can feel like someone has power *over* us, and this tip in the scales means we need to lean in: do more, pay more, be more. Reciprocal relationships are often a foreign experience for fawners. So we find ourselves holding a scorecard, making sure we're always a few points ahead. We do this because there was a time when we needed vital support, protection, or kindness, and we did not receive it. Anxiously measuring how we're relating now is vastly preferable to facing that sort of overwhelm again.

I used to have to respond to texts or voice mails *immediately*. I've felt legitimate fear parking in a spot someone might think was theirs. A friend once asked for a better table in a restaurant, and I basically wanted to die. We don't want to take up space, and we don't want anything hanging over our heads.

Due to our anxiety, fawners overfunction and overcommit. We volunteer, take on extra work, take the load off for others. We can't tolerate the anxiety when no one else steps up, and this leads to—you guessed it—more anxiety. We can't do it all, and while being of service is a wonderful thing, fawners don't know where the line is, when we are of service to others—at the expense of ourselves.

Because we don't know what we believe or feel, we feel anxious instead. Recall that the act of fawning includes both a merging with perceived expectations and a disconnection with ourselves. This overriding of greater authenticity leads to a perpetual debate team in our heads. We try to figure things out, wondering what we should do, but there's as much evidence for one position as for the opposite. Fawners are in fact *looking for ourselves, outside of ourselves,* and it makes us dizzy, confused, and incredibly anxious because there are as many opinions as there are bodies.

Then, when we take prescribed actions like setting boundaries or speaking up to take care of ourselves, we feel more anxious than ever. Without the safety of our fawn response, we are convinced something terrible is certain to happen and we have no protection against it. Thus we fawn again.

For some, fawning renders us incapable of showing up. It's like a paralysis. We can't do anything unless it's endorsed by the powers that be. It's too anxiety-provoking to step outside of prescribed guardrails, so avoidance keeps us safe. But for others, fawning shows up as perfectionism.

Perfectionism, in truth, is anxiety masquerading as discipline. In this context, it aims to keep us relationally safe by ensuring we are "perfect." We achieve in order to please. So many fawners are longing for validation, to be seen, and it seems safe to do it through success, achievement, some obvious marker of our worthiness. But perfectionism is just another way to mask our fears. It ultimately keeps our worries firmly in place because no amount of success erases their origins. And then the perfectionist thinks, *Maybe next time . . .*

No matter how we experience our anxiety or how we attempt to manage it, people are still disappointed. They get mad. They don't accommodate us just because we've accommodated them. And this leads us back to feeling the incongruence in our bodies. The discord between smiling when we're annoyed, doing work that's not ours, being a version of ourselves rather than *ourselves*. This inner conflict is often running just below the surface, below conscious awareness, creating an ever-present anxiety. And we don't know why.

We'll see in later chapters that in order to heal, we have to feel. This includes the underlying anxiety and all the feelings we've been overriding. We have to feel our own bodies, what we are experiencing, even if it's at first devastating. Because ultimately this is the path to gaining actual self-trust. To finding solid ground. To getting out of this anxiety feedback loop and into a larger comfort zone where we can finally like who we are.

It's Not You, It's Me: *The Shame Spiral*

When I was living with a narcissistic stepfather who was grooming me, I didn't have the language of fawning to understand why I responded the way that I did. But I remember feeling like I was prostituting myself—selling my integrity to stay in his good graces.

Randy seemed to have a switch that would flip, and I could never determine when things would change. One moment he'd be icing me out with the silent treatment; the next he'd be lavishing me with gifts. Then I'd have to flip *my* switch. In a matter of moments, I'd go from furious to fawning, saying what I knew he wanted to hear, expressing my gratitude for his generosity while swallowing the rage I'd been feeling so acutely. I felt like two different people: the real me, and the one I had to become to endure my circumstances— funny, curious, singing the songs he wanted me to sing—almost like a performing monkey. I hated myself for it.

That part: hating myself. That is the cost I had to pay to try and stay safe in an unsafe situation. And it perpetuated the **shame spiral**, poisoning my self-perception.

First, we feel shame about the traumatic events we've endured. Isolating Randy's actions for a moment, I was "loved" only in secret, in small doses, intermittently, and only for certain aspects of myself. The withholding of love or the conditional way it was offered was shame inducing. Why couldn't I just be loved like other kids? Why didn't my family look anything like Alex P. Keaton's or the Huxtables on TV? When we are invalidated, abused, neglected, or betrayed, it can induce the shameful, humiliating feeling that *Something is wrong with me.*

Then we feel shamed by people's response to our traumatic events. When I spoke up, things got even worse. I was neither protected nor believed. Like so many trauma survivors, I was told directly and indirectly, *It's no big deal.* I was left alone with my terror and overwhelm. Experiencing a lack of connection, comfort, or resources is further interpreted as *There is something wrong with me.* We feel another layer of even deeper shame.

The way we respond to these harmful conditions—our fawning— has us prioritizing others' needs to such an extent that we behave outside of our value system. Fawning often requires hiding, shapeshifting, and lying, which feels like further proof of our perceived deficiencies. While these habits developed out of necessity, we experience them as personal failings: *I am bad.* Then we carry this shame, a diminished sense of self, into the rest of our lives.

When Randy stole me away to Vegas, telling me to hold his hand because minors weren't allowed in casinos, he also said, "You need to appear older. Let's get you some new clothes."

As a sixteen-year-old, I welcomed the shopping spree. There seemed to be no limit to what he would spend. With new suede boots and a silk blazer, I felt more adult and put together than I ever had, and I liked those feelings.

I knew he was buying my affections and manipulating my perception. I just didn't know what the actual truth was, *Would we get in trouble?* He was confusing me, blaming Vegas for parading me around like his girlfriend. And yet I knew it was a parade. I participated in it. He wanted me to be sexy, and I wore the damn boots.

At the end of the day, all I knew for sure was how I was behaving. Fawning had me saying, "Thank you so much, I'm so grateful." It didn't matter that he was in the wrong (or that I couldn't comprehend the extent of it); his behavior didn't cancel mine out. I held myself to a higher standard, one I literally couldn't meet (*Maybe I'll get in trouble in Vegas or be in worse trouble with him*). Shame is the price I paid.

Shame is a constant thread running through my clients' lived experiences. We can feel humiliated for the ways we seemingly played into our experiences, embarrassed by the truth of what we're tolerating now. We shame ourselves before anyone else has the chance.

If we do go to therapy, it's often for a different, relational concern that seems worthy of our time and resources: "I want to be a better mom," or "I want to be a better partner." It's not that we have a problem; we *are* the problem. We double down on our shame, believing, *I'm too sensitive. I'm asking for too much. Can you help me with that?*

In the shame spiral, many of us lose touch with our innate goodness. This is the reason the why of fawning is so important. We've been called defective when we've simply been adapting to reality— surviving it. This whole book is about destigmatizing and reducing the shame we've inherently felt. It's why I'm so particular about language and tone. Shame has been a huge barrier to our healing. You want to keep a fawner fawning? Tell them they're doing something wrong. We don't pause to reflect on the truth of such statements. Instead, we feel the relational threat and react accordingly, morphing ourselves again, trying to be "better" for the one who is shaming, never authentically healing.

Many mental health experts have been teaching through shame, perpetuating this cycle by saying things like "People pleasers are master manipulators." I think this is, well, *shameful*. What we need is more room to explore what happened in our lives, the impact it's had, how it's manifesting now. We need curiosity, compassion, and vulnerability to heal, and these do not grow in shame. Judging us for the ways in which our nervous systems were hijacked is not only abhorrent but simply doesn't help. Shame holds the need to fawn securely in place. Only when shame has been diminished can we reduce chronic fawning and its consequences.

So Many Masks, so Little Time: *Shapeshifting*

Grace was in her forties when we started working together, and her stated reason for coming to therapy was because she wanted to be a good mother. She knew she'd had a problematic childhood, and she didn't want to repeat the patterns in her own parenting.

With a petite frame and fair skin, Grace has dark brown stick-straight hair that she's professionally straightened her entire life. She wears dark horn-rimmed glasses and very little makeup. We've always commented on each other's wardrobe, starting our sessions with questions like "Where did you get that sweater?" During the sixteen years I've worked with Grace, it's like she hasn't aged a day on the outside, but on the inside, she is almost unrecognizable.

Early on, Grace shared that she wore "different hats" depending on the situation she was in. She was a different person at home, at work, with old friends. She knew if her husband was hanging out with the work version of her, he wouldn't even like her. Her different personalities in various contexts had become so pronounced, when Grace read the book *Sybil*, she wondered if she had dissociative identity disorder.

As she shared the complicated adjustments she had to make to be the right person in each context, I mentioned an analogy that might help her identify how taxing these roles were. "It seems like you're walking a tightrope," I said. Then I asked her if she longed for more freedom.

"It's definitely a tightrope," Grace agreed. "But I love it!"

That wasn't what I was expecting. But Grace explained that knowing where to step made her feel safe. "The idea of having more room, of stepping a millimeter to either side, feels terrifying. Like I'm going to set off a land mine."

The constraints were comforting. She liked it when someone told her what to do, who to be. So she surrounded herself with opinionated people who told her exactly that.

It would take many more months for Grace to realize what all these masks were costing: access to her true self. At the time, she could see her pliability only as helpful, just the way she always was.

Recall that fawners are seeking approval, safety, and connection. **Shapeshifting** isn't always about winning a popularity contest. (Although many of us would like to win it!) Sometimes our shapeshifting looks like doing drugs to stay with the in-crowd. Or gossiping to appease a friend. Shapeshifting is how we learned to manage the relational gap. When we couldn't express or meet our own needs, when we couldn't trust others to do their part, we had to close the gap by morphing into whatever the situation called for.

As Grace and I explored her compulsion to orient toward what others wanted from her, she told a story from her childhood. Her dad was explosive, punishing, with a "You made me do it" attitude. He often told Grace she was stupid, that she wasn't listening or trying hard enough, that it was always her fault.

One morning in high school, her dad said, "Let's order pizza tonight," before she headed out for school. He then asked if Grace wanted onions. She was putting away her cereal bowl when she said no and turned to grab her backpack. Her dad erupted: "You always like onions, and now when I ask you, you say you don't like them?!" He was raging, and Grace was frightened.

To escape further confrontation, she tried to leave through the back door. Her dad came up behind her and grabbed her hair, yelling, "If you want to leave, you'll do it through the front door!" He dragged her by her hair to the front door and then kicked her from behind, ejecting her from the house.

While I'd heard of the volatility in her childhood home before, this scene was clearly painful for Grace to recount. She began to analyze what happened, why her dad reacted that way. "My dad was portraying thoughtfulness, saying he'd order pizza for dinner and asking me what I wanted. But he didn't really care. The truth is, he wanted onions, and my job was to want what he wanted. To know what he wanted. When I didn't do that in childhood, I was punished." She seemed resigned as she presented her analysis.

To this day, sharing food is terrifying for Grace. She hates potlucks, fearing she'll bring the "wrong" thing. Every decision or opinion is an opportunity to upset someone by not doing things their way. As a result, Grace developed a lifelong commitment to become whatever the situation called for. She likes onions because, as she shared, "Everything I do is to de-escalate!"

When we've learned to de-escalate by contorting ourselves, unfawning becomes incredibly difficult. Healthy conflict involves tolerating some upset, but most fawners don't know what healthy conflict feels like. We don't know if we are in relationships that can support it, and we don't want to risk trying. Our bodies are keeping a perpetual eye out for new threats, so even potential upset is overwhelming. We might interpret hints of disappointment as *It's happening again,* and automatically say we like onions rather than face being violently kicked out of the house. Building new capacity means facing the fear and overwhelm we've instinctively turned away from, for good reason.

Noticing all the ways Grace had contorted herself over the years, I said, "It's as though you've never truly been seen. Not by others, not even by yourself." With tears in her eyes, Grace nodded yes.

This is the cost of shapeshifting. We lose access to ourselves. Gabor Maté, MD, an expert in trauma, addiction, and child development, and the author of *The Myth of Normal,* talks about this tension:

> An issue that comes up in a lot of people's lives [is] the conflict we all experience between being ourselves, on the one hand, and being loved and accepted on the other. That's what we want . . . But what if you can't have both and the child can't or perceives that they can't. Then they go for the attachment, and they suppress themselves. Self-expression and authenticity become a threat to them. All our lives we are afraid to be ourselves. It's not a mistake that we give up our authenticity. It's not a weakness. It's not a moral fault. It's a survival mechanism.

While Grace loves the tightrope and the safety it affords her, she hates not being seen. She doesn't want to be told who to be or what she likes. She's tired of wearing a different hat for every occasion, and the inescapable conflict manifests as deep depression.

The adage to "just be yourself" misses the necessity of shapeshifting. How adopting different identities and opinions were required to de-escalate terror. Unfawning involves reclaiming intrinsic parts of ourselves, discovering how to honor them now, but before we can move on or find greater authenticity, we must have compassion for the parts that got lost, for good reason.

Nothing to See Here: *Conflict Avoidance*

It's hard to explain what happens in my body at the first sign of conflict. I'm immediately afraid: *The hammer is going to fall.* In my childhood, when I tried fighting back, asking for help from my mother and school counselor, my mother didn't even respond to what I said; she just called Randy to come and shore up the story. This put me even further at risk. For many of us, fighting back in any form has made things worse. And then it's as though our fight response gets snuffed out because it's safer to drop our grievances and move on.

Recall that Sadie held her breath for much of her childhood. Anytime she tried to stand up for herself, her attempts were thwarted. Defending herself from her mother's abuse, she was often physically attacked. When she stood up to boys at school who taunted her, she was ignored. Even when she tried to defend herself with teachers, she was kicked out of class.

When she was ten years old, Sadie's parents got divorced and she was assigned a guardian ad litem who was tasked with determining what would be best for herself and her twin brother. This woman discovered a collection of drawings that Sadie had made. In each picture, Sadie had drawn herself with no arms. When she described this to me, she said, "This clearly shows how I related to pushing back."

When fawning becomes our go-to trauma response, it's not just our fight response that gets dropped. It's our ability to notice or feel conflict at all. We learn to put on blinders, keeping them firmly in place. We don't even see where harm is done, or if we do, we morph it into something we can tolerate: a story that won't rock the boat.

Growing up, I knew my mother had blinders on. It was as though she could not see Randy's abuse. She adopted his version of every story, thereby eliminating any discord. She didn't see him as cruel or punishing. She believed he was smarter, better at business, better equipped. She didn't know she was abandoning herself; she believed this *was herself.*

Recall Anthony's story, where he could barely own the perpetual invalidation of his upbringing, instead clinging to the "happy family" narrative. Or my experience with my ex-husband taking my Italy savings for his personal use. I saw his behavior as trying to take care of himself, showing up for his career, paying dues that needed paying. He wasn't *stealing* from me.

In our desperate need to belong, fawners become incredible storytellers, endowing others with gifts and motivations they don't possess, writing endings that don't exist, creating redemptive love stories out of utter dysfunction. Then we don't see how much of our lives are dedicated to fantasy. How much energy we're exerting maintaining it.

Hearing me recount the latest family drama back home, my current husband Yancey once said, "Ingrid, the only thing shocking here is that you are shocked about it." What I was sharing was predictable to him. But because I was still in a state of fawning, believing things would get better any minute, my mind was constantly blown. Being blind to conflict lends itself to naivete. We remain trusting, hopeful, almost experiencing the world as a fairy tale, at least until we're shook up once again.

It's no surprise many of us are **conflict avoidant,** as we've never witnessed healthy conflict. I didn't see parents who respected each other, getting closer through the process of shared vulnerability. I saw power dynamics that squashed the soul. Both of my biological parents are fawners who married domineering partners after their divorce from each other. And both of my parents stood in their spouse's shadow. This was the model: You have power *over* someone or you're disempowered, and I knew I did not want to be like my stepparents.

In a healthy system, there is reciprocity and respect. There's tolerance for discord in both directions. But few of us were raised in these settings. From a nervous system perspective, we don't even know it exists.

Avoiding conflict is avoiding intimacy, but it's sometimes the safest bet. And in that initial safety, we can see how perpetual fawning becomes the thing that keeps us stuck. It keeps us from *actual* safety. From enlarging our capacity for healthy conflict. From healthy attachments. From engaging with reality. From healing. We can wear those blinders for decades, and they ultimately conceal a lot more than conflict—they conceal our unprocessed trauma while we're attempting to rise above it. Thinking that we can.

Stuck On Simmer: *Resentment*

Fawning has us avoiding conflict, but it doesn't mean we aren't mad. It means we can't tell you we're mad. We don't feel entitled to anger; in fact, we might not even know it's there. That said, at some point, most fawners become aware of their **resentment,** whether it's from holding all the responsibility in relationships, all the workload in our jobs, or all the caretaking in our families and friendships.

For most fawners, our resentments simmer, right below the boiling point. I once told a therapist, "On the outside, I seem fine. But on the inside, I'm carrying the rage of a three-hundred-pound linebacker." I knew I was angry, but I had no idea what to do with it. The people I was mad at couldn't hear it, that much was clear. So I just held it. Hoping it would eventually go away on its own. News flash . . . that didn't happen. It rarely does.

Fawners sometimes turn to gossip as a release for our resentments that we don't feel we can take to the source. Noticing our tendency to gossip is a powerful way of getting curious: What am I really feeling? Is there a way for me to attend to it more directly? Who or what am I trying to avoid?

We can also take our resentments out on ourselves. Holding so much turmoil that might sacrifice our attachment needs, we must cope somehow, so we turn to drinking or using drugs, disordered eating, or self-harm. Being unable to act directly, we act *out* or we act *in*.

Sadie knew when she was restricting food, bingeing, and purging; something was coming up in her body that she didn't have the capacity for. Bingeing drowned out the noise, and purging got it all *out*. She once said, "My eating disorder and addiction to cigarettes are like dysfunctional parents, telling me, 'You can't feel those things! Let me take them for you.'" She saw how those behaviors were the only protectors she knew for so long. Similar to a chronic fawn response, addictions are often born of trauma, as ways the body found relief. For many of us, once relief is achieved, those defenses remain firmly in place.

Twelve-step recovery has long identified the connection between lingering resentment and being stuck in destructive habits. The main text of Alcoholics Anonymous states, "Resentment is the number one offender. It destroys more alcoholics than anything else." Step 4 is a resentment inventory, seeking to resolve the underlying fuel for one's use. However, the main objective of the inventory is to determine one's personal failings as the root of resentments, seeing where we've been selfish or self-seeking—all roads leading to a "defect of character." While newer twelve-step programs have become trauma-informed, others are still focused on a stance of blaming the victim, one that implies survivors are responsible for the abuse they've endured or that their body's adaptive responses to abuse are selfish.

Sometimes fawners can name our resentments, but we don't *feel* them as much as we think about how they can be fixed. Oriented in the direction of others, instead of ourselves, we think:

Why don't they
. . . do their part?
. . . go to therapy?
. . . apologize?
. . . stop relying on me for everything?

Instead of thinking: *I'm uncomfortable with how much I'm covering for my spouse, taking care of them like another child. Maybe I need firmer boundaries.* A fawner doesn't have boundaries; in fact they don't even think of them as an option. They don't know that they have the power to save themselves after years of orienting solely around others.

This is another opportunity to be labeled as controlling, as fawners get crafty about sharing our opinions, dropping hints, writing letters, asking a million times, calling someone's therapist, sending articles, even talking to other people who might have more sway with the person we are trying to "help." (Spoiler alert: Caretaking is the next section!)

All these strategies are a work-around, trying to solve conflict through a side door. Facing it directly would mean facing the truth of our situations. We might need *more* than boundaries. We might have to leave. This threatens the very relational safety a fawner is seeking—hence the need for managing (and minimizing) our resentments.

This common pattern leaves our needs and feelings unaddressed because the needs of others are thought of as more important. We are quick to assess a hierarchy of need (while surrounding ourselves with people who tend to need *a lot*) and then determine that either our concerns aren't as important or we feel better equipped to handle them on our own.

When fawning works, it can keep us safe in unsafe environments, but long term, it can be like a frog in boiling water. We tolerate things no one should. We become desensitized to bad behavior. And at some point, we need to feel the heat that's been rising if we are going to get out of that bitter stew.

How Can I Help You?: *Caretaking at the Expense of Self*

"Being helpful or useful has been my ticket to love," Sadie said in my office one day. The little girl who drew herself with no arms, who felt like she could not push back, who learned to laugh in the face of abuse, found other ways to make herself safe in a home situation that was anything but.

When she was a child, Sadie and her brother would be watching TV when their mom would come in, yelling, "One of you ungrateful brats left a glass out on the table! How many times do I have to tell you?! I am an amazing mother, and when you do this, it is obvious that you don't care about me."

Sadie never knew when moments like this would turn physically violent. As soon as her mom walked away, Sadie ran to write a note: "Mommy, I am so sorry. I love you so much. I appreciate you and know you are a wonderful mom." And then slipped it under her mother's door.

Relational trauma survivors are often called "old souls," as though our adultlike attitudes and skill sets come from a past life rather than the necessity of our present-day childhoods. Sadie was praised for being wise beyond her years, celebrated in moments where she was **caretaking**, and punished when she tried to voice her needs. "I recall feeling like my sole purpose was to bring comfort to my mother. I could not even feel into my body. Sadie who? I was gone."

It took years of our working together before Sadie became aware of this pattern. But once we identified it, she saw signs of it every-where. "I never felt like my mother was the parent. Maybe when I was sick, she would show up as a caretaker. Otherwise, I was the caretaker. I was the parent."

Because of the necessity for conflict avoidance, it's no surprise that fawning creates a need for caretaking, fixing, and enabling. If there's no room for the mess of real relating, fawners are like Mr. Clean, mopping it all up. We solve all the problems as the only way to attend to our own—through our helpfulness.

Recently Sadie and I commiserated about what happens to us when someone we know faces a crisis. "Oh my gosh, whatever I was doing before that phone call disappears. I morph into whatever that person needs me to be," she explained. I laughed in recognition. "Me too! Anyone's personal emergency feels like a fire, and if I can put it out, of course I should! It would be selfish to even wonder if I had the bandwidth or time to attend to it. IT'S A FIRE."

This kind of helpfulness can get you labeled a good friend. We get rewarded for being the one to step in, to offer help, to take on the job—praised for being a fawner. My client Lily knows this well. With dark brown hair and blunt bangs, she is bubbly and animated. She wants to get things *right* and is often brought to tears when she realizes that she's holding herself to a standard that doesn't exist.

Lily is a perpetual babysitter, party thrower, cheerleader, therapist to everyone in her life, and she recently added pet sitter to the list. Mind you, Lily doesn't own a pet, in part because she'd never want to ask someone to watch it. But when her friend with a very anxious dog, who likes no one but her owner, who drinks *only* from a cup you're holding, asked Lily to watch her dog . . . Lily said yes.

Armed with her friend's jacket, hoping to comfort the dog with her owner's scent, Lily arrived at her friend's house. She grabbed the special goblet and was holding it out, but the dog *wasn't drinking*. Lily tried different glasses. She left the water and walked away. She tried room-temperature water, water with ice. She begged and cajoled, but the dog drank nothing.

Recounting this story, Lily said she was not only worried the dog would become dehydrated but also felt like her entire worth and friendship was on the line. "I could lose my friend forever. How could she trust or depend on me again?"

"Lily, do you even like dogs?" I asked. "Would you say yes to such an impossible task if she asked again? Do you have any feelings about being put in this position?"

"Let's be honest. I'm probably more of a cat person," Lily joked while acknowledging that she hadn't thought about herself in this equation at all.

Fawners have learned that they are the only ones in their family/relationship who can take care of business, metabolize distress. The idea that *This is too much* was a luxury we were never afforded. We have to sacrifice ourselves for attachment or to keep the entire ship afloat. Our only choice was to make things better, to survive, to somehow get everyone out of the fire no matter what we had to face to get there. Or watch it all burn from the inside.

Pick Me!: *The Need to Be Chosen or Liked*

There is one theme underneath almost all the signs of fawning: the need to be **chosen,** the need for external validation, the need to be rescued or picked. This is in fact a counterpoint to self-abandonment. If there is *less* of me, I need *more* of you. So we tolerate abuse and mistreatment and anxiously squash our feelings about it. We become the person others need us to be, do what they need us to do, because we don't want to jeopardize what is ultimately more important: the protection only a seal of approval can provide.

The story I shared at the beginning of this chapter, about my ex-husband using our joint savings for his own personal expenses, was just one of many red flags I blew right past. They were abundant from the beginning, but Mark was the first person I'd dated who seemed open to marrying me.

I'd been vigilant about not marrying for the wrong reasons, writing graduate school papers steeped in feminism on the Cinderella complex—how woman have been expected to be gracious, beautiful, caretaking of others while made to believe they're incapable of taking care of themselves. I'd been taking care of myself quite capably since I left home at seventeen, and if I'm honest, well before then.

But now in my thirties, I'd never broken up with a single boyfriend. I stayed. I hoped and I helped. There was a deeper drive I seemed unable to shake no matter how many papers I wrote, how many therapists' couches I sat on. I *needed*, like my life depended on it, to finally be chosen back.

We'd been dating for two years when Mark proposed with a small silver band he pulled from his pocket. I screamed, "Yes!" and we kissed as though it was the culmination of a great love story, but the ring turned my finger green within an hour. Mark eventually said the band was just temporary and we went shopping for a ring, quickly finding one we both loved. I turned to him with a huge smile. "Is this the one?" as though I were sitting with Neil Lane in an episode of *The Bachelor*.

Standing in front of the salesman, Mark turned to me. "If you can put it on your credit card, I will make the payments."

I wasn't expecting this but couldn't let anything threaten this milestone. I handed my Visa over, and we got on with celebrating. Though he later repeated his promise to pay for the ring, he never made one payment, and neither of us brought it up again.

The truth is, I was shocked when he asked me to pay. I was mad, but I couldn't say I was mad because I was ashamed. I was aware of the salesman as a witness, wondering, *What must he think of me?* as I was thinking less of myself by the second.

I knew if I said no, there would be no ring. Despite all my feelings about the commercialization of love, the ring was important because it was a symbol of being chosen. The ring was almost the whole point. While I wanted it to mean so much more, part of me believed a symbol was all I might ever get.

I also knew that saying no would threaten the engagement itself. Not that I was afraid he would leave, but that I might have to see how bad things were if I didn't keep pushing forward. Bringing down the blinders in that moment would have meant bringing them down on all of it, and I was not ready to see it. I knew he was a liar. I knew his drinking and pot smoking were escalating when he'd originally told me he'd stopped doing both. I couldn't fully address those red flags, so I saw only what I hoped: It was going to get better any minute.

I KEPT PUSHING FORWARD.

This was fawning. This was not cognitive. External validation was like air. We need the safety of others' protection, to be picked for the relationship, the team, the job. It's why we get trapped in over-volunteering and perfectionism. We want to be chosen, to feel safe and loved. Having someone say they wanted to marry me was the ultimate choosing, FOREVER.

I didn't know I had trauma, that I was reenacting it and living in a perpetual fawn response. My body desperately wanted to unlock the prison it was in, but truly believed someone else was holding the key.

The key was someone else's stamp of approval. If Randy never admitted what he'd done, if my mom never admitted what had happened, maybe someone else could choose and believe in me, and this time—I got it. Mark and I got married. And it did not free me like I'd hoped.

It's as though if we can appease enough, turn our cheeks enough, be helpful enough, we hope that eventually we might finally feel worthy. A new form of relational safety might stand in for the safety we'd always lacked. Sometimes it's marriage, sometimes it's the feeling of belonging or getting the job, and sometimes we're stuck still trying to convince our original offenders of our worth. But at the core, we're hoping we can finally stop proving ourselves. The sad reality is that this strategy only invites more of the same.

The only way we get to be ourselves is when we stop self-abandoning. No one can unlock that for us. And it's bigger than one relationship; it's unlocking the door to being ourselves in a million other contexts that might rather we *not*.

A common saying in couples therapy is that water seeks its own level, meaning we tend to partner up with people who are at a similar level of functioning, of emotional awareness and access. Fawners often feel like everyone *else* is emotionally unavailable, but we can't see that we are, too. Fawning precludes being emotionally available to ourselves. The missing link is feeling our own feelings, the ability to speak them, process them, have them at all.

We feel stuck in relationships, solely focused on the other person, not understanding how we are stuck in our own patterns of dysfunction. The fawn response can't provide access to healthy relationships any more than fight, flight, or freeze can. It just feels like it can because the appeasement has us feeling so connected, enmeshed, and consumed. But other people aren't actually the ones who need saving, or at least we aren't the ones to do it. We can only ever truly save ourselves. While I heard that cliché a million times over the years, I never understood how it applied. Understanding fawning finally showed me that I need to shift my focus to myself, and why I wasn't able to do it before.

I used to just feel broken. Like the solutions weren't available to me. But the fact is, chronic fawning was in the driver's seat. I was seeking the solution outside of myself. Trying to solve my dysregulation by attempting to regulate others. Trying to solve it by *looking* as though I had.

Until I looked within, I kept repeating the same patterns. I was always shocked by how each new relationship would wind up largely the same as the one before. Before I met the man who is now my husband, each partner I connected with was unavailable. It just presented differently: alcoholism, immaturity, unresolved trauma, narcissism. But each of these were flavors I grew up with.

I didn't know I'd become fragmented as a trauma survivor, losing access to my whole self. I'd lost myself a little over here, a little over there, over time. It wasn't something I could see. I could see only what was LEFT, and so I thought, *This is me.* And then *This is me trying so hard* to be in relationship, to be "healthy," trying to get some of what I thought we were all meant to have.

We are hardwired to grow in relationship with others. And we're just trying to get those fundamental attachment needs met now. The truth is, though, we are often trying to do it with unavailable people. I believe that healing can absolutely happen in relationship. But it often requires two people who are longing for that, choosing it consciously. It doesn't happen by the simple fact of being in relationship. My first marriage made that abundantly clear.

If you aren't already getting the feedback that you can grow together, and that is the goal, it likely won't happen out of the blue. Our hopes and wishes that *One day they will see how great I am, and they will finally do their own work* will likely stay a fantasy. But one day (maybe today?!) *we* can see how great we are. We can choose ourselves. We can stop doing their work and start doing our own. The deeply rooted work of nervous system regulation. The work of RESCUING OURSELVES. We will look at these strategies in the unfawning section of this book, but here is where there is some good news for fawners: We are brilliant caretakers. We have loads of resourcefulness. We are creative and compassionate and willing to go to any lengths. And when we turn all of that back on ourselves, to rescue all the parts of us that we lost along the way, we can finally get free.

To Tell You the Truth

• • •

If you are reading this book and you don't identify as a fawner, I want to ask you a couple of questions before we dive into storytelling and the fawn response.

- If you had to choose authenticity *or* having your basic needs met, what would you choose?
- If you had to choose physical safety *or* having your feelings and processing them, what would you choose?
- If you had to choose access to a partial life that included appeasing abusive people *or* no life at all, what would you choose?

Fawners have had to disconnect from their feelings, their authenticity, even knowing the scope of what they were living through, as a form of self-preservation. At some point in their lives, it became dangerous to speak up, advocate for themselves, or even be consciously present.

While there is an inherent level of dishonesty with fawning, of changing who we are to become who we need to be, calling us liars or manipulators misinterprets the motivation and necessity. It misses how we needed to lie because honesty invited annihilation. How we had to pretend to be something we weren't because a greater relational need was at stake.

When I use the word *lie* in the context of fawning, it's not in the sense one might imagine, as in true or false, a binary, or a *clear* distinction between something that is honest and dishonest.

With fawning, lying is like tucking pieces of ourselves and our experiences away. Sometimes the tucking is within a safe distance, one we can access and know. We are tucking it in for safekeeping. And sometimes things get tucked so far in, we might never get them back.

When we lie, it's because we are trying to hide something sacred, something that isn't safe in the world. Lying to ourselves and others has been a form of protection. I think of it like a life preserver. No one was throwing us one, so we manufactured one out of thin air. In fact, we became it. I see the fawner's storytelling as a superpower. A genius adaptation that spontaneously came online right when we needed it.

The same thing is true then when I use the word *honesty*. It's less *I'm telling the truth and the whole truth* and more *Is it safe enough to be in contact with what had to be banished?*

Lying to ourselves and others in fawning isn't a moral indiscretion. And it's rarely premeditated.

When my clients have unburdened themselves of the stories they've told to stay safe, they often feel like it's a confession. Where they are so to speak telling on themselves. Consequently, they feel like they are going to be punished, risk my opinion of them, or worse. They brace for impact and so much shame.

Sometimes, once our relationship has been established, I might even ask my clients questions along the lines of "I wonder what we *aren't* we talking about?" Releasing the secrets and the stories we've told is releasing the barriers to the greatest treasure, a reclamation of self. But we can do it only when we recognize that it's finally safe enough to do so. And only when the parts are ready to be known, even to the person who is holding them.

In this way, the lies we've told were our stunt doubles—protecting the parts of ourselves that needed protecting and deceiving others at the same time. They were camouflage.

Knowing we can't be seen for who we are, we become who we need to be. We aren't thinking, *How can I deceive you?* but *How can I be a regular person in the world?* For fawners, the unconscious drive is to present like a regular person, hoping to become a version of a worthy one. It's as though we want to pass as human. As loved. As whole.

I often hear the same language from trauma survivors: "I feel like a ghost, invisible, trapped, unworthy." So much of my own life feels like it was in service of building a case for myself and others that I was real, that I existed, that I was worthy of a life.

Fawners wish we could live with an Instagram filter, but one that actually changes us—removing the shame, giving us safety, blurring the background, cropping what we don't want you to see. Again, for the non-fawners in the house, you might ask yourself what filters you use in your everyday life. The white lies, the stories you've told yourselves . . . What would you have to face if these were completely gone?

Unfawning is the act of finally seeing ourselves and the truth of our lives. When we are fawning, our reality is distorted. We don't see how we really feel, so we don't notice red flags. We keep pieces hidden from the light of day because we don't want to be hurt again. We omit them from our conscious mind and don't share them with others. We can share only safe parts of ourselves with others—our helpfulness, our goodness—and we keep the tender stuff close and concealed.

Sometimes we face how we've embellished stories or made them up completely. When abuse has been hidden, invalidated, and unseen, we can go to great lengths to make it visible, in a way that seems valid. This is an aspect of shapeshifting. We tell stories that show people how we feel, one that gets them to understand. Lying is like a translator, articulating a feeling that is true in a way that feels acceptable to us and others.

My brother once told his teachers at his elementary school that our parents made him sleep outside at night, in the freezing cold. He said he curled up in the empty hot tub with nothing but the cover for a blanket. This is NOT what was happening in our house, but even as a kid, when I heard this, I remember thinking, *That is genius.* Because that loneliness, that fear, that neglect . . . was.

Lily (my perpetually pet-sitting client) started cheerleading at age twelve, and she loved getting thrown in the air, but she hated tumbling on the ground. To avoid this part of training, she faked sprained ankles or left for long bathroom breaks. One day her coach said, "Lily, show me a roundoff, back handspring, tuck!" and Lily, already a full-time fawner, couldn't tell her the truth—that she was afraid.

She started to act like she might faint, sitting down to "catch her breath." When Lily's coach asked what was wrong, she made up another lie, that she'd skipped lunch because she was worried about being too heavy to be a flier, something she knew the coach would take seriously. Recalling this moment from adolescence, how it represented so many others in her life, Lily was heartbroken how often she lied to feel remotely understood in the world. When our actual feelings are constantly overridden—they literally *don't matter* to others—we try to find something that does.

Lastly, sometimes our lying looks like emphasizing the good stuff. The Instagram filter that erases all the wrinkles and then adds professional makeup. Fawners are often caught in constant curation of our lives. Elevating the positives, as though they might erase the rest. We elevate them in our own lives, and we elevate them for *you*.

As someone who was stuck in a fawn response for decades, I spent so much time and energy, not just trying to convince myself I'd had a better past, but that the present moment was better than it really was. Curating moments and events, even capturing them with hundreds of photos to prove that there was sweetness, that there was connection. If I could dress it all up, there was nothing to confront.

I perpetually minimized the impact of trauma, by attempting to rise above it by romanticizing the here and now. Amplifying every little pocket of goodness until I could feel like it was enough. Like it could anesthetize me to the rest. And it did.

I didn't do this consciously. I thought I was just being a good daughter, sister, girlfriend, etc. But I see now how it was curated. And how exhausting it's been. How splitting off from the truth meant I couldn't take care of myself.

It meant I couldn't even know myself. To some extent, we aren't lying as much as we don't know who we are or how we feel. It's not like we start from connection to ourselves and then try to override that. We start from the place of *What do I need to do, who do I need to be, to be relationally safe*? I lied because I needed to maintain someone's perception of me. And because we don't really know another's perception, it was often a guessing game.

As far back as elementary school, I'd tell people I had two solos in my school's choir performance, when I actually had only one, because I thought it would make me cool. Later, I'd say I had a salad for lunch, when really I had spaghetti and meatballs. *Don't want you to think I'm not health conscious!* I'd have no idea what someone was talking about in a conversation, but pretended I'd read the book, understood the reference, nodding my head alongside audible hums to make sure people knew, *I'm not stupid.*

It wasn't even safe to be curious, to learn, to have preferences of my own. So it was a lot to undo. When I was in the early stages of my sobriety, my new friend Frankie and I made a pact to tell the truth no matter what. Initially this meant after almost every phone call between us, one of us would call the other back and admit we'd just lied. The lies always boiled down to some version of "I didn't want you to be mad" or "I felt so ashamed. Please don't think less of me."

While I stopped overtly lying in my twenties, I can see how fawning led to my becoming a therapist in my thirties. It was second nature to "be seen" only when in service to others, but after many years in the field, I felt frustrated and depleted. I wanted to know what it felt like not to censor myself. I wanted to take the "helpful" mask off.

I wondered what it might feel like to paint the entire canvas of my life, not caring how it looked or how it impacted someone else. If my unabashed creativity happened to help somebody, that would be great. But if it didn't, I wanted that to be great, too.

Constantly curating for others' consumption left important pieces out—namely *me*. I don't believe you have to orient this way as a therapist, but it was a natural extension of what I'd always done, so of course it transpired professionally.

I now know that writing my memoir and sharing my true self on social media were huge parts of my unfawning. Self-publishing my book, without anyone's permission, gave me a freedom of expression I'd never had before. When I dropped the mask of "expert" on social media to show that I was additionally someone who was figuring things out, a survivor, and a performer with a sometimes silly and irreverent sense of humor, it felt terrifying and liberating at the same time.

One of the greatest gifts of recognizing fawning is the opportunity to reclaim our true selves. To discover and exert our own opinions. To find out how we feel and learn how we can honor it. We drop the countless masks and finally embody what we've been chasing: self-acceptance and authentic connection.

Because what we all want is a real life. Real moments and relationships. But of course, what comes with facing the truth is the grief of what was never really there unless we were running circles around it, trying to CREATE IT, capture it. Make it so.

It means no more editing, ceasing to idealize others and minimize ourselves. It means speaking narratives that are true, making it safe to do so. Finding safe people to do it with. Particularly when the roots of self-deception are from childhood, being able to stop lying is part of the rescue mission we must go on. WE must go back to the parts of ourselves that are stuck in time and let them know: *I AM HERE. You are safe with* me.

We don't have to tell stories anymore.

Sadie

I met Sadie in 2014. At twenty years old, she was a recovering addict who started using heroin at age twelve. I experienced her as smart, confident, and scrappy—like she'd been plucked straight out of my childhood viewing of the original *Bad News Bears*. She didn't come across as a people pleaser, letting me know on many occasions that she "didn't give a fuck" what people thought about her.

While she held a tough exterior, rebuffing my attempts at gentle concern or education with some version of "I already know," I wondered what it might be like if she didn't *have* to know already. If she knew what that felt like at all.

Most of my early sessions with Sadie were about her relationship with her girlfriend, Margaret. Recall the altercation in which Sadie ran to escape Margaret's yelling, Margaret ripped her shirt, and they both started laughing. Their relationship was rife not just with this kind of physical altercation but with deceptive emotional abuse. If Sadie did something Margaret didn't like, Margaret would punish her—withholding sex or affection until Sadie appeased her the way she wanted. Sadie did not like the cycle she was trapped in, and she was determined to fix it. Skipping over any sort of vulnerability or curiosity, she came in knowing what she needed: "I just need to set better boundaries." She felt certain that if she could learn to speak up for herself, her partner wouldn't treat her in such a demeaning way.

As Sadie presented her goal of wanting to set better boundaries, I could see that it sounded like the right thing to do. Sadie wanted to take better care of herself. She felt tremendous shame for not doing so. But her partner wasn't getting therapy for *her* abusive behavior. Margaret had convinced Sadie that *she* (Sadie) was the one who needed fixing . . . and so here Sadie was, on my couch, trying to save the relationship by doing all the heavy lifting.

Sadie is the little girl who'd drawn herself with no arms, so of course she was going to struggle with boundaries and ways to protect herself. She was trying to solve a relational problem by taking all the blame. It was as though she thought if she could redraw her arms, her boundaries and the abuse would finally stop. It's a conception that many relational trauma survivors initially have of boundaries. If we find the right one, set it in the right way, we can get the other person to finally be good to us. Even our boundaries absolve others of any wrongdoing. For Sadie, this pattern stemmed from her childhood, when no one else took personal responsibility, so she learned to take it all on herself.

Originally from Florida, Sadie had a twin brother and parents who divorced when she was ten. At the time of our first appointment, she hadn't spoken with her neurosurgeon father in many years, saying people often referred to him as narcissistic and revealing that he molested her when she was little. She'd never worked on this in therapy before because she "always bailed" when the subject was brought up. She dissociated when she was made to tell the story. To this day, I don't know the details of Sadie's sexual abuse. But she didn't have to repeat the story to work with it somatically. Somatic Experiencing, a body-oriented trauma therapy we'll discuss more in chapter 6, allowed Sadie to be with the sensations in her body, to work with the energy that was trapped, without retraumatizing her in the process.

When it came to Sadie's mother, who had been a perennial patient for much of Sadie's childhood, Sadie told me her mother was often in bed. Sadie has countless memories of lying down next to her mom, hoping to stroke her hair. Sometimes it was welcomed, but sometimes Sadie was swatted away. If her gestures were allowed, Sadie's mom would praise her for being such a sensitive and wise girl. Then Sadie would stay for as long as her mom would have her, hoping to be held herself and to feel like everything was okay.

When she was twelve, Sadie told her mother about the sexual abuse from her father. Recalling this experience, she said:

> My mother immediately shut down. I called her "therapist" (an unlicensed spiritual healer) who came to the house and pried my mother's body off her bathroom floor. My mother was practically mute for several months. My claim of abuse was never addressed.
>
> When I attempted to confront my father at age fourteen . . . he responded, "I have no idea what you are talking about."
>
> I was often accused of lying or making up stories. After a weekend at my friend's house, my father picked me up and asked, "What lies did you tell about me this time?"

Sadie's experiences were not validated, and in turn she was made the cause of all the drama, turned into a liar, a troublemaker. The one who causes a fuss.

Her eating disorder became one way she coped with all these feelings that had nowhere else to go. She also began to drink and use drugs.

Eventually she found herself in twelve-step recovery.

While Sadie felt perpetually bad in romantic relationships, being a recovering addict allowed her to feel good, or at least like she could be seen as a whole person. Going to rehab and twelve-step groups provided ready-made support and a place to feel her feelings. Sadie thrived in these spaces, giving moving testimony of her transformation. Addiction recovery gave her language for her pain and compassion from people who understood.

The problem was, Sadie wasn't a heroin addict. She'd never tried heroin.

I remember the day she told me. Sitting on my vintage teal couch, her hands tightly tucked between her legs, Sadie said, "I have something to tell you," through a crooked smile that seemed to say, *I'm really nervous. Please don't be mad at me.*

"Okay." I tried to encourage her with a crooked smile of my own: *Let's do this.*

"I'm not a heroin addict. I've been lying about it."

It took me a minute to digest what she'd said. I certainly wasn't expecting this. And yet I understood where she was coming from and how that lie had served her.

As someone who got clean and sober very young myself, I knew what it was like to hear, "I spilled more alcohol than you ever drank." People often implied I couldn't have experienced the same level of devastation as them because of my age, and it infuriated me. It made me feel like I might not belong in the one place that was saving my life. While I never lied about using heroin, I lied about all sorts of other things, all for the same purpose as Sadie. To be seen, heard, valued, or taken care of. I never made up stories about other people. I made them up about me, in order to belong.

When Sadie showed up at rehab for debilitating marijuana use, her heroin-addicted peers and counselors didn't take that seriously. So she eventually shapeshifted into a version of someone who deserved help. She "became" a heroin addict.

She didn't set out to lie. The lies were involuntary—reflexively spilling out as a way to cope with the backlash (her struggles weren't bad enough), and when the body found relief, it wasn't going to let it go. She knew that all her feelings were real. Her pain was real. She just needed other people's opinions and judgment out of the way so she could feel them.

Somehow Sadie's actual story of being sexually abused by her father, being physically beaten by her mother, and attempting suicide several times by age seventeen was never taken that seriously. So she found something that was.

As she sat across from me that day, I felt grateful she felt safe enough to unburden herself of the lie. Safe enough to take this enormous risk, first with me and then with her support group. This is what unfawning often looks like in the beginning, telling a radical truth we didn't think we could tell (once enough internal and external safety has been established). A risk that feels bigger than we might survive. Many of my clients have referred to these moments as "jumping off a cliff," and boy, did Sadie jump.

In the jump, we were able to see what I've seen countless times. She was jumping into *herself.* Other people were becoming less of a necessary safety net. She previously felt, *I will die unless they catch me. I need to help them want to catch me.* She'd made it safe enough to see and own her true experience whether anyone else endorsed it or not. Although it was still incredibly scary, arrival in her true nature was profound.

This recognition allowed her to begin to see how maybe she didn't need Margaret to catch her the way she thought she did. After many months of on-again, off-again, Sadie was still struggling in her relationship, but a tiny opening was emerging. This shift, from *I need [this other person] to save me* to *Maybe I can save myself* can be so hard for trauma survivors to even conceive of, because for so many years, we *did* need others. We needed our parents. But Sadie was now living on her own, reliving the same dynamic of fear and appeasement from her devastating childhood. And she desperately wanted to stop.

During one session my body couldn't remain neutral in the face of what was clearly such a painful and destructive pattern. Sadie was working so hard, had come so far, and yet was still so stuck. I started to cry.

This wasn't some brilliantly timed intervention. This was my humanity bursting forth. I couldn't help myself. I said, "Honey, you aren't safe. You need to end this relationship for good."

She didn't have much reaction in the session. But the next time things escalated with Margaret, she escaped. She got in her car, drove away, and never went back.

Later, Sadie shared how she'd seen me as a motherly figure from the very start of our work together and how complicated that feeling was. Given her difficult relationship with her own mother, she often felt the need to keep me at bay, to be a "good client." Prior to that day, Sadie had never seen me cry, and she said it let her know how serious things were. Deep down she knew they were serious, but she could *feel* it when she saw it in me. I showed her my vulnerability, and it wasn't a ploy to get her to take care of me, like her mom would do. I was showing her how much I cared.

Feeling my genuine concern for her allowed her to know she was worthy of being taken care of. A major aspect of her ability to heal, of her ability to set the ultimate boundary that needed setting, was being seen and cared for by someone who was actually safe. She'd never had that before, and she felt the difference in her body. She felt the difference between setting boundaries to get someone to respect her and setting boundaries that actually protected her.

Although we have great capacity to heal on our own, there is a saying in trauma therapy: "Wounding happens in relationship, and healing happens in relationship."

Sadie recently sent me a quote from *Mother Hunger*, Kelly

McDaniel's book on attachment injury, that captures this beautifully: "the broken maternal relationship *is* the trauma. A safe relationship with one trustworthy adult *is* the cure. Once a safe relationship is established, trauma work might not even be necessary, because attachment healing *is* trauma healing."

Years after shedding the protective layer of "hard-core heroin addict," after leaving her relationship with Margaret, Sadie's tough exterior became softer. She started wearing her hair longer. She stopped rebutting my efforts at connection. Where before it looked like she never quite settled on the couch, she was actually sitting there with me, at ease.

I didn't see her consecutively over the decade I've known her. Whenever she came back, it was amazing to see how much more she'd become *herself*. One day she realized she wasn't an alcoholic, as she'd always thought. The next, she'd begun to date men.

Letting go of false identities eventually brought Sadie what she wanted all along—self-acceptance. In the arc of our therapy, I felt the shift from *my* feeling great affection toward her to her feeling it for herself, too.

Ten years later, Sadie has cut off contact with both parents and is moving in with her boyfriend. It's the loving, reciprocal, healthy relationship she always wanted and honestly thought she'd never have. While her eating disorder has waxed and waned, she can be present in her body, one she no longer hates.

She went back to school and has become a psychotherapist. Today, Sadie identifies as queer and feels she finally gets to be herself. She is living in congruence without lies, overcompensation, or shame.

Four

The Merry-Go-Round of Fawning

Cycles of Trauma Bonds and Reenactment

Like many fawners, I grew up in a dysfunctional family. I always knew this on some level, but I never truly recognized how my circumstances were impacting me and how I had to adapt to exist in the family I was born into. How I made the dysfunctional *functional*.

One of the best descriptions of childhood trauma comes from my friend and colleague Patrick Teahan. He is a fellow childhood trauma survivor, turned expert in the field. In an interview with Dr. Ramani Durvasula, he said, "A definitive symptom of childhood trauma is trying to get a difficult person to be good to us."

While I was growing up in my family, my survival instincts shaped my behavior, which formed my personality, which influenced my way of showing up in relationships. It's as though I was trying to crack a code. I could get the love I needed if I just exhibited the right behavior. I then carried this coping mechanism into all my future relationships.

When we're fawning, it's like we're circling a roundabout we can never get off. We don't see how our exit strategy of needing approval just keeps us stuck in the vortex.

We don't realize we're doing things we don't want to or that we deserve so much better. We're oriented toward the need we are attempting to meet, not the sacrifices we make to get there.

Even if we long for reciprocity and intimacy in our adult relationships, hoping our generosity will come back in some way, we don't notice that when we erase ourselves, the boomerang never comes back. So we offer sex we don't really want to keep the peace, pay for things we can't afford to garner favor, overextend and overfunction in a million different ways, all to feel okay.

Because fawning is a relational trauma response, while it manifests in an individual, it plays out relationally. Fawning perpetuates the patterns in which we learned to fawn. As a short-term intervention, fawning is hard to fault. But when we are stuck in a chronic fawn response, we are turning our lives over to the most primitive part of ourselves. Remaining in survival mode has serious long-term consequences.

There's a saying in trauma therapy: "Red flags don't look like red flags when they feel like home." In this chapter, we'll explore how fawning shows up in our relationship dynamics, how we repeat dysfunctional patterns, how even our relationship to sex becomes distorted through the lens of fawning.

This Time Will Be Different: *Trauma Reenactment*

Trauma reenactment refers to behaviors or relationship patterns associated with our trauma history that we repeat in subsequent relationships and circumstances. As opposed to a trauma trigger, where it *feels* like past traumatic events are happening now, in trauma reenactment, we re-create traumatic elements from our past, often unconsciously.

Some believe we reenact past events as a way to master them. It's like our bodies want a do-over, and we're drawn to the essential building blocks so we might work through past terror and helplessness in the present. However, it's important to note that while reenactment might initially feel hopeful—*this time will be different*—it rarely leads to resolution, as much as the same turmoil.

The brain likes what is familiar. In *How to Change Your Mind*, journalist Michael Pollan writes: "We approach experience much as an AI program does, with our brains continually translating the data of the present into the terms of the past, reaching back in time for the relevant experience, and then using that to make its best guess as to how to predict and navigate the future." This is true whether you have a history of trauma or not. But in my case, my history of dysfunctional relationships finally made sense to me when I could see how I was reenacting my traumatic past. How my body interpreted chaos as home and fawning helped to furnish it.

Sometimes our patterns map out over our specific trauma histories. For example, we're drawn to a particular type in relationships that trigger our attachment wounds. If you were neglected, you might unconsciously be drawn to unavailable partners. Trying to prove your worth, you chase their affections, ultimately pushing the unavailable person away, and the cycle comes full circle. If you were raised with unpredictability or volatility, you might be drawn to partners who are hot and cold, inconsistent, actively engaged in addiction. Again, these relationship patterns feel familiar. Thus they feel safe, even though they are anything but.

Trauma reenactment can also happen in paradoxical ways. In our efforts to prevent the overwhelming experiences of our past, we instinctively make decisions that backfire. For instance, if you were rejected by a primary caregiver, you might try to flip the script by partnering with people you feel are beneath you, warding off the possibility of rejection by someone you truly love. And yet the feelings of disconnection remain, through our unfulfilling relationships and perpetual loneliness.

Additionally, our coping mechanisms get repeated—in this case our fawning—reenacting patterns whether the environment calls for it or not. Trauma responses are like our bodyguards, the greatest protectors. And they legitimately keep us safe. But just as actual bodyguards don't know when the next threat might happen, our fawning stays stuck in the on position, just in case. There is a reason I refer to people stuck in a chronic fawn response as *fawners*. It becomes *who we are,* as protection from further harm.

Recall that an aspect of the fawn response is disconnecting from ourselves, our feelings, and reality. While this numbing leads to an ability to tolerate mistreatment and abuse, it also results in reenacting it, as we habitually block out or minimize bad behavior. While initially adaptive, this inhibits appropriate action in the present, and the past is reenacted again.

Hurts so Good: *Trauma Bonding*

As we read in Francis's story of her abusive relationship with Colin, trauma bonding occurs from intermittent reinforcement, creating a hormonal attachment to the person causing us harm. Fawning for Francis became an attempt to both mitigate the harm and stay attached to her boyfriend at the same time. Dr. Bessel van der Kolk writes about this issue: "Adults, as well as children, may develop strong emotional ties with people who intermittently harass, beat, and threaten them. The persistence of these attachment bonds leads to confusion of pain and love." In other words, survivors of abuse can learn to believe that love and pain go hand in hand. In fact, you saw in both Sadie's and Francis's stories that they were trapped in abusive relationships but couldn't see it. The abuse, the belittling, the pain— it was synonymous with love.

Emotional abuse often perpetuates trauma bonding. Consider the following tactics of emotional abuse:

- **Gaslighting:** Manipulation designed to make someone question their reality.
- **Future faking:** Promises of a better future with no real ability or intention to carry it out.
- **Love bombing:** A barrage of gifts, compliments, and attention, idealizing you and the relationship as "a match made in heaven," whether it's romantic or not.
- **Hoovering:** Behaviors employed to suck a person back into a toxic relationship. These can include love bombing and gaslighting as well as things like using your family and friends to reestablish the relationship, creating a crisis that requires your attention, threatening violence, or making false apologies that sound apologetic but are in truth manipulations to get you back.

Ultimately, we can interpret these tactics as love, thinking we have butterflies, when our unsettling feelings are more related to dysregulation. We are unable to see how we are stuck in a cycle of abuse. Signs of a trauma bond include:

- On-and-off relationships, or with lots of ups and downs.
- Justifying the bad times because the good is "so good."
- Seeking comfort/support/validation from the person who is hurting you.
- Knowing things are bad but waiting/hoping for them to get better.
- Feeling isolated from supportive family or friends.
- Hiding the painful truths of your relationship with others.
- Feeling like you'll die without the other person, like you need them to survive.
- Taking blame for their abuse—for example, "You made me mad because you were so selfish."
- Trying to help the person who is hurting you.

You might notice some of these are also signs of the fawn response. While fawning isn't a necessary component to trauma bonding, I believe it's a common response to it. Our behaviors and self-concept rise and fall along with the intensity of the intermittent reinforcement. In this context, fawning can make us feel like we have the power to shift someone from hating us to loving us. As though we're powerful sorcerers with magical qualities, we can transport ourselves and the other person to another (albeit temporary) reality. This feeling of power, when we feel so powerless in the rest of our lives, is one element that makes trauma bonding so intoxicating.

The truth is, it was easy to hate Randy for ignoring or punishing me. I could see myself strictly as his victim. It was harder to understand my feelings when he stopped. When he brought me back into the fold. I would find myself forgiving his abuses in exchange for moments of his favor. Even then, I was aware that they came at a price, but they were monumentally preferable to feeling invisible and despised.

Fawning didn't just help me survive the bad moments; it made me feel like I could stretch out the good. And it perpetuated my trauma reenactment and trauma bonding cycles.

The Homing Pigeon

Fresh off a failed marriage in my late thirties, I found myself in a familiar—if not heightened—scenario. I was dating a sociopathic lawyer and trying very hard to make him my boyfriend.

He held power over me like a cat's toy, dangling his affections just out of reach while occasionally allowing me to feel victorious. I knew he was playing games, and part of me hated him for it. But another part of me took on the challenge with an instinctual drive to prove my *own* power.

I'd known this man for a couple of weeks when he showed up at the door of my Los Angeles apartment in the middle of the night. With boyish charm, he said, "It's like I was a homing pigeon, and my car started driving instinctively toward your place." His shiny new convertible was parked outside, and he stood before me, sheepishly staring down at his overnight bag.

Flattered by the notion of being his home, I was equally puzzled by his presence. I lingered in the doorway as I saw his innocent blue eyes turn to stone. "Are you going to keep me standing here all night?" he asked, his voice laced with contempt.

Even though I was confused about why he was there, he quickly spun me into self-doubt. *I don't want to be rude.* "Come on in" spilled nervously from my lips. He visibly softened as he crossed the threshold. "I didn't mean to wake you," he cooed. "Let me tuck you in." Relief flooded my body as I welcomed the return of his adoration. *I'm safe.*

I found myself back under the covers as he perched on the side of my bed. Cozy beneath his tender gaze, I noticed his tone becoming confessional. "Most women can't handle my complexity," he said. "You have a rare combination of intellect, empathy, and beauty."

I felt like an irresistible heroine, and it was exhilarating.

The Homing Pigeon shared that he'd been disappointed by countless other women. He thought I might be the one to truly understand him. I was relishing the opportunity when he looked down and said, "I could cut you into a million pieces and have no feelings about it."

He meant it. And faced with his body builder's physique, I had no doubt he could do it. I saw a vision of myself, disassembled like a doll, pieces piled high in my bathtub. But instead of being horrified, I focused on the fact that he could tell me this horrific truth. This was his version of vulnerability. My body interpreted what he was saying as "I want to change, and you're the only one who can help me."

While this experience was deeply disturbing, it was also exciting. Endowed with his trust, I felt like a modern-day Beauty who could tame the unruly Beast with her unconditional love, never understanding how my unresolved trauma formed the basis for this "chemistry." How the trauma bond and my fawn response convinced *me* that I wanted to both help and be with this man.

I genuinely believed—hoped—he could change. Then I would be safe *for good*. All he needed was a genius therapist. Of course it couldn't be me, because I was under some sort of spell, trying to make him my boyfriend. My credentials as a PhD and licensed psychologist with decades of my own introspective work were of no use. Besides, good sense and a proper code of ethics told me he should explore his interest in dismemberment elsewhere.

And then there was the sex. I didn't yet understand how adrenaline from a fight-or-flight response mimics the feelings of sexual desire. Elevated heart rate and blood pressure blur the lines between terror and attraction. The steady course of stress hormones in my bloodstream awakened every nerve ending. Exalted by his attention, I would levitate for prolonged periods—until he withdrew his devotion, reminding me the upper hand belonged solely to him. Then I would plunge down a shame spiral into a reservoir of inadequacy, longing to ascend to great heights once again.

While not all fawners find themselves dating sociopaths, my experience illustrates the self-abandonment that happens so seamlessly in this trauma response. It shows the power I believed I held in moments when I was actually in danger. For so long in my life, my desire to help people who were hurting me seemed like my only defense.

Like many fawners, I couldn't act upon red flags because they were on-ramps to my helpfulness, which was essentially my currency. In the lens and language of trauma, my *safety*.

My body felt like I was always moving toward a finish line—like I'd finally arrive at the healthy relationship of my dreams. But fawning meant most of me was back at the starting line. And although this man was a lawyer, a company vice-president, and his intelligence and success ticked important boxes on my potential partner list, these aspects of who he was would never override the rest.

I knew when the Homing Pigeon was lying or setting emotional traps, but the complexity of our dance felt utterly compelling. I became obsessed with trying to win a game designed to devour me, mistakenly imagining that my awareness of the danger offered immunity to it.

He sent me texts clearly meant for other women but made me feel crazy when I suggested it. One morning he said, "My home is your home, and I have nothing to hide. If you ever need a pen, feel free to look in any drawer." Hours later, I searched for a pen only to find hoop earrings and a note from Maria thanking him for a recent good time.

Humiliated, I texted my girlfriends: *Can you believe this?* Then I promptly tucked away those feelings. I reminded myself he hadn't agreed to exclusivity, so he wasn't technically doing anything wrong. And I didn't dare find out how he'd twist my discovery into a personal failing—likely comparing me to Maria while ridiculing us both.

The Homing Pigeon didn't hide his hatred of women, yet I aspired to be the exception.

Being chosen by someone with this sort of psychopathy can make you feel exceptionally adored—at least in certain moments.

That early morning visit from the Homing Pigeon wasn't the first time I'd heard deeply disturbing things from a man. I was sixteen when I found Randy perched on the side of my parents' waterbed. It was after our trip to Vegas, but before he'd left a note on my pillow and I'd told my school counselor. We were the only two people at home, and he asked me to sit down. Then, seemingly stone cold sober, he began professing his love to me.

I couldn't believe it. I had no idea that he was aware of how fucked up his relationship with me truly was. Until this moment, everything was veiled, he'd always had a simple explanation for his behavior. This was different. My gaze became fixed on my long brown bangs that partially obstructed my view as I heard him say, "We are kindred souls, and I want to give you the world. I know these feelings are wrong. They are not the feelings one has for a daughter."

The wooden bed frame dug into the back of my legs, and I was starting to feel pins and needles in my toes. I hoped the numbness would start spreading toward my chest as he shared that his overwhelming love and longing led him to guilt and despair.

His clarity was astounding, but I knew he wasn't looking for forgiveness. He was looking for permission. "I have feelings for you, too," was the response he'd hoped for. I stared down at my lifeless legs, unable to move. My body was moving deeper into hypoarousal, hopeless, sluggish.

Then, intuitively knowing I couldn't shut down completely—I had to prioritize his needs—I tucked my hair behind my ear, lifted my head, and said, "I'm glad you are talking about these feelings, but I'm probably not the appropriate person to tell."

I still can't believe I spoke those words so articulately, because what I was really thinking was *Go to therapy, fucking asshole! This is the most inappropriate conversation I've ever had!*

This is the incongruence of fawning.

Although it appeared like I was understanding and caring, this was a mask for the terror lying beneath. True self-expression is trapped when we are fawning, or it's allowed only in small doses. Finding a shred of safety in a predatory relationship is always the priority, trumping self-esteem, self-care, or honoring ourselves as separate beings in any way. This is why boundaries don't just feel impossible, they can feel like life-or-death. Setting a boundary would elevate stakes that are already too high. We need to bring the stakes *down* in order to survive.

It's important to note that sometimes we don't just appear to be understanding, we *are* understanding. We are caring, thoughtful, empathic, and patient. But these are still shrouding our own needs. We can't exhibit these same attributes on our own behalf.

Despite my attempts to express gratitude for Randy's candor and to redirect his honesty elsewhere, he was wounded. His emotional pendulum swung to fury, and he stood up to leave, staring back at me through pools of hatred.

This evoked another surprising response: I didn't want him to go. I detested his advances, but the inevitable months of angry silent treatment while he convinced my mother I was the enemy were worse. And I grew into a woman who didn't believe she deserved real kindness or that it came at much too high a price. I chose unkind and unavailable men time and time again, hoping I could convince them to stay and to love me. Hoping I could be enough for them to stop treating me badly. I got off the merry-go-round with my stepdad only to step onto my own ride, unable to see straight for twenty more years.

Dating a sociopath and powerless to stop it, I worried that *I* was the Homing Pigeon, instinctively flying over hundreds of miles and decades of my life directly into a familiar feeling of home. But that home was constantly terrifying. One where I believed I had to save someone in order to be loved.

It wasn't until I sought the guidance of my friend Bill that I finally came out of the Homing Pigeon's spell. Part of me was hoping Bill would say I was being dramatic. "It's unsettling dating someone with that much confidence," he might say, "but it's helping you grow."

"Run," Bill said when I asked for his thoughts. "Run as fast as you can. This man is dangerous, and he will hurt you." Bill said anyone who questioned my worth couldn't see it. My gut knew he was right, but I wasn't ready or able to end it. That's what a spell will do.

"Can you pray for the willingness to let this relationship go?" Bill suggested.

Sitting in a crowded café, I closed my eyes. I took a breath and silently began asking for the willingness to break up with the Homing Pigeon. When I was done, I paused to see if anything had changed. Nope, I felt the exact same way.

"I trust your process," Bill said.

"Great," I responded. "So I can take him to the barbecue tomorrow?"

Three days later, I woke up at two a.m., composing a breakup email in my head. When I realized what was happening—this window of self-worth emerging, my becoming who I needed *me* to be— I went to my desk and started typing while I still had the courage. I was careful with my words, trying to minimize the backlash (more fawning), and then, before I could change my mind, I hit send.

The Homing Pigeon was livid. I knew he would be. I broke up with him by email in the middle of the night. But I couldn't have done it in person. If we were together, the fog would've settled, and I'd have lost myself again.

In his response, he derided me one moment and tried to talk me out of leaving the next. My friends worried about my safety, but I believed he'd never expose a weakness like hurting me over a broken heart. That belief changed when he sent a photograph of his swollen purple hand along with an X-ray from the ER.

"I punched a utility box," he texted.

He was asking for sympathy, and I felt my internal caregiver perking back up, the one who needed to save him in order to save herself.

This childlike part of me truly believed I had to help the people who were hurting me. That I *needed their approval to survive.* So I soaked up the responsibility and shame for the entire system, attempting to raise my caregivers as though I were raising myself. But in this moment, feeling just enough separation from my instinctual drive to fawn, a part of me finally felt like I could cut out the middleman. I could just take care of myself. I could stop proving my worth and step into it.

The very next person I dated was my now-husband, Yancey. When we first met in 2013, I didn't have that "all systems go" spark I was used to experiencing, so I thought we were meant to be friends. Now I understand those particular sparks I'd once thought were essential in a new relationship were better at predicting insanity than healthy chemistry.

I was definitely attracted to Yancey, and I loved being in his presence. Early in our relationship, we took a road trip up to Big Bear for the Fourth of July. After an incredible weekend of relaxing by the lake, experiencing *all* the fireworks, I was dropping him off at home when we turned to each other like, "Well, what are you doing tonight?" Even three days together wasn't enough. We wanted to be together all the time.

With Yancey, there were no games. In fact, I often joked he had no game. After all my relationships with people who were unavailable, often based on distrust and disrespect, this felt so different. Yancey is kind. He is unpretentiously himself. He is funny, curious, and so damn smart. More important, I was not on edge with him, but at ease. I could let go. It was my first time fully experiencing relational safety and reciprocity.

I now know that it's possible to have deep love and companionship—a noncombustible magnetism—without all the madness. I know who I am without the drive to compulsively caretake. It's possible to break free from destructive patterns; it's possible to find a new place within ourselves to call home. It took me years to break free from these trauma bonds, but much of the heaviness of my past is finally where it belongs—*in the past*—and it's like I'm truly soaring.

The F Word: *Sexual Fawning*

When I was a PhD candidate, trauma responses were considered to be fight, flight, and freeze. Long before we had the language of fawning, I was settling in for class one morning when I overheard several students talking.

"You know what the fourth F of trauma responses is, right?"

After some silence, they continued, "Fight, flight, freeze, and fuck."

Our professor was shuffling papers on his desk as he started nodding, "There's truth to that."

Nervous laughter peeled through the early risers, and that was the end of it.

"Let's get started."

The actual material for that day's lecture resembled nothing like this preamble, and it's the only moment in graduate school when I recall such a conversation.

Like many jokes, it was funny only because it was *true*. Everyone in that room knew what those students were talking about. To fuck in the face of fear, to lean into one's sexuality because it's the only power they've experienced having, to have sexual encounters whether one wants them or not—to avoid something worse or gain what they need—these are universal experiences, especially for women who've been taught that sexuality is their only form of power.

Backed into countless corners and then blamed for the ingenious ways we've adapted, women have been sexualized, then called sluts; victimized, then scapegoated; never seen as whole people with bodies reflexively keeping us safe, for good reason.

Fawners in particular can turn to sex as a form of currency, as a way to please, appease, and shapeshift into the ultimate form of desire, often at real costs to their physical bodies, self-esteem, and values. Some fawners have been labeled as promiscuous or sex addicts.

But most weren't desperate for sex as much as they were desperate for subsistence. Wishing to be relieved of their strings, fawners are like Pinocchio—waiting to be made *real*. This makes the entire concept of consent a difficult one. Are we saying yes to a particular sex act or to the possibility of being free?

Although she fawned with everyone in positions of authority, Francis said it happened with boys and men in particular. They *were* the authority by patriarchal standards, so armed with her good looks and ability to be provocative, Francis became who men wanted her to be.

Her sense of self was cobbled together with countless images and examples she'd received on how to be desirable. She noticed how women in music videos touched their hair, what men said in movies about what they thought was sexy. Francis learned to mimic, weaving hundreds of cues from the environment into herself as a masterpiece of magnetism.

Meanwhile, she never knew her own desires—if she even wanted to touch her hair, or what she liked in general—she just needed to be wanted.

Francis tried to be alluring—showing she wasn't afraid to give hand jobs on the party bus to the bar mitzvah. While this could've been budding sexuality and the experimentation arising from puberty, Francis made it clear this didn't come from curiosity or genuine interest in a boy.

She didn't enjoy being touched; she was just relieved to know she had *skin*, like a boy's adoration was the thing that held her together. These exploits were never about shared intimacy or Francis's pleasure. The focus was on the pleasure of the other person, the status or safety their affections might bring, as though Francis couldn't exist without them.

These boys would ghost her for days and then sleep with her on the weekends. They'd be assholes most of the time, and yet she still had to chase. And when she was painfully and awkwardly fingered by them, she made them think it was "amazing."

The truth is, Francis didn't know what physical intimacy was supposed to feel like, what she should ask for, or even that she could ask. She knew only how to perform.

Francis is like so many women who were raised to prioritize the needs of men. Many girls were never taught about *their* right to pleasure. Sex education has been focused on safe sex (also a woman's job) and penetration specifically. Whether women want sex or what kind of sex they might be interested in seems to have entered the chat only quite recently.

Because I had been sexualized by my stepfather in puberty, my sexuality became intrinsically tied to my worth. It often felt like my only power or the sole sure path to acceptance. I would flirt when I wasn't attracted or interested, playing into someone's fantasy while hoping to keep them at bay. This led to countless boundary crossings by older, married, inappropriate men. I was always shocked when they eventually crossed a line, never understanding how or why I was being pursued this way, or how at times I was reenacting my trauma.

I wanted to fawn just enough, as though I could find the sweet spot of proximity, gain their acceptance without their overtures. But I never struck the right balance, at least not for very long.

When I talked with Francis about the extent of her sexual fawning, she mentioned a relationship in her early twenties. Francis was having "great sex," but her boyfriend didn't prioritize or really care for her. He *said* he loved her, but only after he'd cheated.

Fawning sexually as the only way to connect, Francis got recurrent urinary tract infections (UTIs). Even though these caused intense pain, like razor blades were slicing her cervix, she was afraid of losing her boyfriend, so she'd have sex anyway. This led to the equivalent of an ulcer inside her bladder. She was on multiple medications, going for weekly excruciating treatments of bladder installations—but sex was her place of safety. She needed it like oxygen.

Throughout her life, Francis had more sex she didn't want to have than sex she did. She's had sex without protection—so she wouldn't "ruin the moment" or bring down her partner's sensation.

When partners took a condom off without asking or telling her, she was upset but couldn't get mad. She eventually took it as they intended her to—an accident, no big deal.

She couldn't tell future partners she had human papillomavirus (HPV), unable to take care of them because she couldn't take care of herself. Hard conversations fall low on the hierarchy of needs when it comes to finding safety through sex.

Fawners struggle with boundaries because when they do attempt to set these, they are often shamed, harassed, or threatened. Sometimes the person can even turn things around, pretending that the fawner is delusional. "I wasn't hitting on you. Why would you think that?" Additionally, fawners hold a perpetual fear of hurting people's feelings by asserting their own needs or desires. Sacrificing relational harmony, *even in relationships we no longer want,* feels terrifying, so fawners stay. We stay in bed. We sacrifice our bodies for other, vital needs.

With every client, friend, or colleague I've spoken to about sexual fawning, the conversations are animated. "I know what you're talking about" is quickly followed by countless personal examples. Many share the same stories: never having had an orgasm or not for many years into their sexual lives, never masturbating—*does my body even deserve pleasure?* Having sex with a tampon in, pretending to come at the same time as a partner, finding identity in being good in bed.

There is nothing wrong with being sexual or good in bed, but in hindsight, fawners were seeking security more than sexual experience. Seeking a relational need or attention *through* sex.

When I brought up sexual fawning with Grace, my client who loved living as if she were on a tightrope, we were shocked when we realized we'd been working together for sixteen years and hadn't talked about sex the entire time.

Grace remembered an early appointment when I asked about her sex life, and she said, "I have no issues there." She thought, *I like sex, I'm having sex, there's nothing to talk about.* It was only when I brought sex up in the context of fawning that she was like, "Ohhhh, yeah." She'd been managing her sexuality for so long, she couldn't even see where she'd been fawning in that area, too.

While Francis faked a million orgasms, Grace faked *not* having them. But for the same reason: She wanted sex to be all about her partner.

For Grace, it was because she wasn't comfortable having needs. When she was younger, if a partner asked if she came, she'd say, "Don't worry about me, I'm fine." Or she lied, saying, "I don't have orgasms, let's just take care of you," when she'd already had one. She did this to avoid her partner's potential judgment: Did she take too long? Did she come too quickly? Grace is the child who learned not to have preferences, to de-escalate at all costs, to shapeshift to become what the situation warranted. Of course, this manifested in her sex life, too. She didn't want to have needs. She wanted to be the exact person her partner wanted her to be.

While she and I didn't talk about sex, we did talk about body dysmorphia. How she really believed her body was misshapen. Grace remembered her dad walking behind her and her boyfriend when she was a teenager, saying, "How do you feel about your legs being bigger than his?" She consciously thought, *My dad is an asshole.* But she also thought, *He's right.*

She told me she had sex only with the lights off. How when she was younger, she was always happy to perform oral sex but never wanted it in return. She paused and considered this. "You know, I bet all fawners give good head!" We laughed as we acknowledged that yes, that was likely a comfortable state for fawners, on their knees, attending to others, not themselves.

Although the focus on others has fawners feeling *so available*, we were never truly intimate, because we weren't sharing our true selves. Grace was often thinking more about the shape of her body during intimacy, how it might look to others. Fawners are often dissociated from their bodies, from the sex they are having. We can't focus on what might feel good because we aren't fully there.

While sex is often performative, fawners do this to an extreme for the sake of their partner. Sometimes to the exclusion of any sexual pleasure, even during real pain.

In all my years of sitting on therapists' couches, I never knew I needed to work with a trauma therapist. As a young adult, I didn't know how to ask a therapist what they specialized in. I just looked up "therapist" and showed up, like whoever held that title possessed all the answers. But working with therapists who didn't understand trauma meant they couldn't help me make deeper connections to how my current actions were stemming from my troubled past. They couldn't give me accurate language or tools for my life because they saw things through a different lens—like the one that said I had a broken picker.

I've heard the same claim countless times from clients, and they've tried a million remedies. They know their attachment style, have a list of red flags. They've journaled their hearts out and see their patterns. They've highlighted articles about their worth or their power, and it feels empowering until . . . all of it falls flat.

The solutions seemed so practical: Become more self-aware. Prioritize values over common interests. Prioritize friendship over romance. Stay single for a certain amount of time. Keep sex out of a relationship for a time. Write a list of attributes you need in a partner. Say positive affirmations. Go to therapy. And all these efforts can become part of the same vicious cycle.

The idea of a broken picker places the problem, once again, on the individual, as though they are inherently flawed. As if they are a bad apple.

These ideas perpetuate our reenactments. Being told you are broken and then trying to be good plays into the subtle and not-so-subtle power dynamics you are trying to navigate differently. Notions of "You are broken, but I can fix you if you just try a little harder" or "You are unhealed, but I am whole and can help you" imply someone else has all the answers, and that person needs to save you from yourself.

While the problems fawners encounter are very real, labeling them as personal abnormalities hurts those who are looking for help. The *symptoms* of the problem live in us now and we do need to address them, sometimes with the help of other people. But the *origin* of these problems is relational trauma—the operative word being *relational*.

We've spent long enough thinking we are the problem. And we've also wasted a lot of time trying to change the other guy. Though it isn't our fault, we've gotten trapped in the trauma vortex. We have the power to change, and we deserve to feel free.

As we move into the following chapters, we are leaving old methods of chasing our tails behind. Shedding ideas of being the problem and stepping into our own power. Gaining access to our body and our own authority over it. Deciding what we want or don't. Finding the internal safety to say, "No thank you," and mean it. Experiencing relief in not leading with—or being celebrated solely for—our sexuality, our submissiveness, our adaptations.

Fawning

As we lean into the unfawning section of this book, we are moving away from centripetal forces, out of someone else's orbit. We are establishing ourselves as forces of nature. Prioritizing loving relationships with *ourselves* and with *others*, because we have finally found safety within.

For What It's Worth

• • •

Trauma bonds and reenactments occur anywhere there is a power differential, anytime we are *relating*. In other words, everywhere. As safety resides outside of our bodies, fawners struggle to hold on to ourselves: our time, our money, our worth.

It can feel like we are Goldilocks, knowing papa's chair is too big, baby's chair is too small, but the only version of "just right" is when we can see, without a doubt, that no one else wants our chair. No one is more deserving of it or will criticize us for taking it. Everyone must agree: "Go ahead. Take the damn chair."

We don't believe we deserve a chair.

So much of our trauma has been about being unworthy of validation, being seen or believed, being taken care of. Our trauma encompasses being told we were too much, to get over it, to change who we *are*.

We have had to prove ourselves over and over and over again in order to feel worthy of love. Worth is the wound. That *is* the trauma.

It's like someone with a broken arm was never given the support to heal. They have no cast, and their broken arm is just hanging loose, getting hit day in and day out. We look at that person and say, "Why can't you just let it go?"

We don't feel worthy because we were told *YOU AREN'T WORTHY.* This distorts our self-perception.

If we want people to feel worthy, we have to stop asking them to justify their pain. To get over it. To stop saying, "Was it really that bad? Can't you just buck up?"

"Why do you sabotage yourself?"

"Why can't you see how great you are?"

"Why would you care what someone else thinks about you?"

While these phrases may appear caring at first, asking us to get over it again and again is retraumatizing. Yes, we are reenacting our trauma, but let me be clear. So is everyone else.

Feeling like you have to prove your worth isn't just a personal problem. This is a problem that originates in our culture, in our families, in generations of families bucking up and surviving. Only a generation ago teachers physically punished their students, whacking their hands with rulers, and we acted like it was normal. It's like our parents telling us their war stories: "I used to have to walk three miles to school in the pouring rain, so you can wait five minutes at the bus stop!" No, hold up. I'm sorry you had to do that. That must have felt exhausting. Did you ever feel scared? Did you ever get a break? But no, because they don't want to acknowledge their trauma, they won't let us feel ours. And the cycle continues.

Only a generation ago we had separate bathrooms for people of color, separate water fountains, separate places to sit on the bus. And we wonder why some of us struggle with worth? Until 1954, our schools were legally required to be segregated. Feeling inferior was sanctioned by the U.S. government.

My clients have been told in a million ways as children, from breakfast to bedtime, that they were not worthy. Then they stepped into their lives, attempting to meet the demands of being a fully functioning adult in the world. But they'd missed out on a key aspect of a healthy childhood: a secure attachment, knowing that someone loved them just the way they were and that they were inherently safe. While fawning allowed them to become whatever they needed to be to gain attachment and security, it also created an ever-moving finish line. Because their worth remained OUT THERE, they could never fully feel it inside.

It left them striving, hoping to arrive but feeling it was never, ever enough.

I worked to earn a million different degrees, even a PhD, all to show the world that I was okay. But it never fulfilled this deeper need. Some of my clients have been unable to achieve their goals despite their sheer brilliance. They don't understand why they keep hitting a wall. But at either end of the spectrum lies the same issue: *I don't feel worthy.* On one end, we don't feel worthy, so we can't stop succeeding. On the other, we don't feel worthy, so we can't achieve success.

I now see our struggle for worth as two sides of a coin. Fawners are either seeking approval or escaping annihilation . . . and often the coin keeps flipping. We seek approval and then gain it! Yay! Mission accomplished! But right when we feel accepted, we start to fear it will end. Thus we start fawning and contorting ourselves to escape what feels like inevitable criticism or backlash. Back and forth, top to bottom, bottom to top, the coin flips. Because our worth, that tricky, slippery thing, exists outside of us. It is granted only by others, never held by ourselves.

This struggle shows up often in our careers and with our finances. Because we find safety in our smallness, success can make us feel too big. Thus we overwork without compensation. We don't ask for raises or what we're already owed. Just grateful to be part of a team, we allow others to take credit for our work. We can't risk relational safety with bosses or colleagues, so we go along to get along. We don't charge what we are worth. If we ask for something once, we feel that's already too much, so then we shrink. All in fear that people might be mad or think we aren't worth it.

Our blinders have us not seeing toxic workplaces or our lack of connection to a job, not realizing we've disconnected from ourselves to serve a paycheck. We think, *Not everyone gets to work their dream job.* But the truth is, we've never tried. And if we did, we weren't fully online in a regulated way to show up for it.

It's time to stop blaming ourselves for these patterns. This is not a personal failing. This is a reaction to complex trauma.

Fawners often have conflicted relationships with money. We don't know our account balances, our debt, our log-on passwords. We often hold fantasies, just as in relationships, in which our financial status will get better any minute now. Our debts will be forgiven; someone else will manage the money; we will finally BE TAKEN CARE OF FOR REAL. We can't show up as an authority in our financial lives any more than we can anywhere else. Why would we somehow know how to hold, spend, and earn in this one area?

Money signals worth and power, and we equate being big as having power OVER. Power is blended with exploitation, manipulation, abuse. Of course we don't want to step into that energy.

So instead of holding money and accumulating wealth, fawners sometimes shed it like a snake shedding skin. We use money to extend our caretaking and appeasement tendencies, feeling like our relational needs can be met only if we are over-giving. Money is an easy way to take care of people, to show that we care, to show our value in our relationships.

Author Elizabeth Gilbert recently talked about this tendency on Marie Forleo's podcast. Liz, perhaps best known for her mega-bestselling memoir *Eat, Pray, Love,* recalled that she was "such a ferocious black-belt codependent that when I got money, I started wildly giving it away." Like a perpetual fairy godmother to all who entered her orbit, Liz said she "poured a great deal of herself away into the people she loved, and called that love."

Later in her life, attempting to bring more emotional sobriety into her finances, she began working with a financial therapist, someone who could see the numbers, but also what was behind them. After reviewing two years of Liz's spending, the financial therapist asked Liz how much she thought she was giving away. Liz imagined it was 25 percent. In reality? It was 82 percent.

If someone wants to give all their money away, I'm not here to fault them! But like so many themes in this book, it's less about the specific choice as it is making the choice consciously, from a place of agency, self-respect, and wholeness. We aren't being generous if it's at our own expense. Just as it is true in sexual fawning that there is no self in the sex, in financial fawning, there is no self in the spending.

Rather than seeing money and success as a hot potato, we have to learn to hold it, tolerate it, appreciate it as deservedly ours. Just like we need to find our voices, learn to have boundaries, and engage in healthy conflict, we need to grow our capacity to be visible and abundant financially, without its feeling threatening to our emotional well-being. Without its feeling unsafe.

This is easier said than done. The unfawning process is just that, a process. There is no finish line. Unfawning will happen in layers, in stages, an evolution over time of becoming more and more yourself. Unfawning is a lifelong quest to trust what is within more and more.

But feeling worthy in a capitalist society that measures worth in dollars and accolades is a challenge even for those who do not have complex trauma. The journey of unfawning is about tuning less into outward applause and more into inner alignment. That is when we begin to feel our worth, when we can trust that we are already worthy, have always been so at our core—beautiful, brilliant, adaptive creatures that deserve to be loved just the way we are.

Mia

Mia is blond and blue-eyed, with a literal twinkle in her eye. You can tell when you meet her that she's a force to be reckoned with. Often wearing a Patagonia pullover, she obviously possesses great strength, but it's paired with her openheartedness. She is feisty and yet has the sweetest, youngest soul at the very same time.

As one of the first women to summit several peaks as a free soloist, Mia is a total badass. And yet the level of strength and self-assurance it took to accomplish these goals does not align with how she often experiences herself in the world. As we explored these contradictions alongside her trauma history, Mia had a realization: "When I was climbing all alone, it occurred to me that one of the reasons it was so powerful is that it was probably the only time in my life I did not have to fawn. There was no one there for me to fawn for, and I FINALLY got to feel what it was like to truly be myself." Mia is powerful, creative, and bold. She knows she is a force, and yet "I can't be forceful in other areas of my life." Our work has focused on healing this split.

Mia came from a wealthy yet dysfunctional family and a father who gave each of his children a healthy nest egg when they turned twenty-one. She later received a hefty divorce settlement. It was more money than she could ever need. And yet it was largely gone by the time she was fifty and began working with me.

When Mia told me the amount of money she'd been given, along with the fact that she "blew through it," she was mortified. She said something was *wrong with her,* and she was deeply ashamed. As her family expected, she wanted to excel, strive for excellence in every way. There was no reason for her *not* to. And yet her spending and lack of earning over the years were evidence that she was not.

Mia is the only client presented in this book whom I started working with after I published my memoir. She found me online, where I was sharing my story as a therapist, but not with a buttoned-up "all better now" narrative. I was leading with my humanity, the reality of what it means to be living with unresolved trauma and trauma responses, and she was deeply attracted to it. "You had the freedom to be flawed and open about it. I really wanted to live like that."

Mia had previously tried therapy, coaching, online courses, and graduate school. She was obsessed with self-help books. She told me she'd been searching for answers for a long time but was starting to see that "I wasn't actually trying to heal. I was trying to seem better so people would think I was normal."

Much of our therapy has been focused on bringing our attention back to Mia—her body, her sensations, her feelings. Rather than aiming for normal, I would ask her, "What are you noticing now?" Especially in the beginning, she said, "I can't do that." She didn't have the awareness or language to tune in to her body, so the answers weren't available. All of Mia's focus was external. She knew what everyone else was thinking, what they were feeling, what they wanted her to fix.

She intellectually understood the importance of what I was asking. She wanted to connect with herself, but her body did not feel safe. She experienced only her judgment of herself: *You can't luxuriate in your feelings, you have to perform!* In fact, if she was to notice herself, feel her feelings, recall a memory, this inspired the immediate need to root it out! "God, now I have to fix this, too!"

Mia wanted to be normal but had a childhood that was anything but.

She is eldest of five siblings who share the same parents. Her dad additionally had three children in his first marriage. Mia was the golden child of them all, defusing her father's moods. Her dad often said, "I just like you near me. Your presence makes me feel better."

Mia's dad was mercurial and an alcoholic. "You never knew if he was going to be the best, coolest guy or the one who would rip you a new asshole." Physical violence was a real threat in her family. One time she and her siblings had tied a climbing rope to one of the trees in their backyard when her sisters started fighting over who got to go first. One sister started hitting the other with the end of the rope. When their dad heard the yelling, he took the rope, grabbed Mia's eldest sister, and hauled her inside before whipping her with it behind a closed door.

Running to the door, banging as hard as she could, Mia tried to make it stop. Her eldest sister still remembers that Mia was the only one who tried to help, while their mom was hiding in another room.

When I asked Mia about her mother, she said, "Talk about a fawner." Everything she did was to perform, to make her husband happy, to not piss him off or create issues. Mia said her mom is a full-time fawner to this day. She's either shapeshifting or caretaking others, or a hermit in her house to be relieved of those duties.

Mia knew she had a difficult childhood, but she didn't realize how difficult it had been until she was in her twenties. She was watching an episode of *Oprah*, about how Oprah had experienced childhood sexual abuse and how she'd spent so much time and energy overriding, overachieving, being all things to all people.

Listening to Oprah's attempts to feel okay, Mia realized that this had been her experience.

She had not identified herself as a survivor of childhood sexual abuse. But in that moment, a memory resurfaced. Mia's half brother from her father's first marriage, who was ten years older than her, sexually abused her when she was a little girl. At first she thought it had occurred only one time, but then more memories came to her. She now knows the abuse lasted for eight years, starting when Mia was five years old.

It is not uncommon for child sexual abuse survivors to have no explicit memory of their abuse or to recall it only many years later. Most survivors carry implicit memory, sensations, or emotions reminiscent of the events (for Mia, it was a feeling of knowing she wasn't okay).

She didn't tell anyone in her family about the abuse until a year after she'd recalled it. She was hiking a single-track trail directly behind her mom when she revealed the secret that her half brother had molested her. Mia's mom responded, "I'm not surprised. And by the way, you have another brother."

Rather than validate the horrible experience Mia had just divulged, her mother launched into more family secrets: Three years before Mia was born, when her mother was seventeen, she'd had a son. Sent to a home for unwed mothers, she was forced to give the baby up for adoption, then return home like nothing happened.

Her mother's abrupt pivot was a subconscious mandate for Mia to keep on going as if nothing had happened to her, either. Right foot, left foot. Mia abandoned the conversation. She abandoned herself and oriented toward these new revelations her mother was sharing. But Mia never forgot the first sentence out of her mother's mouth. *She wasn't surprised?*

When they got home, Mia's mom went into "drama mode," spreading Mia's admission like wildfire through the family. While her dad yelled, "I'm going to kill your brother!" no one asked if Mia was okay. She just remembers feeling as if she had stressed everyone out.

In fact, the brother who abused her was the only family member who truly checked in with Mia, admitting that it happened and expressing remorse. "I will do anything," he said, "go to therapy, you can beat the shit out of me, whatever you want."

Despite the initial frantic reactions from her parents, nothing changed. Everyone quickly moved on as though one conversation had extracted any hardship from the situation. Mia was expected to attend family gatherings with her brother and eventually leaned into more of a relationship with him. Because he and she were both avid mountaineers, they had interests in common. She was trying to put the past behind them like everyone expected. But then Mia's dad started acting strange. They were talking on the phone one day when she finally confronted him, asking, "What is your problem lately?"

"I think you're attracted to him," her dad replied.

Mia is normally calm and cool, but she lost her shit that day, screaming, "I can't believe you said that to me, can you understand how awful that is!? Fuck you!"

She ripped her phone right off the wall, slamming it to the ground. Here she was doing what was expected, fawning to keep the family peace, and her dad thought she was attracted to the brother who sexually abused her?! The implications ran deep, that she might have wanted what happened, that she was somehow to blame. Was he asking her brother about his attraction?!! It was the biggest betrayal she'd ever experienced by her father.

She didn't speak to him for several weeks. When she did, it was one of the only times he's ever apologized.

When I began therapy with Mia, she had all these voices in her head, variations of her family and friends saying, *Why are you being so dramatic? Aren't you over that by now?*

But again, so often our greatest trauma isn't the thing that happened to us, but the lack of a safe place to turn. It's feeling alone with our wounds. Having them avoided, used against us, or seemingly made about everyone but us.

This was why Mia was still so conflicted. In trying to appear better or over it, she had to abandon herself. She had to pretend she was fine, that she didn't need protection, but the truth was, deep down was a little girl who was still afraid.

This was why she struggled with money. To have wealth was to be visible, and to be visible was to be a target. So she could not get rid of money fast enough. She gave away thousands, always paid for dinner, paid off her friend's student loans. If people wanted something from her and she had the capacity to give it, of course she should! If she saw a need and she could fill it, of course she should!

She let someone live in her back house for free. Her charitable giving was off the charts. In addition, she felt like her wealth was drowning her. She became lost trying to prove she wasn't a rich bitch, a spoiled brat . . . *Please don't hate me!*

When describing her wealth, she said, "It's othering, that kind of money. I didn't want to be other. I wanted to belong." So to shed money was to level the playing field again. To feel like maybe she could fit in.

When we finally tied her issues with money to her trauma history, Mia breathed a visible sigh of relief. She'd been berating herself for how she'd fucked things up, blaming herself for screwing up with money. But the truth was that her body was holding so much shame, such a lack of self-worth and safety, so much relational trauma, it wanted her to get rid of it. Money made her a target, and she needed to stay safe.

Her overspending was a visible symptom of her unresolved trauma. This is where so many people get stuck in their healing. They stop at the symptom, trying to fix that, rather than becoming curious about its function. What it's protecting. What it's afraid of. What lies underneath.

Her wealth also made her feel ashamed that she was still struggling. She felt like everyone was thinking, *What does she have to worry about?*

Mia and I worked together to help her feel in her body that she did not have to tend to everyone else's needs. In one session, it's as though I saw Mia with forty-seven babies attached to her hip, bleeding her dry. She is a calming presence, deeply compassionate and generous. But her constant caretaking/mothering had her surrounded by people who sucked the life out of her. She called it "people eating your soul."

Then there were *Single White Female* types of relationships, new friends who'd become fixated on Mia, as though they wanted to *be* her. She recalls feeling that energy, knowing it was happening, but showing up like it wasn't. Even when they became abusive, she'd still take care of them. Rather than cutting people off to take care of herself, she thought she was supposed to become even more full so they wouldn't take everything from her.

In my work with Mia, which remains ongoing, what matters is not that she is fixed but that she is no longer seeking therapy to appear normal. She is noticing herself. Feeling her feelings in session and taking her ability to name them into her relationships outside of therapy. There is no longer a list of ways she needs to fix herself.

She is becoming a badass in private and in public, not by transcending the human condition, but by sharing it more holistically. She is holding on to herself, her goals, her resources, her truth, and these are allowing her to finally be a force for good in her own life.

PART TWO

The Journey of Unfawning

Five

The Magic of Trusting Yourself

The work of unfawning is about building a new relationship to ourselves, establishing both trust and connection. We must reset our compass from an external orientation to one focused on ourselves as the authority. We learn to look within. This can be deeply uncomfortable, and it takes some serious reconditioning. I want us to be gentle with ourselves as we explore an entirely new way of showing up in the world.

We can't just dismantle old beliefs and behaviors. Healing isn't a hammer. Remember that fawning has long been a protector. Many of my clients talk about fawning not just as their personality, but as if it were the only thing holding them together. So unfawning tends to start with self-compassion rather than stripping things away.

The truth is, only *you* know how to embark on this unfawning journey. While I share various practices in the chapters to come, each person's unfawning is unique. Coming out of a chronic trauma response—in fact, healing from trauma generally—is never a one-size-fits-all endeavor. But that is part of the magic. Unfawning can take surprising shapes.

The only thing required to begin is a new inner focus. Unfawning is reconnecting with your intuition and answering what calls to you, even if it feels like small nudges of guidance. Unfawning starts when we direct our sensitivity, empathy, patience, and all the goodwill and wisdom we've given to others back at ourselves.

It wasn't until I began writing my history, upon Randy's death, that I began to unpack and recognize my own complex trauma. From the moment the writing began, I felt its importance to me. I kept telling friends and my husband, Yancey, "This is the most healing and helpful thing I've ever done."

Seeing my experiences and my responses in black and white on the page allowed me to understand that my entire life had been mired in trauma response. I had just been blind to it before. Up to this point in my life, I had never visited a trauma therapist for *myself*. (I had learned about various trauma modalities but only to better serve my clients. Have I mentioned I'm a fawner?)

I didn't identify as a trauma survivor. The shame those words inspired was too great. What trauma? I felt only what I'd been made to feel: dramatic, selfish, like I just hadn't tried hard enough to get over it. And those feelings informed my attempts to heal. I'd been trying to get better for a lifetime. But all the talk therapy, education, self-help—while it was beneficial to a degree—wasn't moving the needle. None of it allowed me to identify I had relational trauma, nor did it give me the tools to recover from it.

Writing was different. In the years-long process of writing what became my memoir, I retreated from the spaces and places that had previously given me support. I wasn't in therapy. I wasn't seeking outside answers, prescriptions, or finish lines. I didn't make this choice consciously; it just felt right. Part of what was so helpful about my process was that I didn't even know what was unfolding, so my defenses couldn't be two steps ahead, dictating what was and what wasn't going to happen.

Instead, when I was writing, I was connecting directly with *me*. With my own internal wisdom. With what *needed* to happen more than with what I wanted to happen. I wasn't seeking external validation. (Okay, maybe I was secretly hoping for a book deal!) But what that process eventually offered me was something much richer: a new perspective on my life that only I could offer. And a new path to healing that only I could follow.

My life became the perfect container for my unfawning when I stopped looking for someone else to give me the answers.

We are the only ones who know how to heal ourselves.

This is why I teach through personal story, mine and my clients', rather than focusing on particular theories. It's also why there is no step-by-step guide to unfawning. As you'll read in the chapters to come, only *you* will know what comes next, what direction your compass is pointing toward. But a great way to start on the journey is to learn to connect with yourself.

What Do You Notice?: *Orienting*

When working with trauma, therapists are encouraged to steer away from questions like "What do you think about that?" Rather, in almost every training I've attended for various trauma therapies, they use language along the lines of "What do you notice? What are you experiencing? What are you aware of now?" An important part of trauma healing is moving away from a strictly cognitive relationship with ourselves, centered in the brain—what we know, or what we *think* we know—toward what we are sensing, feeling, dreaming, intuiting in our bodies. That is where the work of unfawning resides.

Dr. Peter Levine's body-based model of trauma resolution, Somatic Experiencing (which we'll learn more about in the next chapter), was inspired by the realization that animals in the wild are constantly under threat, but their nervous systems don't hold trauma the way humans' do. He wanted to understand why.

Dr. Levine realized that animals are constantly oriented to the environment through sight, sound, smell, taste, and touch—in other words, their senses, which are the language of the nervous system. In this way, animals are always connected to themselves and their surroundings, aware of their environment and their place in it.

But with our busy lives and big brains, humans have found all kinds of ways to disconnect from the world around us. Our feet rarely touch the actual earth. We're constantly distracted, looking at our phones, at traffic, at our to-do lists. We are overriding our bodily wisdom and don't even know it, living on autopilot, a partial dissociation at all times. Unresolved trauma further disconnects us, making the past feel intrusive, removing us from the experience of *right now*.

One of Dr. Levine's simple yet extremely helpful tools to reconnect us with ourselves and the world is called **orienting.** Orienting is something I do with just about every client, and you can practice it right now. Wherever you are, look around and notice what you see. Slowly move your head to the right, to the left, and up and down as you take in your environment visually.

After you've taken a minute to scan what's around you, see if your eyes are drawn to any particular place. This could be an object, light, or a shadow. It might feel pleasant or neutral. I often find myself orienting to nature or natural objects, but it's really up to your body. Allow your gaze to settle and just notice what you are experiencing.

As I invite clients to try this exercise, I almost always witness a shift. There is a softening of their shoulders or jaws. They often take a spontaneous deeper breath, signaling more safety and regulation in their body. There's a physiological reason for this. When we are in survival mode, we don't have the luxury of slowing down, widening our perspective, or taking in additional sensory input. Consciously engaging in this practice signals safety in the body. We aren't repeating, "I am safe," like a mandate we are trying to follow. By looking around and engaging the senses, our nervous system experiences more safety by moving us into present time and place. Just a few moments of orienting are enough to bring us back to center.

We aren't *trying* to be more present. We just are, and that's the difference.

Notice what happens in your body as you orient visually to your surroundings. You might also notice what you hear. The hum of the air-conditioning. Traffic outside. Ambient sounds or loud ones. See if you can notice how it feels in your body to hear them.

Try orienting with each sense separately, one at a time. Some people find that one connects them with their body more than others. It could be touch, the feeling of your hands rubbing together, or the fabric of your sweater. It could be smell or taste.

Orienting is a helpful daily practice, but I also find it particularly useful when I'm feeling anxious or triggered.

It's also what I was spontaneously doing in my writing. In order to write a scene, I used my senses to map it out. What did I see? What was I feeling? It's like those younger parts of myself, trapped in time and disconnected, were regaining their senses, too. Even all these years later, I was coloring in the lines. I had the capacity to feel now what I had to disconnect from then.

What Do You Need Right Now?: *Resourcing*

What aids you to feel more present, connected, or safe? Before you go making a list, these are not cognitive questions. I want you to tune in to what your body knows to be true.

Resourcing is about finding tools to help us connect with ourselves. It's a process of discovery rather than having things already figured out. When we resource, we enlarge our capacity to feel our feelings, manage stress, build resilience, and stay present. Finding resources that help us get in touch with our body and sense of self is essential to the healing journey.

I always marvel that what works for one person does not work for another. Some people love weighted blankets. (I adore one on the couch, but do *not* want one on my bed.) Some love water: swimming, baths, showers, or spas. Some love heat, and some love the cold. And the truth is, what you need at this moment might not be what's helpful at a different time.

Ask yourself not just *What do I need?* but *What do I need right now?*

Though it may seem like a simple question, *What do I need right now?* is likely one you haven't often asked. When we learn to attune to others, we look outside of ourselves for answers. We often don't know what we want, have no connection to what we need. This is why orienting can be a simple practice of slowing down and dropping in. Let that wave of finally being present come over you and then ask yourself, *What do I notice? What might I need?*

It might be something like yoga, or maybe you're just hungry. The magic of unfawning is found in this inner attunement. In these moments when you ask yourself what you need, listen, and then do. Follow the clues. You don't have to understand them. But they often lead to the next thing.

So many fawners don't know what their favorite foods are, what hobbies they might like to try, because their lives have been dictated by external markers of what is okay. I remember asking Anthony what he liked to do for fun, and he was like, "What are you talking about?" The only prescription was work or maybe working out, but anything outside of those activities felt taboo, frivolous, unsafe because he would be ridiculed or judged. By starting to look at art, buying pieces he loved, surrounding himself with more things that reflected his interests, he started a ripple effect that continues to this day. It's what led him to the men's retreat, to his connection with the bears.

We might remember what we used to enjoy, what we were drawn to as children. When Davis, who was taught that "smiley is weird," was trying to figure out how to attune to himself and build internal safety, he brought out his old comic books. He watched TV commercials from the eighties on YouTube. The smell of the books and the jingles from his childhood reconnected him to vital pieces of himself. He then deepened these connections through meditation, in silence, finding ways to take one afternoon off just to be with himself.

It can take time to get our bearings, to determine when our bodies are saying yes or no. There's a reason we use the phrase "trust your gut." Widely considered our second brain, the gut carries a deep intelligence, our gut feelings, our internal compass. It doesn't care about the *why*. The gut knows something the intellect might not even understand.

Two of my favorite resources are walking and nature. Even in my Los Angeles neighborhood, very much a city climate, I orient to the clouds in the sky as I stroll, to the living things I see along the way. I've never regretted movement outside—especially when I can get out to the trails or the trees. Fresh air, birdsong, communing with the forest—all of this is shown to lower our levels of cortisol, the stress hormone, and is probably why my husband never hesitates to watch our son as I go out for a long hike. I'm practically a different person when I come home.

Expressive arts can be immensely healing. What music do you love? When was the last time you listened to or sang your favorite song? I recently had a Prince dance party for one in my living room. I looked RIDICULOUS, but I was reminded of the countless routines I made up to Prince as a girl, and it was so powerful to be with that part of me now.

Break out the paint, clay, or crayons. See what colors you are drawn to. Move the materials without thinking about it or trying to create a masterpiece. I usually encourage the cheapest art supplies available to lower the bar on making something perfect. It's less about the outcome than it is the process of creating. About getting in touch with the essence of you, which for so long had to go into hiding.

A word of warning: I think we can often make these types of experiences another thing on our to-do list. Going to yoga, CHECK! Purchasing scented candles, CHECK! But sometimes the right thing might be *not* going to yoga. Not spending on another tool of healing. This is why this work of listening to our bodies is so important. Whether it's on your calendar or not, what do you need right now?

The goal is gaining new perspective. Getting to know yourself outside the need to behave a certain way, breaking free from the rules you don't even know you're living by. Reconnecting with your body and learning to listen to its cues. Nurturing a deeper connection to *you*.

Francis recently went to the woods by herself. For a couple of months, she felt the pull to stay in her friend's cabin that was sitting empty. She had an open invitation and really wanted to go. But even though she was in her late thirties, Francis had never traveled any-where alone. She was hoping her current partner would come. She asked several friends, waiting for their schedules to align. Time kept passing, and she still couldn't find someone to go with her, so she de-cided to face her fears and go by herself.

We had a Zoom session while she was there, and as I logged on, I immediately saw the difference in her. She was so INSIDE herself. She was cooking what she wanted when she wanted it. Setting the temperature to whatever she desired. She was lighting fires, doing things she'd never done before, and finding that she *could*.

She was fully inhabiting her space and body, and we both felt the difference. Although she lives alone, she spoke about a tether she feels in her regular life, attached from her body to others. She literally can't be herself or orient to herself completely when the tether is attached. But in going away, she severed the tether, even temporarily, and she felt the freedom from it. This allowed her to feel more of her innate resources, her goodness, her wholeness, releasing her to trust the next nudge of guidance that came her way.

This part of the continual unfawning process—learning how to trust our own intuition—is so foundational. Once we know what guidance actually feels like in our body, we start to recognize it more and more. It's a stirring of excitement in our belly at the thought of an idea. It's a warm feeling of recognition and rightness. It's making time for what nourishes us so that we have the capacity to do the next thing that unlocks the next level of our freedom.

Give Yourself Permission: *Taking Space*

I often encourage fawners to **take some space,** wherever they can. It could mean intentionally taking an extra ten minutes in the car before going in the house. It might mean taking a whole afternoon for yourself. Notice what it feels like to put a little space between you and the people who trigger you. This is helpful for nervous system regulation generally and for unfawning specifically.

Before I asked my ex-husband for a divorce, I had to cut through a TON of fawning. That involved distancing myself from my husband's expectations (*What will he think of me?*) and my community's expectations (*What will they think of me?*) and focusing on what I needed (*What do I think of me?*). I especially worried about what my clients would think of me. A divorced therapist seemed like a terrible calling card at the time. One particularly frazzled day, I realized I just needed some space. From everything—my relationship, my job, and the expectations that were wrapped up in all of it.

I had a friend who had offered me a visit to her condo in Palm Springs. I wasn't even thinking about divorce; I just knew I needed some space from Mark. He was annoyed I was going away for a long weekend alone. He wanted to come along, and it was hard not to give in. "Why don't you want to go away with your husband?" But I held firm, and I honestly didn't go to make a decision, I just went to be by myself. I knew it was important.

I read by the pool. I called old friends. I was in a different space physically, which gave me different space internally. I wasn't trying to convince myself of anything or sort anything out, but by the time I got back in my car to drive home . . . I just knew. It was over. At least I needed him to move out. I didn't decide; my body had the chance to know.

Fawners have a hard time taking up space without some sort of permission from others. I remember when I was newly sober in my early twenties, I committed to take myself on a date to a coffee shop and do some writing. I drank my coffee slowly, worried they would kick me out once I finished my drink. If I had been there with a friend, I would have felt fine; *we* were allowed to take up space. And if someone was to get mad at us, my friend could have acted like a shield, helping to take the heat. But being alone in a public place made me feel vulnerable, like anyone at any moment could think I was doing something wrong.

Just *existing* feels assertive for a fawner. We have to practice making our own decisions. Rather than our first reflex of *I'm good—you can decide,* we must wonder, *Where do I want to go?* But this might invite opposition. *What will they think of my choice?* Even if our mind is telling us that we did something wrong or will be punished, this is patterning from our trauma. Learning to take up space requires learning to tolerate discomfort.

And here's what you'll find: Not every situation requires fawning. Not every person is waiting to criticize or belittle us. In fact, practicing taking up space in other places can help us wake up to how small we feel in relationships that may be hurting us. When we start feeling cramped, it's an indicator that we've outgrown our situation.

Listen to Yourself: *Noticing the Nudges*

Healing from trauma is often less about solving a problem (although we might *want* to solve some things) and more about opening to new perspectives, narratives, resources. It's less of a prescription and more of an exploration.

Notice the things you feel drawn to or curious about. Notice your dreams—the ones at night and your waking ones. You might even notice what you feel jealous about in someone else's path (*I wish I could do that . . .*) These are all clues of where you might want to be. This is all pivotal information.

You might initially feel like you're being noncompliant or you're going to get in trouble. Unfawning can feel contrary to the rules you've followed your entire life. The hierarchies we are living in have reinforced the idea that we can't trust ourselves. That we are bad, sinful, or selfish, that we have to be controlled. So moving out of chronic fawning means restoring the sacred relationship to ourselves. Our bodies have an inherent wisdom that truly wants us to heal.

I think magic happens in part because we start looking for it. We stop focusing on what we *think* the problem is in our lives, what we *think* the solution is, and start orienting toward a bigger picture.

I thought I needed to stay in a broken relationship to be whole.

Mia thought she needed to overcome her trauma *for good*.

Francis thought she needed to save her partner to save herself.

Anthony thought he needed a perfect career to gain his family's love.

Sadie thought she could learn the right boundaries to stop her girlfriend's abuse.

When we unfawn, we stop focusing solely on our triggers and start orienting toward our glimmers, sparks that call our attention. I call this *authenticity unplugged*. Often we can look at moments from our past, memories of times when we were strongly connected to ourselves, and try and bring those feelings into the present.

These are moments when you felt your "me-ness," whether it was a solo dance party in your bedroom or writing in a journal, or when you found the perfect hide-and-seek spot and felt proud of your ingenuity. Moments without an agenda, which encompass unfiltered, pure contact with self. This is the opposite of being on autopilot! Where we feel so connected that sometimes there is even a moment of *Holy shit! I'm here!* Moments of inner attunement, authenticity, acceptance, joy.

Take a moment. Let your mind drift back. See if any of those memories surface for you now.

Before we dive into more tools of unfawning, perhaps at this point in the book you can pause and appreciate the magic that has been in you all along. The way your system adapted to protect you. Fought for you. Even when it led to some behaviors you aren't proud of, there were genius intentions, and they came online without your express permission.

Perhaps you can pause and put your hand on your heart, a posture of self-compassion and gratitude. Feel what you've come through already and how you came through it. How you see it . . . Maybe a little differently now.

Notice what you've resonated with so far in this book. See if you can slow down and appreciate that. Not just with a quick *Yeah, yeah, I get it.* But more of a *Where do I feel it? In my body? With whatever this new awareness evokes in me, where does it want me to go next?*

When Mia saw my posts on social media, she knew that she had to reach out to me. She thought, *There is no way I'll ever hear back from her,* but the nudge was so strong she eventually followed it. I had just one opening, and she was able to fill it. And now that my work is pivoting toward writing, she is the last new client I've taken on. Yes, a course or teacher or book on Instagram can be the next nudge you've been needing!

What are some nudges that you've been noticing? Even if they feel out of left field, impossible or absurd, I suggest you write them down. Maybe it's a dance class or a restaurant you've wanted to check out. Maybe there is a retreat you've always wanted to go on, but the timing never seemed right or you couldn't justify the expense. Maybe it's a travel destination you've always felt called to, a movie you've been meaning to watch, or a book you want to check out from the library. It doesn't matter how big or small the nudge is, what matters is that it is there, and it has stuck around. That is a sign. These nudges and body-based wisdom become the springboard to do the inner and outer work that comes next.

What are some resources that you know help you connect with yourself? What are some things you'd like to try? It might be journaling, taking hot baths, going for a walk. Write those down, too. When we are dysregulated, disconnected, it's hard to think of the things that connect us back to ourselves, but if you have a list, you can choose something from it to try.

This work is not a shift in mindset, but a shift in orienting from everything external that told us who to be and how to override our experience to anything that helps us be with ourselves now. A shift from reflexively doing to actually being.

Trigger City

• • •

I get it. The word *trigger* is overused. It's become synonymous with *upset*. And yet who am I to say if something is triggering for another person or not?

A trigger is a felt reminder of a traumatic event. Because of the way traumatic memory is encoded, we often hold no narrative memory of a specific event when we were harmed. As our brain was flooded with neurochemicals, we paid attention only to what we needed to survive. As a result, memory was encoded at the sensory level. This is why we often can't recognize what is triggering us: a sound, a smell, a touch . . . Our body just recognizes the sense and reacts accordingly.

Triggers can be external: loud noises, anniversaries, or scenes from a movie. And they can be internal: feelings of powerlessness, loneliness, or physical tension. Sometimes we're aware of a trigger, and sometimes we aren't. While they range in severity from mild to overwhelming, they make us feel as though previous threats are happening *now*.

Triggers don't feel good, and I would rather not have them. But if we zoom out a bit, we can see them as the body's way of getting our conscious attention. Like windows to our wounds, triggers can signal where we need more healing.

This is another area where we move out of the old mental health paradigm that implies symptoms are a problem we must solve to be normal. Triggers are normal. Symptoms are a wise communication, conveying what we've been through and how we learned to cope. To feel better doesn't mean eradicating all signs of embodiment, but bringing more attention, compassion, and safety to wounds that never received them before.

In this way, triggers are similar to our nudges, calling for our attention. Sometimes we are called with curiosity or inspiration, and sometimes it's with an urgent ringing of the doorbell. "HELLOOO!"

Although triggers happen to us, we can bring more conscious awareness to what tends to be triggering as a way to meet our needs in the present. For instance, look at the objects you keep. This is deeper than wondering if they spark joy. Instead, ask yourself if they contain a trigger. Do they make you feel *bad* about yourself? Do they remind you of something horrific?

I once kept a French press coffeemaker that belonged to an abusive ex-boyfriend. It was durable and functional, and I liked it. And yet every morning I held it in my hands and noticed the cobalt-blue cover on the carafe, it reminded me of how that man treated me. How he told me I wasn't smart enough to be his girlfriend. How he cheated and lied, and how I felt about myself as a result.

I did this every morning for YEARS until the French press broke.

The day I bought my own damn French press changed my life. Every cup of coffee felt like fresh-brewed self-esteem. I didn't realize how tormented I'd been every morning until the physical object was gone.

Don't wait until what sparks your own terror happens to break! This is what our local Buy Nothing groups are for. If you can, send your own triggering objects off to a new home without further angst or regret.

Then there's the stuff we can't get rid of. The fact is, we *will* get triggered, and our lives are not meant to be in service of avoiding them. While some obvious icky things can be weeded out, other times it's just *life*. It's more information, more opportunity to be with ourselves directly and to heal our deeper wounds.

For many of us with relational trauma, triggers can send us into what Pete Walker calls *emotional flashbacks,* "sudden and often prolonged regressions ('amygdala hijackings') to the frightening and abandoned feeling-states of childhood."

I used to think I'd never experienced a flashback. I thought they were all like the ones we see in the movies, with a specific memory and visual reexperiencing. But flashbacks are any way we reexperience events as though they are happening now. They may or may not be tied to a specific memory, because many of us are flashing back to daily life rather than discrete points in time.

They can arise in a fight, when you are in conflict with someone who treats you in a way that evokes your childhood. In that moment, your body time-travels and gets flooded with feelings from the past. Your brain goes into survival mode. You are acting out from the reptilian brain instead of from the more advanced prefrontal cortex. You can't have a rational conversation or even clearly articulate your thoughts. The person you are fighting with might think you are just being an asshole in your inability to engage. But the truth is, that part of you is offline.

Sometimes I can pinpoint the trigger for an emotional flashback, but many times I can't. Over time, I've started to recognize the quality of the flashbacks when they happen. As the name implies, they are emotional. I feel young, afraid, like I'm bad and going to get in trouble, like I'm guarding against brutal shame. I feel defensive and like there's no way out, all at once.

These flashbacks can arise at any point, and when they swoop in, they completely cloud the present moment. They become the lens I'm looking through no matter what's actually in front of me.

They feel real.

Something in our current situation is igniting the pain of our past.

While pain is not pleasant, I encourage you to reframe its existence from, *Ugh, I'm triggered again,* to *I wonder what this is evoking?*

Becoming a parent sent me to Trigger City. Remember that conflict for fawners often feels like the world is about to end. Yelling truly terrifies me. And yet parenting called on me to deal with my own child's occasional yelling/biting/kicking on a not-too-infrequent basis. Yes, that behavior is developmentally appropriate. No, it's not pleasant for any parent—and it was excruciating for me. My rational brain understood that the angry outburst was coming from a child, but that didn't matter. Just like veterans flash back to active combat when they hear fireworks, my child's tantrums felt like terror.

Children can't regulate their own emotions. Sometimes this is really messy. And sometimes I couldn't cope. I felt like *I* was never allowed to throw a tantrum, particularly in adolescence, when no one held that kind of space for me. So although I never imagined having such feelings, I found myself resenting my son's ability to outwardly express it all.

I became flooded—with my child's feelings and my own. I felt out of control, and this was the scariest feeling of all. I didn't know what was happening, and it felt like there was no way out because strategies aimed at parenting weren't solving the real problem: *my* dysregulation. All of this exposed my powerlessness . . . and when you have lived a life trying to get control, this is terror personified.

I now know that having a child can be deeply triggering for people with unresolved trauma. And those of us with an overactive fawn response might unconsciously *want our children to fawn.* That is how we survived, so it can feel like our children won't be safe in the world without learning to appease, get quiet, and comply, all under the guise of respect. When they don't shapeshift for our benefit, we simply don't have the skills to help because we haven't learned regulation ourselves.

This is why it's so important for parents to address their own fawning. By doing so, we can take responsibility for our dysregulation and break the cycle of living in survival mode, teaching our children a different path forward. Not only is unfawning setting future generations up for emotional maturity and success, but it can also heal previous generations . . . if they are willing to do the work.

The key to coping with triggers is learning to respect the messages they transmit and then responding with compassion and resourcing. I didn't need to beat myself up for being a bad mom (which of course, I did). I didn't need to see my child as a problem (I also did this). I needed to see that something in me needed real help, and to respect that there was a reason for my upset that was deeper than I could understand at the time. My triggers were in fact indicators of unresolved trauma.

Sometimes simply saying to ourselves "I am triggered" or "This is an emotional flashback" can help our rational brain see things more concretely. Sometimes looking in the mirror, seeing our adult face, or looking down at our adult hand can be a physical reminder that we are all grown up, not in present danger. Remember the orienting exercise we discussed earlier in this chapter. Grounding ourselves in the here and now can help us move beyond our triggering past.

When we feel triggers, remember how far we have come from the traumas of our past and how much healing we have begun to access. You'll read in the following chapters how we can heal these wounded parts and bring ourselves more into the present.

Davis

Davis was referred to me by a couples therapist, whom he saw with his wife, to work on childhood trauma. The first day we met, he said, "I have all these boxes, and I don't even know what they contain. I'm too afraid to open them."

He was pointing across my office, at a pile of invisible boxes that followed him everywhere he went. Although Davis didn't know what was inside, I would soon get to know the mastery with which he conceptualized and organized his world.

Davis's mind is extraordinary. He and I can geek out on language in session—getting swept up in understanding something, articulating the granular aspects of it. Davis is a graphic novelist, where his command of language serves him well, and his career is a bit like his boxes. He has an underground, cultlike following, and his books layer complex meaning, comedy, and social commentary in tiny packages of brilliance.

Compartmentalization or fragmentation is a common feature of complex trauma. As a way to protect ourselves from overwhelm, we split off from what happened, from the parts of ourselves that were wounded along the way. That's what Davis was trying to communicate with the boxes. Parts of him were trapped in unprocessed experiences from his past. But so much of him was lost during that process that almost nothing of him remained in the outside world. His fawning self, a false self, seemed like the only safe way to navigate his life.

Some people fawn in the face of danger, when triggered, or in certain relationships. But Davis's trauma started so early that he fawned *all the time*. He didn't self-abandon on occasion, he self-abandoned as a condition of having to associate with other human beings.

Trauma healing is never linear. We work with what's available to us at the time, so in the years I've known Davis, we've unpacked his boxes slowly. Although I share aspects of his story as unified parcels of content and time periods, this is not how they were presented. Discovering what happened to him and getting in touch with his true self has occurred piecemeal over time.

Davis grew up in West Baltimore. When in fifth grade he tested into a magnet elementary school for gifted students on the other side of town, his social interactions went from easy to overwhelming. Every day, he took the long bus ride from his all-Black neighborhood to a predominantly white and privileged community.

As accomplished as he was academically, with test scores in the 99th percentile, he was struggling socially. When we spoke about the challenges he faced in those days, Davis describes his unease: "Listen, I had nappy hair and kept wondering what it would look like straight. I saved all my money to buy one nice brand-name shirt. But I never thought the problem was the *place*," he said. "I just thought it was *me*."

Showing up to class, Davis raised his hand every time he knew an answer (and he knew the answer a lot). He didn't understand why he wasn't being called on as much as at his old school. As we unpacked his struggles, we recognized he'd likely be considered Twice Exceptional (2E) by today's standards, a term that denotes academic giftedness in addition to another form of neurodiversity, like having ADHD or being on the autism spectrum. A lot of Davis's journey has been about feeling like an outsider and trying to understand social dynamics so that he can feel comfortable within them.

Davis lived with his mom's sister in one of the large housing projects of Baltimore. He'd been with her since he was five years old and remembers feeling safe and cared for.

It was a welcomed respite from the years prior. When Davis was in preschool, he'd lived with his mom in a house belonging to a religious cult, a house full of people coming and going at all hours. Davis had been on constant high alert. Though he now knows there was criminal activity going on, at the time he just knew there was no structure or boundaries. As is true of all children, Davis craved both.

On a trip to Florida with his mom—a trip that Davis later came to understand as running from the FBI—they were pulled over by the police. He watched his mother get arrested for selling drugs, and the next time he saw her was in a Baltimore jail.

This is when his aunt took custody. But in the summers, Davis traveled to Texas and stayed with his father, stepmother, and stepsister, who was five years his senior. Davis does not consider his deepest trauma to be losing contact with his mom. Instead, it is what happened during these summer breaks, starting when he was nine years old.

At first it was innocent enough—his stepsister was affectionate, offering secret indulgences while their parents were at work. Having considered himself to be girl crazy since kindergarten, Davis was interested in these daytime experiments. Their relationship and what happened between them existed in its own time and space, separate from what felt like an idyllic family life otherwise, happy conversations at the dinner table every night.

But as they escalated in frequency and nature, his curiosity and interest vanished. He said no. Told her he didn't want to do it anymore, but she insisted, and things progressed to daily sexual experiences no child should have.

Today, he resonates with the language of being groomed and sexual abuse, but he told me about these experiences from the perspective of initially wanting them. Much of our work has been about reconnecting with the parts of himself that did not. Trying to regain access to the parts of him that felt sad and scared, that felt abandoned and alone, and that knew he was powerless to stop the horror.

To withstand such frightening abuse at such a young age, Davis learned to shut off access to the parts of him experiencing these horrible things. When he left Texas for the school year, he didn't consider telling his aunt; he just stepped into his persona as the smartest boy in his class. He pretended things were fine so he could keep going. Then he'd have to face the same terror again next summer. It lasted for five years.

Davis had never unpacked this trauma with anyone. These parts of himself and the memories of these unspeakable events lived in these boxes. In his present life, this need to compartmentalize eventually led to separate lives. Davis told me about his multiple affairs. He'd found himself obsessed with flirting, with massage parlors, seeking the familiar ache of his childhood days. *Will this lead to a sexual encounter? Will I get in trouble?* The shame/pleasure pathways became so fused, he struggled to locate his sexuality outside of forbidden circumstances.

While he wasn't proud of his behaviors, he was aware of their *importance*. He knew they were serving him in some way. His separate boxes, what he later called "pocket dimensions," were the only places he could access the truest parts of himself. These periods in secret, ideally with women who were disconnected from his actual life, were the times when he truly *lived*. The rest of his life, he was only fawning, even in his marriage.

This was why his couples therapist had referred him to me. Everyone sensed the disconnect. He wasn't having sex with his wife. They were living separate emotional lives. Davis didn't want a divorce, but he didn't know if he could be all of himself in his marriage, either.

Remember that we initially fawn our way *out* of danger, which results in leaving behind parts of our true self. As we continue to fawn, perpetuating this disconnection, the body reenacts elements of our traumatic past in the hopes of gaining mastery. This often means working our way back *into* danger and dysfunction, hoping to find the lost parts of ourselves again. This is what Davis was doing. He was trying to get access to the past so that he could choose differently this time—be able to set boundaries and trust his no, or at least connect with the parts of himself that were still tethered to those familiar circumstances. All his affairs were really, sadly, an attempt to heal.

Davis had no practice being in real relationship in his everyday life. And yet he offered pieces of himself through his writing. In his work, in a witty phrase or complex theme, he put his heart out into the world. But it was still coded. It was still hidden. It was still in a box.

It wasn't enough to connect with readers in this way. Davis needed to learn how to be himself in his real life. To slowly extract, piece by piece, what remained boxed up. To bring containment to these fragile and frightened parts without hiding so he could live fully, out in the open.

It's difficult for people, therapists included, to see the function of present-day behavior that can appear so dysfunctional. But we must. Before we rush in to fix the bad behavior, we must honor the purpose it has served. We must be curious about its function. We can't just bulldoze the secrecy or affairs, get rid of the boxes. *Davis* was in those boxes. Our job was to make it safe enough for him to come out.

We had to respect the fragmentation that happened and where it took him. Only then could he begin to reconnect with himself in the present. The terror this inspires, however, is no joke. His shame and anxiety would rise to the surface. I would see him, in real time, in my office, turn into that little boy, so afraid of being found out. He would say, "Even as I'm talking right now, I'm worried my phone might be on, someone might hear." His constant fear was that he would hurt somebody if he was fully honest, if he had to set a boundary. These were hot fires he did *not* want to touch.

He recently shared with me that he is so conflict avoidant, he doesn't allow himself to even *think* about what he feels because he's too busy thinking what someone else might think or how he should respond if they ask.

So a part of Davis's trauma healing and ultimately his unfawning is making it safe to know what he is feeling. It's not about letting others know. But can he just *feel* the feeling? It is so helpful for him to think about it this way, breaking it down into manageable steps, and it's working.

We used Davis's own strategy of compartmentalization, isolating all the parts in order to understand their function, their needs, what they were protecting him from. And it's been a game changer. He basically now points to a box and asks it to tell us what's in it, and that's how he bypasses the separation he's always experienced. But it's still a practice.

A couple of years into therapy, Davis left his marriage. While there was love, he had to step out of the cycles that necessitated more fawning—*We are good, I am good*, family dinners resembling summer breaks at his father's house. He had to divorce himself from his wife and from all of *that* to find more of *him*.

Davis began to see a woman he had seen while he was married. He is in a monogamous relationship with her now, without boxes, without secrecy. This is what attracted him to her, as she drew him out of hiding.

For a long time, he didn't use her name in session. Then one day he said he wanted to. He made it clear, he was stepping into making that relationship more real, making her more real, so he could be more real, too. To no longer keep these vital parts of him secret.

This is the joy and pain of this work, being with people as they become acquainted with themselves, learn to love and honor themselves—while facing the truth of how they got lost to begin with. Facing the grief of what they lost long ago, and from that point until now. I've said it a million times and know that it's true: Reclaiming our whole self is the bravest, hardest work anyone can do. While some of Davis remains in boxes, he's no longer confused as to why. He remains committed to being in relationship with everything that got tucked away, feeling everything he wasn't capable of before. He has already done so much of this work—in the box of my office. He has shown all of himself in there, and as we look around together, I see more light pouring in.

Six

Blinders Off

How to Do the Inner Work of Unfawning

The process of unfawning is a paradigm shift. It's not about *never* fawning. We are moving out of a binary, black-or-white orientation to life. The focus is no longer simply:

Safe *or* Unsafe
Me *or* You
Healed *or* Unhealed

Unfawning is an expansion. We are broadening our vision to see more choices and have greater flexibility. When we expand our bandwidth, we can finally break free of the old narratives and patterns that once defined our lives. We don't have to tell stories that erase aspects of ourselves or of our reality. We instead learn to write new ones that include *all* of who we are. And the truth about everyone else, as well.

When we begin to unfawn, we find we can get off the tightropes we've been on for so long and finally roam free. We experience nuance, wholeness, self-love. Unfawning means taking up more space, taking deeper breaths. We are reclaiming our voices, opinions, preferences, and desires.

If you've been following someone else's script for years, you'll start to hear your own voice. If you've been a perpetual problem solver for others, you'll finally direct your focus back to yourself. If you've been shortchanging your whole self for the sake of everyone else, this is where you start to reclaim it.

Unfawning is a balance of processing what's happened in our lives, honoring the shifts we want to make, and knowing that fawning will remain a protector. There will still be contexts where fawning is *appropriate.* Just as a fight response is appropriate at times but not *all* the time. As we become aware of our fawning, it can become more conscious. Sometimes we will flatter, other times appease. This isn't inherently bad. As we notice our instinct to fawn, we might even choose it. Coming deeper into our bodies does not mean eliminating our instincts. Unfawning means that we don't live in a trauma response 24-7, self-abandoning at every turn.

Just like with the signs of fawning in chapter 3, there is no precise order to this process. Every nervous system is different, and opportunities will arise for different people at different times. But the inner work will likely involve learning to regulate your nervous system, reprocessing your trauma, and reparenting yourself. It will mean feeling your feelings, not just the hard ones—but learning to hold the good, the abundance, the growth and lightness we all deserve.

Regulating Your Nervous System

Recall that fawning stems from a lack of safety in our bodies. We instinctively mitigate danger by meeting the perceived demands of others—whether that's placating an angry spouse or taking abuse from an irate colleague after a botched presentation. We meet their energy where they are and then try to defuse it, because going *against* them (and standing up for ourselves) would invite greater harm.

We aren't meant to live in this state of perpetual activation and ongoing instability. Being in a chronic trauma response is a form of nervous system dysregulation. A major component of unfawning is learning to quell the constant arousal, regulating our nervous system in order to foster more internal safety. To regulate our responses instead of reacting in the moment.

Understanding Regulation

While nervous system regulation is often equated with being calm, it's not about remaining Zen at all times. That's just not realistic. A regulated nervous system is *flexible*. It means our sympathetic (fight or flight) and parasympathetic (rest and digest) nervous systems are working together, in harmony.

When we are regulated, we are better able to cope with stressors, interact with people without becoming overwhelmed, and maintain emotional stability. In this state, we connect with and operate from our internal compass. Noticing the physical nature of our feelings, we are *embodied*.

Becoming more regulated allows for more space, in ourselves and in our relationships. It makes it possible to pause, to say "Maybe" or "Let me think about that." We often need space in between the instinct to fawn and the discovery of how we actually feel.

Dysregulation, as we've covered, comes in various forms. *Hyperarousal* involves overstimulation. Some signs are:

- We feel irritable, angry, or anxious.
- Our bodies are jittery, on edge, easily startled.
- We might have obsessive thoughts or difficulty concentrating or sleeping.

- We might feel physically hot or notice an elevated heart rate.
- Our feelings are deep and intense. We feel overwhelmed.

Hypoarousal is the state of being understimulated. We are disconnected from feeling or underaroused. Some signs are:

- We feel foggy or dissociated.
- We have low energy or physical weakness.
- We feel numb, depressed, empty, or shut down.
- We tend to isolate, feeling bored and under-responsive.

Remember, fawning is a combination of *hyper-* and *hypo*arousal. You see the lies but don't call them out. You respond to threats with compassion and reason. You dance, sing, and perform through every storm. As we've seen, it's an uncomfortable push-pull. So the work of unfawning starts with regulating our nervous systems through practices and activities that help bring us back to center. Some are about slowing down, and some are about moving the energy through. I often suggest people try several different activities, listening to their body to see what it might need in the moment.

However, if you are in an ongoing threatening or abusive situation, regulating your nervous system will not make that threat go away. It will not change your external circumstances. But we can respect our current realities while becoming more in tune with ourselves, increasing our clarity, which allows for more conscious choices—big or small. In the end, maybe nothing changes on the outside, but we can still strive for an authentic relationship *with ourselves*.

Many of the actions we'll learn about in this chapter can become daily practices. Don't wait to feel overwhelmed to move into more regulation. There are cumulative effects to nervous system regulation, similar to the benefits of working out. We don't do it once and get fit. These are lifestyle choices along with practices for when we need additional support.

It's All about the Body, Baby

There is a theme in almost all the inner unfawning processes. They happen in our bodies. That's right. Unfawning is about going in. Not to our overactive minds, which can argue for any side, second-guess, or insert opinions that have nothing to do with what we actually need. (That's part of what's kept us stuck.)

Trauma is trapped in the body. Our unexpressed feelings are stuck there, too. So this is body-focused work, stepping away from the desk and our phones, stepping out of autopilot. The work of unfawning requires us to feel our bodies, move our bodies, notice sensations and nudges. We prioritize our relationship to self by being with whatever is happening in the body, to the degree that we can, and building from there.

Getting Back to Center

Here are some examples from my clients of how they have learned to regulate their nervous systems.

- Anthony lies on his acupressure/massage mat almost every day. With tiny pressure points, the mat offers physical stimulation that he finds physically and mentally beneficial. This is something he does by himself at home, but many people find body work of all kinds immensely helpful. Reiki, massage therapy, acupuncture, and yoga are all useful methods of tuning in to and taking care of your body.
- Francis wears a breathing necklace, which looks like a tiny whistle, slowing her exhales and reducing her anxiety. When

we are dysregulated, we tend not to take full breaths. Many people find that breathing exercises are a powerful way to access themselves and the present moment.

- Sadie loves to hike with her dog. Connecting with a pet is a powerful form of co-regulation—feeling aligned with and supported by a pet's energy and love. Additionally, when Sadie hikes, she is out in nature, orienting to her surroundings. Just going outside and breathing fresh air and letting your eyes rest on the horizon have healing properties. The Japanese call this forest bathing, and it is proven to lower your heart rate, your blood pressure, and your cortisol levels. All from going out and being in nature.

- Mia uses expressive arts to paint, draw, write her way through. She has an art journaling practice. She creates tiny collages and draws images along with inner reflections to get what she is feeling onto the page. She'll also paint large canvases—whatever her body calls her to in the moment. Many people find knitting or crafting with their hands meditative or cathartic. What matters is getting out of our brains and into our bodies, tapping into our creativity that feeds and regulates us in a way our to-do lists cannot.

- Davis breaks out his old comic books, watches animated shows that connect him viscerally to himself. He sketches and has a long-standing meditation practice. Additionally, he knows that he needs alone time to decompress and *really* be with himself.

- Grace takes long walks, often with friends, during which she practices sharing what's really going on. She has a personal stretching routine. Organically moving her body allows her to listen to and honor herself. She loves shopping by herself, wandering through department stores at her own pace, with her own thoughts.

- Lily loves to write, dance, and create. She is playful and finds that being silly, dressing up with her goddaughter drops her into her body. Play, joy, and laughter are so crucial in our unfawning process. We fawners have worked incredibly hard throughout our lives, hoping to be validated and seen, so we need to be careful not to bring a relentless overdoing to our path of healing. There can be a lightness to it! While this is serious business, being overly serious can shield us from what we are seeking. *Take it easy.*

- My friend Elizabeth loves to hum, under water ideally, but any humming will do. The sensory experience of immersing ourselves in water and the way that humming stimulates the vagus nerve both activate the parasympathetic nervous system. These immediately help my friend feel more relaxed and in her body. Singing can do the same.

- I like hot baths and my weighted blanket, scented candles and music. My editor and I want to make an unfawning playlist so we can dance and sing to powerful anthems, or even tune in to the sadder songs that facilitate getting in touch with those feelings and needs.

You might try any of the above or a host of other things, like giving yourself a full body shake, from head to toe. Drinking from a straw. Throwing a ball against the wall and playing catch with yourself. Jumping rope or on a trampoline. Splashing cold water on your face. Try the restorative yoga pose Viparita Karani, Legs Up the Wall, or guided imagery—your own or prerecorded. Work out. Eat food that brings nourishment and comfort.

Be creative. Turn to your own life experience and ask, *What feels helpful when I'm out of sorts?*

And remember, it's not about becoming a chemist to always find the perfect state. *We will be out of sorts.* We will feel triggered. We will feel low and/or anxious. We aren't bypassing the human condition. We are being a bit more in it. Which is why I always encourage the return to self-compassion. We are not fixing ourselves but being with ourselves.

That is in fact the *key*.

Fawners are habituated to regulate *others* in an attempt to regulate themselves: gaining others' approval, making them happy so we can be happy. Part of the paradigm shift is finding our center, our safety, without the middleman. This shift is major.

And it's also scary! Not privileging someone else's discomfort tends to set off the old alarms: *You are moving in the wrong direction, abort abort!* This is where we might reflexively return to the old behaviors we know so well: helping, appeasing, taking the blame . . . you know the drill. So part of gaining more regulation, then, is tolerating the discomfort of doing things a different way.

Mia used to have trouble bringing up any issues with her boyfriend. When she summoned the bravery to voice her discomfort, she would see him leave his body, dissociating as she tried to speak up. It was like he disappeared. Then she'd immediately think, *Ugh, see! You cannot bring things like this to him! This is what happens when you do!*

Once the other person feels impacted by us, fawners feel like it's game over. We shut it down, retract, or diminish our needs. We feel like we've fucked things up.

While our discomfort and their reaction might need attention, it doesn't mean we shouldn't have spoken up. We have to learn to slow things down. See the discomfort and count to ten or orient to our surroundings. We put our hands on our heart, say to ourselves, "I'm allowed to share what works for me," and breathe through the growing pains.

Although I wish this weren't true, you can see how not shrinking, hiding, or finding your sweet spot of existence can elicit, dare I say, terror. And yet that is the direction we are asking our bodies to go in. The compass is steering us toward greater autonomy and authenticity, but attempting to move more freely directly hits a nerve.

So an important question we must learn to ask is, *Am I in danger, or is this discomfort?*

Our bodies may be screaming danger, recalling previous threats to our well-being. Moving out of survival mode then means moving into the present time and place. Situations that provoke our triggers provide an opportunity to go inside, feel, and be present with our emotions. We aren't meant to avoid discomfort; we are growing our capacity to tolerate it.

While upsetting her father might have put Mia in immediate danger during her abusive childhood, Mia's partner today is not abusive. And even if her partner lacks the language or capacity to stay present to their conversation, bringing things up to him *isn't* dangerous. It may be disappointing. Their dynamic likely needs more attention. But it will not devastate her.

Initially, most of us find that the needle points to fawn no matter which direction we are trying to go. The needle doesn't even know there are other directions. We don't get immediate access to the entire circumference; we are working with degrees.

Not immediately collapsing in the face of conflict is a huge degree.

Not immediately rescuing someone from their own pain is a huge degree.

Asking ourselves what we want or need and then meeting these to the best of our ability . . . I mean, this moves the needle at least several degrees. And eventually we find that we have the full range of motion we've been seeking. It's a process of gaining internal support so fawning can step back.

Reprocessing Your Trauma

Recall that not all traumatic events lead to an experience of trauma. Sometimes our body has the internal and external resources to move through a situation largely unscathed. Other times, it's like we're stuck at the top of the roller coaster and our body has never been able to come down. This is called *unprocessed trauma*. It can be from our childhoods, from years ago, even from last week. It remains trapped in the body, keeping us in a chronic trauma response. We believe we still need constant defending, even when the immediate danger has passed.

Unfawning requires getting unstuck. Remember the analogy we discussed in chapter 1, how animals instinctively shake off a fight-or-flight response to threat with a full-body shudder? Yep, we're animals, too, and we need to get what happened to us out of our bodies.

Most trauma therapies are designed to help a client reprocess their trauma. This means revisiting and working through traumatic events in ways that feel safe, allowing us to feel our feelings and integrate what happened so it's no longer running our lives.

Think of it this way: For *years,* many of us have bypassed our deeper feelings through our trauma responses. Additionally, in trauma that stems from childhood, we weren't developmentally capable of processing overwhelming feelings, so they've remained untouched ever since. Luckily, we have the capacity to process them now. We just need to know how.

There are as many ways to reprocess trauma as there are ways of being traumatized, so this is hardly a complete list of modalities. But I will cover several trauma therapies I've experienced as a client and utilized as a therapist, as they are extremely effective in this work. These are well-established modalities, so trained professionals shouldn't be difficult to find. That said, you can find healing even through digesting the work that follows on these pages. Similar to group work, where someone else's therapeutic process elucidates your own, the session material presented is meant to evoke your own experiences with these themes. Perhaps as you've seen yourself reflected in the personal stories in this book thus far, you might also see yourself through our healing. Witnessing someone else break through old patterns can begin the process of breaking your own.

Many trauma therapies have ancient origins; healing has always tended toward similar themes and practices, no matter what system it is now categorized under. Furthermore, like body workers who use a little Swedish massage and a little deep tissue work, each practitioner of trauma healing has a different way of interpreting and working with the magic of each system, often incorporating different models into one cohesive experience. Just as trauma survivors are encouraged to lean into intuition and the present moment, so do the best trauma practitioners.

If you are seeking therapy, I'd like to suggest a few guidelines.

- **Strictly cognitive modalities are often not successful in working with trauma.** Referred to as top-down approaches that rely on our thinking brain, they can keep us in our head when we need embodied, experiential, subconscious work. So finding a therapist who is trauma informed is a must. Finding someone who is trauma *trained* is ideal. That means they have specific bottom-up trauma modalities in their tool kit.
- **Purely analytic strategies, in which a therapist is a blank slate—answering a client's questions with more questions (think Freud)—can be terrifying for relational trauma survivors**. I recall when I was twenty, feeling so confused, attempting to come out from under years of gaslighting and being the scapegoat. I was trying to understand what was *real,* asking my therapist questions I sincerely wanted answers for. But she'd never tell me her thoughts, responding only

with "How do *you* feel about that?" It was maddening! I needed someone to be with me, to be sturdy, to help me see the truth. Most people with complex trauma will do better with a relational approach, where a therapist offers more of themselves in the relationship, building authentic, healthy attachments with their clients.

· **Fawners often come to therapy wanting to change, but their appeasement—even of their therapist—can get in the way.** As a therapist, over the years I've had many clients admit to wanting to "be my favorite," pretending interventions were helpful when they weren't or outright lying about the details of their lives. Clients have also shared stories of previous therapy, where much of the work was spent in avoidance with a therapist who never caught on. This dynamic can happen no matter what a therapist's theoretical orientation is, and when it does, a therapist might mistake compliance (or silence) for progress. Once again, fawning is perpetuated as a solution when in fact it is part of the problem.

More on that last point, because it's so important. As I mentioned in chapter 5, *you* are the expert in the room. This means if something isn't working, fawners need to practice saying it. Risk hurting the therapist's feelings! As therapists, we don't know how to help if we don't get real feedback on what is beneficial and what isn't. Remember that every nervous system is different. A specific tool might work great for one person and not at all for another. This doesn't mean you—or your therapist—are doing something wrong; it might mean you should try slowing things down and going back a step. Don't feel like you have to keep plowing forward.

I recall a therapist once asked me to try an exercise. Rather than telling her what was happening, which was that I was feeling a lot of resistance, I closed my eyes and sat there wondering, *How long should*

I sit here so she knows that I tried? Now I know I need to say exactly what I'm experiencing, even if it's "I hate this and here's why." A good therapist can work with you, make adjustments, at the very least validate your experience. If they are just saying you aren't willing, you are stuck in avoidance, while asking you to try again and again, let them know, "This isn't working for me!"

If you have been transparent and have asked for your needs to be met, and you find that the therapy still isn't helpful (and you should know if it is or isn't), it's okay to move on. I say this knowing how hard it is to find the first therapist, much less another one! But the fact remains that we came to this work to GET OFF THE HAMSTER WHEEL. Sometimes therapy can feel like we are still on it.

Making Sense of Yourself: *Internal Family Systems*

Even though I unpacked most of my trauma while writing my memoir, I finally sought out a trauma therapist, not for training purposes but because I realized I needed one. My therapist, Holly, works with several modalities, and the one we spend the most time using is **Internal Family System (IFS).**

IFS has surged in popularity in recent years. *Parts work,* as it is also called, is most closely associated with therapist Dr. Richard C. Schwartz. It's a therapeutic model based on the idea that our internal structure or psyche is made up of different parts that were developed in our childhoods to help us survive. Many people find the language of parts familiar, as they've long said, "A part of me feels . . ."

To echo Dr. Schwartz's book title, there are *No Bad Parts*. Each part serves a purpose. You may have parts that are extremely rewarded and thus tend to get a lot of airtime, like the good girl or the scholar. You might have others that are in direct conflict with these parts, like the bad girl or the lazy one. Parts work is about listening to these different parts of you, trying to separate from them, and meeting their needs so you can ultimately meet your own.

At the center of our parts is a Self, the real you. The Self should be at the head of the table, calling the shots. But often we become *blended* with various parts. We think we ARE the good girl, we think we ARE the scholar. Consequently, they are calling the shots, and we aren't making conscious decisions. In other words, our personalities and choices are being dictated by very young, even primitive parts of ourselves.

Because these parts developed in childhood, they still have that mindset. Many parts don't even realize that we have grown up, that we don't need their brand of coping so desperately.

Many parts are *protectors,* working hard to protect us from intolerable feelings or experiences that were too overwhelming. A powerful feature of this work is thanking these parts for how they have served us for so long. When they feel seen and validated, then they can stand back, take a break, allow other parts to play a bigger role.

Fawning is a protector. For me, she takes different forms in different environments, but her protective nature remains the same. When I see her as such, I immediately feel less shame. I see how and why she came online so forcefully, rushing to my aid. Sadie similarly talks about fawning as a constellation of parts that were developed at different points in time. She refers to them as her "little fawners."

For me and many of my clients, when fawning gets ignited and we see it as a part of ourselves (not all of us), we can create a little separation between us and the response. We can be in relationship with it. We become curious: *What is this part afraid will happen if we don't fawn?* We can see how hard it has been working and share gratitude with it for its efforts and good intentions. We can wonder if it can see our newfound capacity, our chronological age, notice that we are capable of taking care of ourselves differently. We can be curious if the fawning part needs or wants anything from us now.

I first learned about parts work when I was in graduate school. But it wasn't until I was writing my memoir that my parts came to *me*. When I felt the pull to the page, it was like my parts were demanding to be heard and attended to. The essays and stories that were pouring out of me were fully formed aspects of my experience and yet completely disconnected. I wondered, *Why am I writing about being thirteen and then my first marriage?* It didn't make any sense.

I now see this as different parts of me coming to the surface, ready to speak, be heard, and be recognized.

My memory of being thirteen and alone with Randy in the hot tub was one of the first stories that emerged. As I wrote it, it was as if it had happened yesterday. What was said in our conversation, how I felt in that bubbling water—it was crystal clear. That thirteen-year-old part of me had been holding that experience this entire time.

Although getting her story down on paper was one step, advocating for her by naming what actually happened, it wasn't until later that I returned to her in parts work. Or rather, she came back to me again.

I was in a session with Holly, describing my daily headaches. As usual, I was trying to figure out why, when Holly suggested I pause and turn my attention to my body, my *system,* to notice if there were any parts that needed my attention.

To my surprise, as soon as I closed my eyes, I was brought back to the hot tub. While I'd previously connected with my thirteen-year-old self, transcribing her experience word for word, I now realized that I had never let her connect with me. She was still alone out there, standing on that deck. Outside of the sliding glass door, she was wet and shivering. That part was still trapped in that moment.

As I saw her there, I invited her to see me. For her to witness all the internal safety I'd built, to see my chronological age, that *we* were now a certifiable adult. I let her see how we were no longer helpless, at the mercy of that man or any other. And from this place of agency, I asked her directly what she needed from me now.

At first she just wanted to go inside. I watched as she opened the sliding glass door and entered the house. She took me back to my old bedroom. As she began to look around that room, orienting to what made her feel safe back then—little toys I was obsessed with, posters on my wall—her overwhelm was beginning to abate.

As she felt a little less frightened, I wondered if she could feel my presence. She let me know that she could. And we both felt relieved. We both knew I was the one she was waiting for. It was time for her to finally feel safe.

I asked if she wanted to stay in that room with the things that gave her comfort, but it was very clear that she wanted to leave. At that moment, my inner thirteen-year-old wanted to go to Rocky Mountain National Park, Colorado, somewhere I'd felt safe as a child. She wanted to run with the majestic elk. And I let her go, running through the fall colors of my favorite place up to the highest peaks and beyond.

At last that thirteen-year-old part of me was free.

This is what reprocessing can look like in IFS. While I tend to process in a very visual way, others find that different senses emerge. It's a sensation, a knowing, a voice. Finding a trapped part of you and setting them free from the past, from the wounding they'd been carrying for so long.

Dr. Schwartz describes this kind of reprocessing in *No Bad Parts*. And it can feel, I know, a bit woo-woo. Like, *Really, we are going in and seeing visions?* Yes. Yes we are. We are going back to the past and changing the ending. Even if it didn't happen at the time, we can make it happen now.

Neuroscience shows us that the brain lights up in the same areas when it's engaged in an activity and when it's imagining doing that same thing. Sports medicine uses this knowledge in training athletes, encouraging them to imagine the perfect race, seeing themselves at every turn, visualizing their performance, and then noticing how it correlates to the actual one. We can use this same tool in reprocessing trauma. As it happens in our imagination, our body processes it as real. And this is what allows our trauma responses to recede. As we are no longer stuck in the past, we no longer need their constant defending.

The Only Way Out Is Through: *Somatic Experiencing*

We talked about **Somatic Experiencing (SE)** in chapter 5, where we learned about Dr. Peter Levine's tool of orienting to help bring us back into our bodily and present-day awareness. At its heart, SE aims to complete the body's natural response to trauma. In other words, we're working to get off the roller coaster.

Simply put, SE is a bottom-up modality that focuses on body memory and physical sensation to resolve chronic and post-traumatic stress. Some practitioners are psychotherapists, and the work can look like talk therapy, but it might also involve physical props like weighted beanbags or blankets. Some practitioners are body workers. They use a massage table and have direct contact with your body. Either way, SE focuses on bodily sensations and what actions our bodies want/need us to take that we weren't able to in the moment. We don't always understand why these actions feel necessary, and sometimes clarity doesn't come until much later. But what matters is completing the cycle, processing traumatic memory and sensation in the body to return us to a more regulated state. No matter what memory we may be working with, after SE there is often a feeling of release, like something long blocked is now able to flow. By identifying and releasing these physical sensations, a discharge process can occur, restoring the nervous system to its natural rhythms.

As part of our training in SE, we had to see a practitioner ourselves. And in one powerful session, I moved through feelings that had been stuck since the early nineties.

My SE session began with me telling my therapist Kristi about a recent phone call with my mom. It was after Randy passed away, and I was trying to support my mom in her grief, in starting a life on her own. As soon as I heard her voice, I knew she'd been drinking. She started going on and on about how proud she was of my brother. "I honestly don't know what I would do without him. I'm just so proud of how he's turned his life around." She was effusive about how much she loved him and how amazed she was by his sobriety.

The way my brother turned his life around *was* amazing. For decades he'd vacillated between jail and homelessness until, shortly after Randy got sick, he checked himself in to the Salvation Army Rehabilitation Center. Right when I thought my brother would never get sober, he did.

In the year since Randy had died, he'd been there for our mom in ways I could never be. But listening to her on the phone, I could practically see her beaming with pride. I became more and more irritated, something welling up from deep within. I've been sober for half of my life, and I'd never heard her talk about me the way she talked about him. The disparity was agonizing. I pursed my lips to keep from blurting out: "I know, Mom, he is your beloved and favorite child."

As though she finally had a moment of self-awareness or noticed my silence, her tone changed. "And you know, I love you, too," she said awkwardly.

I wanted to throw my phone down and scream. But instead, I said, "Yes, Mom, I know. I love you, too. I actually have to get going for preschool pickup."

Recounting all of this to my therapist, I felt the same flash of rage I'd felt on the phone. "I feel *so angry!*" I said, and then quickly returned to the story I was telling.

Kristi had me pause. "I'm wondering if you would be willing to return to the feeling for a moment?" *Ugh, I don't want to return to the feeling; just let me tell you what happened and then we can move on!*

I tried to set aside my disgust (and the thought I'd done something wrong by fleeing the feeling in the first place). Closing my eyes, I became curious about what was happening in my body: the heat that was on my shoulders, the fire raging in my belly. "This is so fucking annoying!" I said with as much volume as I allowed myself in her office.

I then opened my eyes and looked around. I saw a coaster sitting on her side table I'd never seen before. It was imprinted with the red rays of the New Mexico state flag. Randy was from Albuquerque, and we had the same coasters in my house growing up. It was strange seeing an artifact from my childhood resting in my therapist's office.

The visual seemed to amplify the unbelievable anger that had been brewing for a lifetime. I verbalized the feelings that were coming. "If I couldn't get validation from my parents, then I was going to find it *somewhere* . . . maybe in achievement after achievement," I said, turning my attention back to Kristi. "I've run a marathon, received three college degrees, started a private practice, and none of these has been a teeny-tiny drop in the bucket of acceptance I was striving for."

I paused.

"I'm not saying these things weren't worthy of my time," I said. "But the part of me that was doing these things to *be worthy* is pissed it didn't work!"

The rage that welled up inside me as I said these words was a rare glimpse of what I knew was *always* there, conscious-adjacent. As I closed my eyes and allowed myself to feel even a fraction of it, I saw an image of my fist punching the air.

I told Kristi what I was seeing, and she suggested I hold that image, slow it down, and see what wanted to happen next. I began to see my fist striking a metal wall. The impact shattered the wall into millions of pieces. I continued to narrate my experience, telling Kristi what was appearing. "I can see pieces of metal starting to fly in every direction," I said.

"Keep going. Notice what you're experiencing as you feel that punch and see the wall shatter."

Though she wanted me to stay with my body, I went back into my head and analyzed the fantasy as a representation of what I was sure would happen if I actually felt my anger: It would come back to hurt me. The shards represented the repercussions to letting my anger out.

But in this visualization, when I returned to what my body was telling me, it didn't feel afraid. My body didn't want me to stop. It needed to keep going. It wanted me to keep punching.

Kristi trusted my process and asked, "Is there anything that can protect you from the shards of metal?"

I saw myself covered in ancient armor. I checked in with my body to see if the image felt sufficient. Once I was safe behind the chain mail that covered my face and the metal breastplate that secured my torso, I saw the shards flying at me faster and harder, almost like I was a magnet. I was no longer punching the wall, but pieces were originating out of thin air, like a summer rain was coming down hard and horizontal.

The fragments were coming directly for me, and the harder they landed, the louder the sound of metal on metal. I could hear it in my mind and feel it reverberating throughout my body. It was visceral, exhilarating, the pounding and vibrating like a tribal dance on my chest. The rhythms tapped into something deeper, guttural, parts I hadn't tapped into for decades. As though they were pounding me back into my body, I was being reanimated, and it felt *so good*.

Feeling the contact, *the conflict*, was like an explosion, and I began to chant: "I am here, I am here, I am here."

Permitting myself to let my fist punch, an outward manifestation of all the anger and rage I'd felt throughout my childhood, allowed parts of me I'd long exiled to come back online. My whole self was awakening. I was breathing life back into my existence, letting my anger bloom and grow, to take up all the space it needed so I could take up all the space I needed.

I felt compelled to intensify the energy and asked Kristi if I could throw the small beanbag I'd been holding. Sensory props are often used in SE, and she said it was fine, so I launched the beanbag across the room. This was the action I'd wanted to take when I was triggered by my mom, what my body wanted to do when I was on the phone. I'd tamped it down in the moment, but now it was being released.

I closed my eyes and started sobbing. A lifetime's worth of anger, sadness, feelings of abandonment, not being chosen—they were starting to release, too.

I felt like I was no longer carrying something I'd been holding for years.

As I left the session, I knew it had been profound and exhilarating, but it wasn't until I started writing this book that I came to understand what happened in that session more clearly.

That phone conversation with my mom after Randy died was in 2018. But when she praised my brother, it triggered something that had happened years ago, in 1991, during our mandated family therapy. During those sessions, after my intervention, Randy said he never took me to Vegas. That it was a "figment of my imagination." Then he turned to his youngest son, my stepbrother, and said, "You've always been my favorite child."

In response, my mom turned to my brother, repeating those words: "You've always been *my* favorite child." When she finally turned to me, it was to say, "Ingrid, I believe that you *believe* those things happened with Randy, but I don't believe they did."

In the moment, I tried to fight back. I yelled, "Mom, why would I make this all up?! I wouldn't have *anything* to gain!" I told her that women threw their panties onstage at Wayne Newton, that our fingers turned black from the slot machines. "How would I know any of these things if I'd never been to Vegas?!"

It fell on deaf ears. And twenty-seven years later, I was still holding all of my rage. Not just from the invalidation, but from the evisceration. How no one ever stood up for or praised me.

So as I recounted that phone call to Kristi and felt just a smidgen of the anger that was waiting for me, she helped me stay with it. I didn't know I'd been triggered, only that I was annoyed. In fact, I felt shame that I was annoyed about my mom's love for my brother: *What is wrong with me?* But with a little feedback from Kristi to tune in, to slow down, to stay with what my body was experiencing, I was able to feel and process the anger I'd been holding for nearly thirty years. It was like the healing was right there, waiting for me under the surface.

It's a theme running through all the modalities in trauma healing: We don't need to analyze what's happening or receive a therapist's interpretation. Instead we need to trust the truth in our bodies so we can begin to reclaim it. We need to let the feelings come. Discover that we can feel them. Allow natural processes to finally resolve.

Moving the Past to the Past: *EMDR*

A modality that has surged in popularity as an evidence-based treatment is **Eye Movement Desensitization and Reprocessing,** or **EMDR.** Yes, it's a mouthful. But it is an incredibly useful model for releasing the traumatic charge from previous experiences that hold great emotional distress.

The model was originated and developed by Dr. Francine Shapiro, a psychologist and educator. Its most well-known concept is bilateral stimulation, the left-right rhythmic pattern of moving your eyes back and forth. While originally conducted solely with eye movements, bilateral stimulation now includes any rhythmic left-right pattern such as crossing your arms over your chest and tapping your shoulders, often called the butterfly hug.

No one quite understands why EMDR works. One theory is that bilateral stimulation mimics REM sleep, helping the body process and consolidate memories and emotions. Another is that it encourages better communication between the right and left hemispheres of the brain.

Prince Harry famously used EMDR to treat his trauma surrounding the death of his mother, even allowing a camera to film one of his sessions for his documentary with Oprah, *The Me You Can't See*.

In the session, the memory he wants to work with is a trigger. He's never understood it, but every time he flies into London, he feels tense and afraid. He and his therapist work with a memory of sitting in an airplane, waiting to descend. "What do you feel?" his therapist asks.

"A hollow, empty feeling of nervousness . . . everything feels tense."

"When you feel those feelings, what is the message you are getting about yourself?"

"I'm the hunted," Harry says. "I'm helpless and there is no escape."

"When you think back on that moment, what would you prefer to think about now?"

"I'm not helpless . . . this is just a brief moment in time."

The therapist then asks Harry what he is feeling. He says sadness. When asked where that comes up in the body, he points to his belly.

This is when Harry begins bilateral stimulation and is encouraged to let any memories, associations, or feelings arise.

He becomes aware that his feelings of tension and fear stem from the time right after his mom died. Shortly after her death, he traveled to Africa for two weeks and said he felt so much lighter there. But upon his return to London, the home where his mother was no longer alive, he was watched, pitied, and tormented by the press. He never realized this was where the fear came from, that first time he flew back home.

As Harry continues bilateral stimulation, he describes the process as a "clearing of his hard drive. . . . Every time something comes up, it's like whoosh . . . we're done with that. Whoosh . . . we're done with that."

After a few minutes of this process, his therapist asks him to go back to that airplane seat and see what he notices now.

"I feel calm. Calm and therefore strong."

That is the end of the session.

Now, this session was actually phase four of an eight-phase process. There is much we don't see, but what is key is noticing how his previous beliefs about the situation—*I'm feeling hunted and helpless*—get replaced with a more positive belief: *I'm calm and strong.* Now, when descending into Heathrow, he can face it in his present-day circumstances, rather than be fueled by the fear of the past.

I am an EMDR therapist and often use it in my practice. During a session with Sadie, she shared that it felt like her body was holding a secret related to why she was still struggling with her eating disorder. "I know everything there is to know about eating disorders, and yet here I am, still bingeing and purging. I'm SO ready to release it!"

There was a tension between what she knew and what her body was allowing. So she wanted her body to tell her: *Why are we still hanging on to this?* She sat with her eyes closed and let her mind travel back in time, trying to find a specific charged memory. But the charge was in the present, with her frustration of having tried *everything*. She was tired of looking for answers, even of searching for where to begin in EMDR, so we began from a place that was previously intolerable for Sadie: *not knowing*.

Sadie had been solving her own problems since she was a child. It wasn't safe not to know, and so we connected with her feelings of overwhelm when she couldn't figure something out. "Notice if there are any sensations, feelings, or memories associated with *not knowing*," I suggested.

Sadie closed her eyes, checking in. Then she nodded her head to let me know, *I've got something*. She noticed physical sensations in her body, pain and anguish that reminded her, *I am powerless. I am broken*. Then Sadie began bilateral stimulation with the butterfly hug, slowly tapping one hand, then the other.

The idea in EMDR is to notice what you notice. It's not about telling a story; it's being an audience member of your own mind and body. Letting whatever comes, come. No more blinders. No more resistance.

As Sadie continued to tap, she kept going back to her head, thinking—figuring things out, so things weren't *moving*. I suggested she try opening her eyes, curious if bringing a little attention to the room (orienting herself) could offer more containment.

Sadie gazed toward my bookshelf, and I suggested she connect with the last thing that felt resonant before continuing with bilateral stimulation.

Within minutes, she burst into tears. She was nodding, crying, taking so much in as she continued to tap, back and forth. Sadie shared that a Rolodex of EVERYTHING that had happened in her life was playing on a screen before her eyes. Every moment she had been touched in a way she didn't want to be touched, every time she fawned when she wanted to exert power. She saw that her eating disorder had been holding everything she wasn't able to. Anytime something happened in her life she couldn't handle, she would turn to bingeing and purging. The bingeing initially numbed her feelings, and the purging knocked her out.

Her eating disorder was her longest-known experience of being protected from her pain, relieved from figuring things out, of being responsible for every awful thing in her life. It was holding it all. There wasn't enough knowledge in the world that could have arrested her bingeing and purging when it was responsible for holding *everything*.

Getting rid of those behaviors would have meant getting rid of her life, her memories, the closest thing she felt in childhood to being held and protected. Until she could tap into her body, see and feel this enormous truth, she couldn't let those behaviors go. She had to take her memories back, let them play out on a reel in her mind, feel the feelings they held. Let them move through her body.

A dam had been broken, and Sadie witnessed every last drop pouring over it. Like a final, enormous purge, everything her eating disorder had been holding was released.

She'd become internally safe enough to contain it and was finally able to process what had happened. Instead of feeling powerless and broken, I asked her how she felt now. "Liberated," she said. "Free."

Sadie always felt like her body wasn't hers. Like she wasn't the only one inhabiting it. We'd done previous EMDR sessions related to her father's hands on her body, as though they belonged there more than her own. But in this session, she knew: Her body was hers. She felt more embodied than she'd ever felt. EMDR purged what her eating disorder was always trying to but never could. Sadie hasn't binged or purged since. She hasn't even felt the urge.

While EMDR is conducted by a trained professional, bilateral stimulation can be used as a form of nervous system regulation.

Other forms of bilateral stimulation are drumming, dancing, and even walking. I now see the action of typing as I wrote my memoir as bilateral stimulation, so even as I remembered those moments from my past, I was also reprocessing them with the left-right tapping of my fingers and bilateral eye movement as I reread the sentences on the screen.

We can use bilateral stimulation when we feel overwhelmed or are experiencing something distressing.

In all these modalities, and many others not mentioned, reprocessing means we can finally see what is true. We can feel it. We connect with radical acceptance. We release the hope of what we wanted things to be, the outcomes that seemed easier to tolerate.

No longer holding things at arm's length, we notice that the answers aren't up to our conscious mind, but that doesn't mean there aren't answers. This is why the idea of choosing to be happy, for people with unresolved trauma, never works. *Choosing* means overriding something else. It turns out that this stuff is pretty important.

Unfawning is a process of being with whatever is there. We can't advocate for ourselves or find our center without it. Then, eventually, we might get to happy. But for me and many of my clients, happy was no longer the point. Being real, being in our actual lives, becoming free—that's what we were seeking.

Medicine to Heal

I am licensed as a psychologist, not as a medical doctor or psychiatrist. Prescribing or managing medication is not in my scope of practice. However, I would be remiss not to mention that several of my clients are currently taking or have taken medication as a helpful bridge to more regulation and freedom from their trauma symptoms. If you are seeking psychopharmacological solutions, please consult a psychiatrist who is familiar with complex trauma.

Additionally, another form of trauma therapy is gaining popularity: psychedelic-assisted psychotherapy. This healing work has ancient roots but was pushed underground by the FDA in the 1970s when it banned substances like psilocybin, MDMA, and LSD in the wake of the movement to "Turn on, tune in, drop out," a phase credited to Timothy Leary, the Harvard professor and psychologist who urged people to detach from social conventions and hierarchies through the use of psychedelics.

Despite federal regulations, these substances have continued to be used to expand one's consciousness and specifically to treat trauma. Recent studies show promising results. In particular, one study on the effectiveness of MDMA on women who suffered sexual assault showed 83 percent who received treatment no longer met the criteria for PTSD after treatment versus 25 percent of the placebo group. Psilocybin is being studied for its ability to treat depression, anxiety, and trauma. The theme among all these medicines, though they have different properties, is they allow people to access difficult memories without the same emotional charge. Thus people are able to see and process trauma with some distance. It is also believed that these medicines can rewire circuitry in the brain, breaking long-standing connections to forge new ones, sometimes in as few as one or two sessions.

Journalist Michael Pollan's tome *How to Change Your Mind* brought this underground work to the public as he unpacked the research behind and power of these therapies, and his Netflix documentary series based on the book is a good primer. However, some psychologists caution that particularly in the case of serious trauma, the course of treatment tends to be longer-term trauma therapy, and it is less predictable than the documentary implies. Much work is being done to legalize these substances, though right now one of the only legal psychedelics in every state is ketamine. Known for fostering feelings of well-being while creating an emotional distance from negative, repetitive thoughts and feelings, ketamine is a dissociative anesthetic with powerful psychedelic effects. Ketamine-assisted psychotherapy (KAP) is being used to treat depression, anxiety, PTSD, OCD, and eating disorders.

Psychedelics should be imbibed in a therapeutic setting, with therapists specifically trained in their healing properties, in a space that is safe and contained. While we cannot control where we go in a psychedelic journey, we can create the conditions for safety no matter what comes up in the medicine.

While psychedelic therapy can seem like the darling of the therapy world right now, it is important to proceed with caution. One of the reasons many therapists are advocating for legalization is to ensure more oversight. To use these treatments effectively, parameters must be in place. Without protections, such therapies can do more harm than good.

Accepting Your Reality

Like so much other unfinished business, trauma inhibits our ability to grieve. When fawners remain stuck in time, seeking endings that don't exist, we can't grieve the wounds in our lives, much less all the time we lost trying to avoid them.

Much of the regulating and reprocessing work is preparing us to finally feel and cope with loss, grieving both what happened and what didn't. We grieve:

- The loss of years lived behind a mask.
- The loss of self, in service to others.

- Time spent on toxic hope.
- Inadequate and painful relationships.
- Feeling truly abandoned by our loved ones.
- The lack of success, freedom, and joy from staying small to make others comfortable.
- So many unmet needs.
- Perpetually trying to be better when we were never guided to the source of our pain.

Grieving allows for closure on our own terms. So many of us have been waiting for a harmonious end, one where everyone understands and no one is mad, where we have permission to leave. Not every story ends neatly. We have to grieve that, too.

Grieving drops us into *reality*. This can be painful, but it's also where we have real choices. The more Anthony saw the origins of his trauma, the more he had to come to terms with who his parents actually were. Anthony never felt loved. His weekly phone calls with his parents never revealed their genuine interest in his life; instead they were about fulfilling his mother's need to appear loving and interested. When he felt and processed that loss, he could set boundaries with his parents: not immediately returning their calls or participating in family gossip and showing up only to events he wanted to, and doing so only on his own terms.

Fawners have felt invisible and undeserving for so long, but grieving can restore our voices. It opens the door to a healthy fight response where we build our capacity for anger and asserting ourselves. It holds the seeds of reciprocal relationships. We'll cover more of this in chapter 7.

My clients and I have discovered our healing often entails leaving a trauma-bonded relationship. This type of grief can feel especially painful. It moves beyond the loss of the person or the relationship to feeling like *you* are dying. For this reason, there is a saying in trauma work: Healing can hurt worse than the original wounding. In my experience, as we'll see in the pages to come, this was abundantly true.

When Francis left Colin, she felt for the first time the debilitating pain that *no one was coming to save her.* Fawners spend their lives looking outside of themselves for answers and for the love they are lacking. When we wake up to how fawning is no longer working, when we realize the person or situation that we thought would save us is gone or will never do what we thought they would, we feel a complete loss of hope. Unbelievable despair.

Sadie remembers when she left Margaret for the last time. She didn't think she could withstand the pain. It made her tap into all her unprocessed feelings of her dad leaving to start another family when she was little. While she hated his abuse, the pain of being abandoned by a parent is brutal. Sadie said, "It felt like my dad was leaving us all over again. I felt like I was dying."

Mia had to grieve who she wanted her dad to be, the parts of him she overlooked to feel close, to remain his golden child.

Davis is aware that there is more to grieve from his childhood, everything he went through as a little boy.

I've had to grieve my mother. We will speak to more of that process in chapter 7.

We've had to grieve not just what happened in the past, but also the loss of self the original wounding required. We must grieve the fact that the people who were meant to be closest to us, to love us the most, hurt us the most.

This kind of grieving opens the floodgates. As we seek closure from a trauma bond, our current pain opens the door for all the unprocessed grief that has been waiting behind it. In this way, we begin to see that a part of us *is* dying. The part that was fiercely protecting others. Fighting for them and abandoning us. In facing what feels like disloyalty to ourselves and others, we become more honest than we ever were before, and this begins our rebirth.

This means, like we talked about in reprocessing, *feeling* our pain. But not all pain is equal. Resmaa Menakem writes in *My Grandmother's Hands*:

> There are two kinds of pain. *Clean pain* is pain that mends and can build your capacity for growth. It's the pain you feel when you know what to say or do; when you really, really don't want to say or do it; and when you do it anyway, responding from the best parts of yourself. *Dirty pain* is the pain of avoidance, blame, or denial—when you respond from your most wounded parts.

As we'll read in the next chapter, clean pain often requires action. It hurts in the moment, but it also transforms us. Menakem continues: "Paradoxically, only by walking into our pain or discomfort—experiencing it, moving through it, and metabolizing it—can we grow. It's how the human body works."

Unfawning means grieving the loss of our childhood beliefs. For me, it meant losing the belief that the people who were harming me would one day wake up or see the light, take care of themselves, and take care of me, too. But I also believed that outside my personal scope of dysfunction was a largely good world, full of functional and healthy relationships. A world full of kindness. I thought if I could survive my family, I would arrive in this larger, healthier family of all things. That if I was good (fawning), it would dictate my outcomes. In other words, I would be the only variable in what is otherwise a largely stable, predictable environment.

Eventually I realized that the world wasn't full of rainbows and sunshine. So many of us created magical world views in response to the toxic environments we had to survive in. We created world views as children who were parenting ourselves. So now when people are cruel or selfish, it's like we don't have a place to put it. We feel truly blindsided.

Rituals can be a profound way to mark transitions and honor grief. They can hold aspects of the grieving process and make it visible while we are building our new sense of self. Perhaps you might write out all the things you are letting go of, then set the list afire and watch it slowly burn. Go to the ocean and watch the waves roll in and out. Light a candle symbolizing the new you, the new hope and light of this chapter.

Anthony marks his big moments with tattoos. Mia creates art. Sometimes we have a spiritual or movement practice that holds the weight of our grief. Allow yourself to lean into these containers, visible markers of all that is passing and what it's awakening in you.

When these veils are lifted, we can sit with feelings we never wanted to sit with. In a world that feels more threatening than we ever realized. In both small and grander scales, we can find a way to stop making things pretty, stop insisting on silver linings. Because we realize that THIS is what we've been fighting for, too. To live in reality. Not the magical thinking of a child's mind, but the full expanse of what it means to be human. To enlarge our capacity to tolerate, metabolize, create, thrive, and truly participate in life. Our newfound connection to reality means that we can see the good stuff, too. We own our worth and gifts just as we own our pain. We stop playing life and start living it.

Reparenting Ourselves

● ● ●

Are You My Mother? by P. D. Eastman is a well-known children's book from the 1960s. As I came across it recently, I couldn't help but read it as though it were about childhood trauma survivors, stuck in a fawn response.

When a baby bird cracks through its shell to find she's all alone, she travels far and wide, asking all she meets: "Are you my mother?" Searching for nurturance, unconditional love, she turns to a kitten. "Are you my mother?" She asks a dog, a cow, even flies to the top of a giant excavator, hoping to be scooped up and chosen, not knowing she is actually in harm's way.

So many of us are like this bird, constantly searching—in places and faces that can never give us what we need and deserve. We turn to our bosses, our friends, a lover: "Are you my mother?" All in the search of protection, belonging, and love.

No matter how much we've tried to purr, bark, or please and appease, we never experience the true connection we are seeking.

This is the path of the fawner. So a key pivot point in our healing is realizing that we can become the parents we always longed for. This process is called *reparenting*.

In essence, reparenting is parenting ourselves. It's becoming the parent we needed back then. When we can provide the care and nurturance we always deserved, our needs can finally be met. We can validate our own existence, marvel at our beautiful wings, and the past can begin to reside in the past.

While there is no such thing as perfect parenting, the fact is that children need co-regulation. Parents bounce babies because they literally can't self-soothe. Babies can't get up, walk away, feed themselves, even burp! They must borrow their caregiver's functioning for quite some time.

And yet so many adults are still unable to regulate their own emotions! In fact, this is an aspect of generational trauma. Our parents carry the coping of their parents, and generation after generation, we are handing down our wounds. This truth has led to a movement of cycle breakers, parents who want to do their own work so they might spare their children some of this ongoing burden.

People often become aware of their difficult childhood only when they become a parent themselves. Anthony held his family's party line—*we are a happy, loving family*—but found that he was parenting his son in radically different ways. The incongruity between how Anthony's parents showed up for him and he showed up for his son eventually led him to see what he'd always been lacking.

So how do we reparent ourselves? First, we have to take those blinders off and recognize where our parents didn't meet our needs, where they outright failed us. We allow ourselves to put down our stories and admit what our childhood was really like. This doesn't have to be about blame, it's about clarity.

Reparenting Journal Prompts

We might begin to see what we need in the reparenting process by asking the following questions:

- What do I continually seek in others but find lacking/impossible? Worth, an invitation, validation?
- What fantasies have I been striving for to set me free? An achievement, someone's apology, being chosen?
- Fill in the blank: If _____ could happen, I would finally be okay. What does that represent for me? Why do I think that this is the finish line? Is there a way to grant myself that now?
- What negative beliefs do I hold about myself, such as, *I am unlovable and unworthy*? Where did those come from? If I saw a photo of myself as a child, would I say that directly to them?
- If people finally saw my worth, what would they see? How does it feel to see my own worth now?
- Are my basic needs of rest, nourishing foods, connection, and movement being met? How can I take small steps toward meeting these now?
- Where can I add more playfulness, creativity, music, and nature to my life? Lean toward these experiences, as they embody the opposite of survival mode: afraid, helpless, and isolated.

Reparenting might mean inner child work. To be honest, that phrase had me rolling my eyes for most of my life. It felt *cheesy*, insufficient. I couldn't personally connect with the idea. (Likely because I still wanted YOU to be my mother, but let's not digress.)

Inner child work can mean whatever you want it to mean. It can mean bathing your inner child in white light or writing letters to your young self. In fact, lots of trauma work feels like inner child work, as the core is related to seeing and soothing ourselves. Inner child work means validating ourselves, creating internal safety. Inner child work is seeing the little you who was neglected and trying to give them all the love, rest, and relaxation that was so lacking all those years ago. I've often encouraged clients to check out trauma-informed parenting content or books. I find that the way people talk about parenting their children now is a helpful way to see what we might have been missing. Then we can grant it to ourselves in the present.

Since I was twenty-one and newly sober, I've been carrying a photo of myself from preschool in my wallet, like parents used to do before they had cell phones. It's nice to have a visual reminder that *she* is why I'm taking good care of myself now.

In a recent session with Francis, she connected with a part of herself that was stuck in her old house with Colin. She was depressed, lying in bed, crying. She couldn't motivate herself to get out of the house. Her hypoarousal was shielding her from the overwhelm of her life, leaving her practically lifeless. As we worked with this memory, Francis saw herself going back to that house, back to that old bedroom, taking her own face in her hands. Eye to eye, nose to nose, she said to herself, "I've got you. I've got you. I've got you." She did not have to give up; it was not time to die.

The fact is, even adults need parenting! The notion that we turn eighteen and lose the need for mothering or fathering is absurd, and yet many of us still don't have those supportive connections. Additionally, the part of Francis who was still stuck in the house with Colin was the same little girl who was stuck in her mother's house, years ago. As long as I've known Francis, she has used that exact language: "I feel STUCK." She needed a loving, capable presence to help get her unstuck, and that loving presence was *her*.

Her younger self (likely every age she'd ever been) was finally able to move. She got out of that bed, and Francis saw two of them getting in her car. Her younger self was sitting in the passenger seat, feet on the dash, and Francis was in the driver's seat. Moving them both away from harm.

For me, reparenting meant, *I had to choose me even though no one else ever did.* I had to love myself unconditionally, see my worth, stop waiting for other people to see it first. A key part of healing trauma means we become the person we needed as a child. This means showing up for them, connecting with them, loving them, and letting them feel that they are no longer alone.

Lily

Lily came to see me because she struggled in her dating life. She explained her conundrum: "If I don't end up liking the dude, I won't be able to break up with him. And then I'll probably just marry him." She was laughing as she said this, passing it off as a joke. But it was *true*. She was petrified to start dating because saying yes to a first date meant losing her no.

I started working with Lily when she was in her late thirties, longing for companionship and romance. As Lily explored her relationship history, she talked about the one serious boyfriend she'd had in adulthood who was possessive and insecure, always making her feel small so he could feel better. She knew she felt anxious around him but wasn't sure why.

In working with her therapist at that point, Lily shared how she'd been paying her boyfriend's rent, that she had planned a trip to the Midwest for them so he could visit his dog—putting her own job on hold to be the *best girlfriend ever.*

The therapist noticed the red flags and suggested she read *Codependent No More.* But after reading the book, Lily arrived at the conclusion that her boyfriend was the codependent one. He had the alcoholic father. She wasn't trying to control him, and she *totally* cared about herself, so much so she was starting therapy! After learning about codependence, Lily felt *more* inclined to help. *He must be going through so much!*

She didn't share any of this with her therapist. *She just doesn't get it,* Lily thought. *I don't want to disappoint her.*

Meanwhile, Lily told her boyfriend he could move in with her, thinking he'd get back on his feet and be in a better mood without all the financial stress. He in turn gave notice at his apartment complex immediately. So she cleaned his entire apartment, helped him paint the walls, and then thought, *HOLY SHIT, HE WILL BE LIVING WITH ME!*

She wasn't even sure she wanted to *be* with him, let alone live with him. She'd gone too far, hoping things would get better if she doubled down. But with the stakes this high and after another incident where he belittled her, she found the courage to end it.

"I'm so glad you were able to take care of yourself in the end!" I said, hearing this story. "I wonder if you can trace any of this back to your childhood. Where did you learn that you can't say no or take care of yourself?"

Growing up in Florida, Lily was constantly reminded how lucky she was: "There are starving children in Venezuela." This wasn't just something *all* parents said. Lily's parents immigrated from there.

She recalled a vivid memory from when she was maybe five years old. Sitting on the floor, crisscross applesauce, she was watching *Care Bears* when her mom placed a clothespin on her nose.

"Mommy, that hurts!" she said with a cry.

"I know it does, honey," her mom said in a soothing voice. "But it will help thin your nose. You'll thank me later."

Lily felt helpless. Like being herself was letting her mother down. So she kept the clothespin on, time and again. She covered her nose every time she laughed, preferred taking photos of her side profile where the width of her nose was less pronounced, and eventually got a nose job in her twenties because, as she said, "A good girl has to make good."

So many of the messages she picked up on during her childhood had this undertone: Don't be too dark, don't be too ethnic, don't . . . *be*.

When you believe you are bad, wrong, or not enough right out of the gate, it can inspire a need to please, to be better, to "overcome." It can disconnect you from your inherent worth, your sense of agency or choice. The clothespin really bothered Lily, but she knew her mother was bothered even more. By who her daughter was.

Lily was often told in a teasing manner that she was meant to "*adelantar la raza*" (advance the race). She explained that beyond needing to assimilate, she should marry a man with lighter skin, so their children would be lighter, too. It was confusing to hear such things from people she loved. She internalized these statements as *Something is wrong with me* and *I have value only based on my proximity to whiteness.*

Lily's mom never intended to shame her. Having had her own experience of what it means to be a Latina immigrant, she believed she was doing the right thing. Lily's fawn response didn't develop in an overtly abusive environment. And yet it became a primary mover in her life.

She never asked for what she felt was too much, and she was overly responsible for other people's feelings. Someone once said to Lily, "You're so agreeable." She smiled and responded, "Thank you!" In some way, this reflected her kindhearted nature. But as we viewed her experiences in the context of trauma and trauma responses, complicated feelings began to arise—how she'd unintentionally abandoned her values, career and relationship goals, even her self-worth.

"I just thought I was being a nice person," Lily shared during one session, when she was beginning to realize how widespread her fawning was. "I thought I was doing what I was supposed to do to make sure everyone was okay and that everyone liked me . . . Looking back, I think I felt the need to prove that I was a good person because something inside me felt like I was bad."

I wanted to better understand this root belief, including where it came from. I asked, "I wonder if we might connect with this part of you, the one who believes she is bad? What else does she want us to know?"

Lily paused. And then shared a painful memory. "The one time I wasn't in control and let my guard down, I lost my virginity when I was blackout drunk."

It was Memorial Day weekend, at a sandbar in the Florida Keys. She was nineteen and partying with friends on someone's boat when she passed out on the couch. She was later nudged awake to find her friends had disappeared.

The guy who nudged her was good-looking, and they started dancing before he asked, "You want to go downstairs?"

Lily was attracted to him, she wanted him to like her, so she said, "Sure."

Arriving in the downstairs cabin, he opened a door to the tiny bathroom and told her to go inside. Her first thought was, *You said yes to going downstairs, you MADE him think this would happen, and if you say no now, you'll make him mad.*

Lily told me that she didn't remember much of what happened next, just that she came to when he started screaming, "Are you a fucking virgin?!"

Lily panicked, trying to figure out the right answer. *Being a virgin is a good thing, right?* Also, it was true, so she said yes.

He looked at her, disgusted, while washing the blood off his body. "What the FUCK?!" he screamed. She immediately wanted to backpedal, thinking, *I gave the wrong answer. What did I do?*

She did not think, *What did* he *just do?* She thought, *What did* I *do?* And then he rushed out of the bathroom and slammed the door behind him.

Now alone, Lily sat on the toilet as blood kept running from her body. A part of her hoped to stay hidden in that bathroom forever, but a friend eventually found her and wrapped her in a towel. He took her back to her friends at the shore. She told me she felt like a zombie for the rest of the day, even joining her girlfriends at the tiki bar that night, where she ran into the chance of seeing that guy again. Lily was in a state of shock when someone finally asked, "What's wrong?"

Lily was obviously not herself, so her friend suggested they leave. She nodded. She thought he meant leave the tiki bar, but he meant did she want to go *home.* He then drove two hours in the middle of the night to get her there safely.

I was horrified on Lily's behalf hearing the details of her experience. Both for what happened to her and for how she seemed to be presenting it now. *Lost her virginity while blackout drunk? There was no consent, this was rape.* But she was NOT using that word.

I shared how sorry I was and wondered how she was feeling in this moment. With tears in her eyes and mine, we oriented to the present time and place. I was cautious how I proceeded, but knew these details weren't adding up. "Lily, you were raped."

Her eyes glossed over, and she said matter-of-factly, "Well, my friend took me to the hospital the next day, and the doctor who examined me said it was rape. I'd been torn so badly because I obviously didn't want to have sex, but I was like, 'No, my parents will be ashamed of me. They'll be upset with me, or people will just see me as a rape victim, as weak.' I was already struggling with not being good enough. I couldn't have that, too."

We paused. Maybe longer than was comfortable. But I wanted to take a beat, for her to feel the space that I was holding, even if it was almost too much to bear.

Lily agreed that it was a sexual assault. But the blackout story always came first, forcing her to take the blame. She remembered when she originally told her girlfriend on the boat what had happened, her friend said, "Well you were lying down with your butt in the air, what did you expect?"

That day with me, she was testing the waters. Maybe I would think it was her fault, too. For Lily, either it needed to be her fault or she told herself she wanted it to happen. Or she had to forget that it happened altogether.

The more we explored what had really happened, the more she could see that she had more memory than she was allowing herself to hold. Yes, there was a loss of consciousness for a time, but it was dissociation after the assault began.

Dissociation is a common experience for trauma survivors, one that protects us when we get overwhelmed. The body detaches from what is happening when it is too much to handle.

She came to see how the appeasement of fawning was less about being interested in him ("I was dancing with him, I thought he was cute, I said I'd go downstairs") and more about not wanting him to be mad or to hurt her. She was pumping the brakes that day. He wasn't listening. He kept going. And she left her body.

Owning the truth of what happened made it all a little less scary and a lot less shameful. The fogginess of the story started to have a beginning, a middle, and an end—it felt more contained.

I asked if she was okay if I called it a rape now. She nodded. "Yes, but what gets me is the fact that he never will. He will never think he raped someone. And that still makes me feel weird." So many fawners remain trapped by the need for external validation. We want our abusers to validate the abuse. And most of them never will. So Lily remained trapped all these years. Trapped in her head and in that tiny bathroom.

Now, there is a part of her that feels powerful, recognizing that

"THIS IS MY STORY, there is nothing wrong with me. There was nothing wrong with me then." She's found compassion for herself. She also understands why no felt impossible in her dating life. Her no was taken from her years ago, and seeing this experience for what it was for the first time allowed her to get it back.

After we'd worked together for a time, Lily finally felt ready to go on a first date. He wasn't showing much interest until she mentioned she was going to bake a pie with a friend the next day. "He seemed more interested in the chocolate banana cream than in me," Lily said, "and he asked if I'd save him a piece." It turns out that not only did Lily struggle to maintain access to her no after saying yes, but the inverse was also true. If she liked someone and they weren't interested, she'd do anything she could to get their affection, anything she could to turn their no to a yes. She continued her story. "Of course I laughed and said I would bring him a piece. But the next day, we never made the pie, and I thought, OH NO!"

Having discussed her fawn response previously, Lily and I started laughing at what was unfolding in real time, the way fawners immediately orient to the needs and wants of others as though it's our job. In my experience as a fawner and a therapist, sometimes laughter is the best medicine.

She continued with her perceived dilemma. "I promised this dude I hardly know, who doesn't seem to care if I live or die, a slice of damn pie! What's a girl to do?! Now I'm going to have to bake one all by myself, just to give him a piece!"

Lily is genuinely funny, a comedic actress, and we were both in stitches as she continued: "But thanks to therapy, I realized how nuts this was. I thought, *You should* not *spend your entire day baking a pie. You should buy one instead.*"

Calling every bakery in town, Lily found banana cream—no chocolate, but close enough. Then she paused. She witnessed what she was doing, the frantic feeling behind it. She realized, *This man hasn't bothered to text or make another date, and . . . who eats a whole damn pie?*

Obviously, she should buy a slice, because as she shared, "I'm learning to take care of myself!"

Off she went for the perfect piece. Surely this would win him over—a sign of how adorable, how thoughtful she was. But driving home, she saw that slice in the passenger seat. It didn't look adorable. It looked like she was trying to convince this man that she was enough, like she was as sweet as pie. And when she got home, she ate every last bite of that pie herself. *Progress!*

So often the answer isn't stopping our fawning behavior altogether. It is about noticing when we fawn. It's an "Oops, I did it again!" followed by another "Oops, I did it again." Eventually we'll get to the point where we say, "Oops, I *almost* did it." That doesn't mean we won't ever fawn, but we begin to notice the instinct as it arises, allowing for greater consciousness and flexibility overall.

On the last day of shooting for a recent acting job, Lily thought, *I should get everyone a present!* She even had the perfect gift in mind when she suddenly caught herself: *What am I doing?* She reminded herself that the work she did, the way she had already showed up, was enough. She now asks herself the question, "Am I doing this only so they will like me more?" If the answer is yes, then it's a no for her.

Now Lily is taking up more space and speaking up for herself. She used to not have opinions, being afraid that outspokenness on her part would invite ridicule. But now she is voicing her thoughts. She's excited to continue being herself in her career, in dating, in all her friendships. Lily wants to be *in,* but she doesn't want to be *inauthentic.* She is practicing boundaries, including saying no, even in dating—things that felt impossible before. The more she gets to know who she is, the harder she leans into that.

Seven

Opening Up

Tackling the Relational (Outer)
Work of Unfawning

While so much of unfawning is about listening to ourselves, building self-trust, and allowing it to become our guide, the work can't stay totally internal. It inevitably impacts the world around us. In fact, you might have noticed a theme running through the experiences presented in this book: Unfawning changes our relationships.

No matter how much healing I did on the inside, when I was trying to maintain the same relationship dynamics with the people who hurt me, I stepped right back on the merry-go-round.

All the self-care I loaded onto one side of the scale was counterbalanced by engaging with the same people in the same ways. When I put myself in situations where they continued to ignore what I'd been through, I abandoned myself—and this reinforced all my negative beliefs: *I am unworthy. I don't deserve love. Dysfunction is relationship.*

As we have gained more access to ourselves, continuing to grow means sharing our newfound capacity with others. It means changing the way we show up in relationships, resetting the terms. We carry the notion that *wounding happens in relationship, and healing happens in relationship* into the world. We don't wait for it to happen—we make it happen.

We practice sharing our preferences, opinions, what we like—and conversely, what we don't. We take up more space in our relationships. Sometimes by asserting ourselves, and sometimes by taking up literal space in the world. We practice *not* being the first one to volunteer, to offer to pay, to jump in to help, or to rescue another person when things go wrong. Rather than always orienting ourselves toward others, we practice letting others lean in toward *us* if they are able. And if they choose not to—well, that's good information, too, that allows us to make informed choices from there.

Waking Up Our Healthy Fight Response: *Anger and Assertiveness*

Some of our relationships need rebalancing—more of our authentic and whole self, less of our managing the whole kit and caboodle. But sometimes others aren't ready or willing to change with us, and some of those relationships may need to end.

Anger—Igniting the Fire within

Many fawners have lost access to their fight response. As fighting back was never safe, we disconnected from everything related to it, sacrificing our ability to feel our angry feelings, communicate them, or speak up for ourselves at all. Therefore, part of the unfawning process requires that we awaken this dormant part of us so that we can embrace the agency, autonomy, and authority it provides.

For most fawners, when we were in touch with our hurt or anger, our feelings were invalidated and we were steamrolled: "Calm down. Don't be so ridiculous, you're so sensitive . . ." Over time we learned to repress our feelings and needs, believing it was our job to let it all go. Like pebbles in a river, the currents had been sweeping us downstream for so long, we eventually told ourselves we're just really good swimmers.

But imagine if you didn't *want* to swim, didn't want to go along to get along. Imagine for a moment being a boulder in that same river. Watching the currents make their way around you while you remain, unwavering. Not being a pushover. Holding your own. In this image we can see that the boulder isn't stopping the river by not rolling with the tide. Every element, including the boulder, gets to be exactly what it is.

We are meant to experience the full range of emotions, and **anger** is a valuable member of the team. Just as for Riley in the movie *Inside Out*, whose fiery anger helped her mobilize at the hockey rink, anger can be a guide. It can let us know, *I'm not okay*. It can give us a voice. Anger is a bridge, connecting our deeper feelings of hurt, pain, and sadness with the ability to assert ourselves and set boundaries in the world.

For many fawners, our healthy fight response got snuffed out. At the age of twelve I was told by a social worker: "Emotional abuse isn't *reportable*." Later my parents said, "You are being dramatic. You're a selfish liar." Attempting to advocate for myself and be in touch with the fire in my belly got me burned. So *tsssssssss*. Out the fire went, for good.

A key aspect of unfawning, then, is cultivating a new relationship with fire. Learning how to tend to it safely. Learning to hold the fire within allows us to become sturdy, stand upright, stand up for ourselves. Moving from passivity to activity—anger allows mobilization. And this is part of what helps the roller coaster come down. We can move through a fixed fawn response by saying, "Hey, I didn't like that!"

Many fawners fear their own anger because they've faced unhealthy anger from others. Unhealthy anger is violent, selfish, used for dominance or control: "I am right, no matter what!" Spiritual teachings have disavowed anger, and we've all heard about anger management, interpreting these messages to mean that *everyone* needs to quell their internal fire. But fawners need to stoke it. Blow on the baby embers. I know this can *feel* like we're gonna burn the whole forest down, but most of us are lucky to light a birthday candle.

We don't sacrifice ourselves to anger, impulsively reacting in a rage. We learn to feel our anger and be in relationship with it. In that Somatic Experiencing session, for example, I noticed where my anger resided in my body and what it needed from me to authentically resolve. Feeling our anger isn't always relational; we're not necessarily channeling it *at* others. We might instead notice it moving in and then out of our bodies—like a weather pattern bringing vital nutrients to the soil. After I felt my anger, throwing that beanbag across the room, I dropped into what was beneath. The tears finally came. No one else was even involved. But as you'll read later, finally feeling the anger and then letting it release allow us to access the appropriate actions we need to take.

We can't take care of ourselves if we can't feel our anger, and we can't be truly intimate or vulnerable in our relationships, either. Healthy anger is about respect—respecting ourselves and respecting others by letting them know our boundaries, who we are, and what we need. Then they can decide for themselves how to interact or respond. We stop pretending or trying to manage our feelings, and we let *all* of them be.

Yancey, my husband, is a big stomper when he's angry. I named his actions *big stomping* in a less-than-compassionate moment one day. But now I do it, too. Sometimes when we are mad, we recognize that we can't have a real conversation with each other. We are too dysregulated, so as a way to move that energy through, we big stomp.

Like a cartoon character, huffing and puffing, big knees in the air, hearing the sound of your feet as they land. I often have a bit of a scowl on my face. I'm sure I look rather hilarious in my flip-flops, big stomping down our block.

But fifteen minutes later, I am back in my body in a more regulated way. We can return to our conversation. This doesn't mean I've gotten over my anger. It means I can communicate it in a more compassionate way. A way in which my husband can hear me, *receive* me—which is what we both really want.

Fawners often found alternative ways to channel their anger because it wasn't safe to express it directly. Mia remembers turning her anger on herself from a very young age. She punched and scratched herself or pulled her own hair. Her anger couldn't be expressed to others, so it went to her body. But even this didn't evaporate her anger. Because "then, I was not only angry, I was angry that I *got angry*." As though anger itself was the problem, she became flooded with shame.

Today, Mia recognizes the buildup in her body when anger wants to be recognized. She has learned to respond kindly to herself when she sees it coming. "You don't have to do that anymore. You can scream if you want, but we aren't going to hurt ourselves." Then she often does scream, in her car or into a pillow. Or she takes a lot of deep breaths, almost yelling sighs. Talking out loud to herself: "I am so fucking frustrated right now!"

She has taken martial arts, which involves actually kicking or punching in safe ways. And now she can do these same practices at home.

Like with many of her other feelings, she channels anger through art journaling. While this practice has always been an outlet, she uses it even more intentionally for this purpose now. Translating anger into art feels less scary than expressing it with words. She loves using a chunky graphite pencil, and then she scribbles, *really* hard.

Sometimes she makes noises as she goes, and it feels like taking the anger out of her body and transferring it onto the page. Being with her anger in this way allows her to see it in a healthy way. It removes the blinders and the shame.

Leaning into healthy anger provides a gateway to appropriate response. We turn from how others might be impacted to what we actually need. But we don't go from zero to ten. It's a process.

Assertiveness—Finding Your Voice

For many fawners, being assertive feels *aggressive*. Standing up for ourselves can feel *mean*. I've additionally felt *selfish* (the one word consistently thrown at me when I tried asserting myself as a child). These are the barriers to taking care of ourselves, and let's not sugar-coat this . . . they are painful!

Part of learning a healthy fight response means feeling the boiling point we've been avoiding for good reason. Along these lines, there's a saying: When we stop people-pleasing . . . people will not be pleased. I wish it wasn't true! Much of unfawning is about tolerating the responses we get when we stop fawning. It's a package deal. Expressing our feelings increases the chances that people will express theirs back. Speaking up for ourselves can invite criticism.

Many people talk about the work of asserting ourselves like it's a YOU GO, GIRL victory lap: "You are WORTHY!" or as simple as "Just take care of yourself and set healthy boundaries." I use the word *tolerate* on purpose. For fawners, asserting ourselves doesn't initially feel like a victory. It feels exhausting and it feels like CRAP.

Healing trauma is some of the bravest work we can do. Put your hand on your heart. Remind yourself that taking care of yourself is not selfish. You are allowed to exist. And in our existing, we can practice new ways of regulating our nervous system. Remember those tools and strategies we learned in chapter 6? We're gonna need them!

Eventually, I promise, we'll discover that it's all worth it. Because this is where we really begin to find our true selves, not the overcompensating version. This is where we find our voice, our joy, our creativity. There is so much we gain access to when we aren't cut off from who we truly are.

Unfawning is about coming home to ourselves. Our true nature, our delights, our desires. Ultimately, this will feel better than anything in the world.

When we assert ourselves, we tap into the ability to speak up with clear, respectful language. It doesn't mean we stop considering other people's needs; it means our needs matter, too. Stepping out of the safety of submission feels aggressive because we don't have this new territory mapped out in our bodies yet. But asserting ourselves is not threatening. We can ask questions; we can state our needs. This is the work of becoming a real live human.

This is where we feel the change we've been longing for our whole lives. When we allow ourselves to be truly seen, we can allow others the opportunity to show up for us when we need it. We can experience vulnerability not solely as danger and fragility, but as open-hearted bravery.

As we find our emotional availability, we find it in others, too. We don't just lose some relationships, we gain new ones. As our capacity grows, we are drawn to different types of people, and they are drawn to us.

For Lily, assertiveness always meant being rude or entitled, as though she were saying, "I matter more than anything else." Being assertive wasn't *polite*; it made you stand out, which meant potential danger. She didn't want to appear ungrateful for what she already had. A lot of this was cultural for Lily, as she came from an immigrant community. Instead of being assertive, she was encouraged to work harder without complaint.

She avoided assertiveness, which meant avoiding *herself.* When I asked her how this felt, when she was angry but couldn't address it, she described the experience: "My heart starts beating faster. I feel an intense heat and an uncomfortable tingle on the back of my neck and in my ears. I feel a heaviness in my chest. Like I'm being weighed down, but also like I'm gonna float away. I'm totally outside of my body and desperately trying to grab hold of something that will bring me back down, yet unburden me, too."

This is the moment in fawning when she would lie or start backpedaling. She'd throw herself under the bus and take responsibility for things she didn't even do. All to avoid her anger, all to avoid the need to assert herself.

A friend recently asked Lily why they weren't hanging out as often. Instead of saying, "I'm focusing on myself and my mental health right now," she immediately apologized. Said, "I'm being a bad friend," then promised to be better. But that's not how she felt or what she wanted. She wanted the space, not just from her friend but from everyone. But she didn't know how to hold her boundary.

Before we started working together, Lily felt like apologizing or backpedaling worked. She felt relieved once the other person was relieved. But now the heat on her neck wasn't going away. Taking the blame *stopped working*.

This is what I mean by our bodies will tell us what they need. Lily didn't shame herself into having a voice. As she came into her body, she could hear and feel its feedback. *This does not feel right for me.*

It can take a while to notice what we feel in the moment, so at first we might catch it only after the fact. But this doesn't mean it's too late. It means after we've processed how we feel, we can go back and say, "I wish I would have handled that differently." Or "I realize now I wasn't completely honest. Can we talk about it again?" We can ask for a do-over!

Alternatively, we can lower the stakes and simply imagine being assertive, in relationships that aren't as close. Don't do anything just yet! How does it feel in your body to *think* about returning an item to a store? Telling the waiter they brought the wrong order?

Notice the sensations you're experiencing in your body and place your hand on your heart. See if you want to deepen your breath. Orient to your surroundings through your senses. Then see how these impact whatever sensations you were feeling moments before. See how it feels to be an advocate for yourself even in your mind. Notice if a particular part of you needs attention. This practice can aid us when we move closer to taking action in real time.

Sometimes it's helpful to write a script of what you'd say if it felt possible. This can help you find your voice privately. Perhaps you might share it with a trusted friend or someone who understands, so they can validate your feelings and support you in sharing your truth more directly.

Bookending our actions can be helpful, too. This means taking care of ourselves both before and after we lean into new spicy territory. We learn to regulate ourselves on both sides of big moments, because doing something new can leave us dysregulated. It might look like taking a walk before we have a hard conversation, and additionally planning another activity for after, like taking a warm bath or listening to music.

Igniting a healthy fight response is a necessary component of unfawning. But we can do it at our own pace, with supportive community, and alongside growing a self that can tolerate all the feelings that arise.

Here I Am: *Setting Boundaries*

Before a fawner can *conceive* of setting healthy boundaries, we have to know and have compassion for the parts of ourselves that never saw boundaries as an option. We must realize that boundary-setting is less about what boundary to set or how to express it, and more about acknowledging the triggered parts of ourselves that are still afraid . . . and showing them that we have the capacity to set boundaries *now*.

Many of us are just learning what a boundary means for the first time, so it's useful to think about boundaries in the context of fawning, in all its many flavors. Remember that fawning can look like caretaking (or leaning in), or fawning can look like appeasement (or leaning away). As both flavors pull us from our center, establishing boundaries is a way to repossess it. Boundaries are about taking personal responsibility while also holding others accountable.

Finding Your No

When our fawning leans in the direction of caretaking, we've loaned out parts of ourselves as though we're a hardware store. "How can I help you? Have you tried this new tool?" We've drawn up plans for others they know nothing about.

Compensating for neglect, invisibility, and never having our needs met, we've attempted to meet everyone else's needs as the route to self-care. Boundaries in this context means discovering where we end and where someone else begins. We stop overextending, overfunctioning, never asking people to show up for themselves, too. If you have felt a tether from your body to theirs, pulling you toward their perpetual need . . . this is where you cut it (or at least make it an elastic band rather than a rope).

In practice, this means not saving people, perpetually solving their problems, or being a parent if that's not your actual role. Boundary-setting looks like sitting on our hands and not putting out their fires, even if it feels like an emergency. Are you a firefighter? An ER doctor, a rehab, their therapist? You get the idea.

We have to enlarge our ability to tolerate discomfort here, too. It's *hard* not to jump in when we think we can help. They might be looking you right in the eyes, begging, and yet fawners need to know: Just because you think you can help doesn't mean you should.

This can feel *mean*. So here's a reminder: In your attempts to save others, you have gone down with the ship. In not holding others accountable, your own needs have not been met. Additionally, as we stop enabling and infantilizing, we free up space people need to step into and step up in their own lives. It doesn't mean they will. It means we are getting out of the way so that they can. Fawners need to find their no. When we've perpetually overextended ourselves, finding our no means, "I won't be more responsible for your life than you."

When our fawning leans in the direction of appeasement (smiling as we're being steamrolled, unable to stand up for ourselves), establishing boundaries is about deciding what we will and won't accommodate. It's as though we're building a wall around our bodies, keeping us safe. While there is a door, only *we* can open it.

Fawners are accustomed to letting people into our space who don't deserve to be there. Then we spend our time and energy trying to manage the harm they cause on the inside, rather than simply asking them to leave. So instead of attempting to minimize the hurt and chaos, finding our no means, "I won't let you infringe on me in this way." It means closing the door, walking away, disengaging.

Of course, there is overlap in these two categories, and boundaries aren't always a hard line. They can be flexible; they can be negotiated. They aren't just related to abuse and neglect. Boundaries are essential in any relationship, whether it is a boss who expects too many late nights, a friend who always stops by unannounced, or a mom friend who never returns the favor. In fact, sometimes starting with a more casual relationship can help us learn to eventually set boundaries in relationships where more is at stake.

Boundaries Don't Guarantee Outcomes

Fawners have often believed that setting a boundary in the right way (fawning) would elicit a positive outcome. But now that we've established more internal safety, we can see that boundaries are not, in fact, about changing the other person. Getting them to finally take care of themselves (or us). Getting them to stop being bullies or abusers. These aren't boundaries. Rather, boundaries are a continuation of how we take care of ourselves—whether the other person changes or not.

We don't have control over outcomes. In other words, you can assert yourself ("These late nights aren't working for me"), but you can't make your boss agree with you. The step isn't about making them change; it's learning to voice the problem. When we do, a million things can happen. Maybe we voice our concern and receive validation, and that is all we needed. Maybe we have a specific request: "Can I get some overtime?" The boss may say yes, or she may say, "That isn't in the budget, but if you get me through this project, I'll give you three days off." Sometimes they say, "Are you kidding me? Who do you think you are?" Setting boundaries isn't about trying to control the situation but rather about speaking up for your needs. All the different responses give you more information and the ability to make decisions from there. It allows you to enter into the real negotiation of human relationships.

Fawners fear: *If I have the conversation, it's going to go badly.* But we don't know if that's true! We have to practice having these conversations. Sometimes people surprise us and show up in ways we never could have imagined. It isn't just about having hard conversations, it's about recognizing all the possibilities that can unfold.

I know setting boundaries can feel terrifying, and you likely want to stay in chapter 6, doing inner work that feels more under your control. We'd rather sign up for another session of EMDR or try another reparenting technique in the hope of removing the need for boundaries. While that inner work is key, we can't stay there.

I tried as hard as anyone to try and solve my trauma 100 percent on my own, taking responsibility for my part in it. But sadly, eventually, some things had to change in my outer world if I was going to stay true to myself.

When I'd first started writing after Randy died, I'd been shameless about calling anyone I could think of to corroborate my story, make sure I was remembering things right. I called social services to see if they could find any physical paperwork from the nineties related to the case. I called one of Randy's ex-wives. I spoke to all three of his biological children. I tried to talk to the family therapist who'd done those mandated sessions. I was so desperate to hear how other people experienced what happened, to gut-check what I remembered and how fucked up I thought it was. And I received so much validation. "Oh, yeah, he was like that. He did that with me, too." His ex-wife even mentioned a friend of hers and Randy's who had seen us in Vegas, visited us at our hotel room, and got out of there as fast as he could because he could tell something was seriously wrong.

But in all my interrogations and investigations, I never asked my mom. In fact, I avoided talking to her about my writing, until one day I decided it was time.

We were on the phone when I nervously shared what I'd been processing, which was a lifetime of pain inflicted by her husband. I tried to keep my voice steady, even as tears began to trickle down my cheeks.

"After Randy died, I felt like I finally had a voice again. I was flooded with memories that would wake me in the middle of the night, and I'd rush to write them down. I've talked with everyone else, all of his kids, even his ex-wife, as I've been working on this manuscript."

She was quiet, so I kept going.

"I've honestly felt freer since he passed. And I'm tired of having his version of the story be the only one. I need to tell my side. You and I have not talked about any of this since I was in high school, and I guess I want to give you an opportunity from this place in your life to tell me what you understand about that time."

"Well . . ." There was a long pause. "I'd have to think about it some. I don't know what to say right now."

I knew she wasn't expecting this confrontation, that she felt overwhelmed. I told her how I was originally thinking I would just send her the book when it was finished, but I didn't want to ambush her with an entire text. "I don't know what depth of conversation you and I will ever have about it," I said. "But I don't feel okay with the elephant in the room anymore."

Caution crept into her voice as she replied, "I can understand that. And I can understand where you are coming from. It's just something that I don't feel comfortable with. I don't know if I want to bring up all those *feelings* in me."

"But never talking about it is impacting our relationship," I said as I tried to keep my temper from flaring. "It feels dishonest to me. Now that Randy's gone, I was hoping we might have a different relationship, that we could finally be close. But that can't happen until we acknowledge what happened in the past."

The more we talked, the more I felt like I was trying to swim against a current of polite but stubborn resistance. She kept saying, "I understand . . . if that's what you feel you need to do . . . if it makes you feel better, then I suppose that's good . . ." Never once getting in the water with me, never acknowledging that anything I was saying was real.

I finally said, "I've been holding a lot of hurt for a long time because nobody else could see it, witness it, and believe it. And I'm finally saying *this is real*. It happened. It's pretty fucked up and I'm not going to keep it a secret anymore. At some point, I need us to address things more directly. At least that's my hope. Why don't you think about it."

She agreed and we hung up. I let out a long breath I didn't know I'd been holding. I felt a little lighter and proud of myself for being so bold.

But our second phone call wasn't any more productive. My mom seemed even more determined to put off any hard conversations, with a harder edge to her tone, saying, "My psyche is pretty fragile right now, Ingrid. I've had a hard time getting through this last year since Randy died, and I just don't know if I can even go there right now. This is stuff that happened twenty-five years ago, and I understand that you need to do what you need to do, but I don't know that I'm ready."

She wasn't ready? After twenty-five years? "Mom, I've been holding in my side of the story, feeling like no one believed me. I can't do that anymore. If you want to maintain that none of it happened, I'm going to have a really hard time with that."

"I can't do anything about the past. I can only do something about today and tomorrow," she said. Then she started to cry. "I love you very much . . ." She paused for a long time, her voice so shaky and soft she was barely able to finish. "I hope that we can still have a halfway decent relationship. Maybe we can have that conversation somewhere down the road. But I just can't do it now."

My heart sank, but I said I understood. I told her I would just keep writing until the time came when she felt ready to talk about it. She took another long pause and said, "Well, I'll probably try and go to yoga this afternoon. I haven't done anything like that in weeks, and I really need it."

"That sounds like a good idea, Mom," I said. And we hung up.

I initially felt some relief after that conversation. At least I wasn't keeping my writing a secret. Then I returned to the comfort of my longing: *Maybe one day she'll face the truth.* I carried that hope around like a time capsule for another three and a half years.

We entered a global pandemic, and Henry graduated from kindergarten. As we'd done for decades, I talked to my mom a few times a month about comfortable topics in the present tense. I would occasionally feel her support, but mostly the same emotional distance.

The longer Randy was gone, the more my mom seemed to revere him. Yancey and I didn't see family for a long while due to COVID-19, but we finally made it back to Colorado. My mom had moved in with her friend Kathy, and we spent several days with them in the mountains.

As my mom showed me to her bedroom, where Yancey and I were meant to sleep, it was like walking into Randy's shrine. The old posters that used to hang above his piano were looming large over her bed. The sight of his things made my skin crawl, but I didn't say a word. At least not to my mom.

While my mom was at the doctor, I took a moment to talk to Kathy about my book, and we sat crying in her bathroom. "I'll do whatever I can to help your mom see the truth," she said.

We took family photos, ate lovely meals, and played Uno as a family. My mom drank in the evenings, seeming annoyed that Henry didn't show her love the way she wanted, and I felt the same way I always had—like being with her was an obligation. Like my mom didn't know me at all, but this was what it looked like to be a good daughter. You show up. You accept your mother's limitations, privilege her wounds. You understand that she's doing the best she can. Only now I felt angry about it.

I finished my manuscript and showed it to a few key people in my life . . . including Kathy. I'd sent her a copy, hoping she could be a bridge of understanding between my mom and me. A few months later, a message popped up on Facebook from Kathy; I was terrified to open it.

"I wish I never read your book, because I have no respect for your mom now."

A knot formed in my stomach. It never occurred to me that my mom might be affected by blowback from my book. I had been so nervous about the wrath that could come for me, I didn't see the possibility that my mom might face her own consequences.

Kathy's message continued: "I just can't understand how she didn't advocate for you. Whenever I bring it up, she just screams that you are a liar. She won't even acknowledge it, and it really bothers me. Whenever we have a conversation about it, she wakes up the next day like nothing happened. Just like in your book. Head in the sand. I'm so sorry."

The knot in my stomach turned to nausea. "Yancey," I said, "can you please come here?" As I read him Kathy's message, I started to cry as though I were choking. Coughing tears that had been lodged in my throat. *I can't believe it. My mom's not just refusing to acknowledge my experience. She's screaming that I'm a liar.*

Yancey hugged me hard. I was stunned, fighting to figure this all out, like a math problem my life depended on. It had been five years since Randy died. Whatever I had perceived as a possible window to that conversation with my mom was clearly a closed door. It was never going to open. I felt forced to see something I had never seen this clearly. I had always looked at my mother's denial as the issue, but I was the one with blinders on.

My mother had abandoned me. She did it back then, and she was still doing it now. Prioritizing that man and his story over the truth of my experience. Not only that, she was hurting me. Defaming me by calling me a liar. It hurt now just as much as it did back then.

It was humiliating.

"If she still thinks I'm a liar, I can't be in relationship with her anymore," I responded to Kathy. I meant it. I was surprised how much I meant it. It didn't feel like a choice, as though my body was revolting and letting me know it would not stand being in a relationship with my mother for one more minute.

I went numb and curled up on the couch next to Yancey. We tucked ourselves under a weighted blanket and watched mindless TV before going to bed. When I woke up early the next morning, I composed a text to my mom. It flew out of me without too much thought, but it said everything. Then I did not send it. I wanted to sit with it. I wanted to know what it would feel like to say goodbye to my mom. To feel the weight of that decision, for myself and for my family.

Initially, I noticed some relief. I was fiercely advocating for myself, and that felt like the right thing to do. I felt my strength. I thought of all the obligatory calls and visits, and the idea of never doing that again was liberating. I felt more authentic.

I was lying in bed a couple of days after Kathy's message and I couldn't sleep—tossing and turning, the tears starting to come. I didn't want to cry. *Please don't cry. Please don't feel this, it's too much, I can't do it.*

I wanted to tell Yancey what was going on, but I couldn't. The kid in me who saw that her mother had given up on her was too embarrassed. I felt worthless, even with the person I knew loved me the most.

I went to the bathroom and sat in the dark, my body on the cold toilet seat and my face in my hands. I cried as I rocked back and forth, the sobs relentless.

The clarity I had gained through my writing, sharing, and heal-ing had led to this? My hopelessness was like a blackout. *I don't want to kill myself, but it would be okay if I died.*

Decades of devastation were coming for me. Years of pent-up pain. I cried for over an hour, until I was too tired to weep. The feel-ings were still with me, but all my energy was gone. I crawled back to bed, feeling gravely alone.

The next morning, I told Yancey what had happened. The look on his face, indicating he felt so much sadness but didn't know how to say it, shattered me. I knew he was coming from a loving place, but I couldn't feel it. I only felt pathetic, and that made me feel everything all over again.

And then somehow we got Henry ready for school, and I showed up for six clients over Zoom. I did what I had always done, said the things I needed to hear. Felt the hope I needed to feel—not the hope that someone else might change, but that I could feel better even when they didn't.

One week after I received Kathy's message, I opened my phone and saw comments my mom had made on my personal Facebook page. Lovely comments, ones you would imagine a grandmother to make. But they just made me angry. *She can't keep pretending to be loving when she's screaming that I'm a liar.* I opened the message I had written for my mom a week earlier and hit send.

> Staying in relationship with you, knowing you believe I'm manipulative—has kept me from healing—from ever being my true self. I am finally choosing to love myself no matter what you or anyone else thinks of me. I never wanted it to come to this. But I can no longer have you in my life while you hold Randy in such esteem and continue to view me as delusional. It doesn't feel like a choice anymore. It feels like I should have done this a long time ago . . .

I didn't want to have another conversation. I didn't want to hear her defense or allow anything to change my mind. I just wanted it to be done.

As I reread the message, I felt dizzy. I couldn't think straight, but I suddenly realized it was Randy's birthday. I couldn't believe I sent that text on his birthday.

My mom didn't text back immediately, an hour later, or even that same evening. However, my stepbrother John told me she'd sent him a text that night. Their annual "raising a glass to Randy" for his birthday message. The contrast was striking. Right as I told my mom she was losing me by choosing Randy, she was celebrating him.

The next day, I started to wonder whether she'd received my text at all when I saw a message on my phone.

Dear Ingrid, I am so sorry. Hope your book helps you heal. Personally I choose to not live in the past. I cannot change it. Everyone makes mistakes. I am sorry for mine. I love and care about you and your family. I pray for you every night. Love Mom.

On the surface, some of it seemed loving. But I turned my attention away from her words and toward their impact. I asked myself questions I might have asked a client:

Do I feel seen, heard, or respected? No.

Do I feel understood or validated? No.

Do I feel like she wants to make things right? No.

Do I feel overridden, blamed, shamed, or manipulated? Yes.

When I answered these questions, it was clear. My mom was saying nothing at all in her message. I'd never heard her mention a single mistake she claimed she was sorry for. Was it when she abandoned me thirty years ago, or was it last week when she called me a liar?

I noticed her comment about not living in the past. It's one trauma survivors get all the time, and it's a gross misrepresentation of trauma. Being traumatized is not a choice. Trauma is not something that happened back then; it's not in the past at all. It's an ongoing experience of feeling deeply unsafe and terrorized, over and over, in the present moment.

My mother's need to stay in denial was understandable. She would have to admit her entire life was a lie, that she put me in harm's way, left me there, and then blamed me for it. But understanding *why* she did it didn't mean I needed to stay in relationship.

I finally realized that if I *had* to choose (and I did), I would rather have me in my life than her in my life. What a horrible choice, but I was making it. Ironically, this was all happening the week of Mother's Day. With a mix of sadness and self-respect, I was saying *Happy Mother's Day* to me. I was breaking a cycle, doing the brave and brutal work of healing trauma.

I had been a good girl for decades, living with my mother's alcoholism and denial, connecting with the best parts of her, thinking they were enough. What I never understood was how that kept me in harm's way. I had to leave the most important parts of myself at the door, never able to claim them as my own. I never realized that staying in relationship with a mother who saw me as broken made me believe I actually was.

Now it's over two years later. I still haven't spoken with my mom, but I feel sturdier than ever. Kathy and I keep in touch, and she shared that my mom read my memoir when it was published. She could hear her crying in her bedroom. My mom told Kathy one morning, "I believe her."

My mom has not told me these things. But over time, I've realized I don't need her to.

I have no regrets cutting off contact with my mom. Taking that space and giving a voice to my pain were necessary for me to heal. I had to put her needs aside to finally take care of my own.

But I wonder if I still need such firm boundaries now. Sometimes a hard boundary is necessary. I have no judgment there. At other times, boundaries become more flexible. Only we can know if we are putting ourselves in harm's way. Only we get to decide how to best take care of ourselves with the resources we have at the time.

I always knew my mother didn't have the capacity to show up for me, and I had compassion for her. I understood her predicament. But before I did the work of unfawning, I didn't factor myself into the equation at all. Seeing her pain meant I had to deny my own. Her struggle was always more important, because I thought she needed to get unstuck in order for me to get unstuck. But when I finally stopped waiting for her to get it and *I* set those boundaries, it gave me the room I needed to gain a new perspective about myself. Nothing has changed about how I see my mom. I didn't need to figure her out in order to heal. I had done that work years ago and it didn't heal me. Today I still see my mom as a woman who was stuck and have compassion for her. But I see myself completely differently. I can speak my truth. I can get all my needs met. And now I can approach all my relationships from a completely different angle.

Time does not heal all wounds.

But I think setting boundaries can get us at least halfway there.

Breaking Down Boundaries

I believe the real work of boundary-setting is everything we've reviewed up to this point, but here are some additional suggestions I share with clients that might be helpful to you, too.

· Start small! When someone asks what you'd like to do, check in with yourself and answer honestly instead of orienting to their needs with a go-to "Whatever you want is fine."

- Write a list of your values. What is important to you? It's difficult to set boundaries if we don't know what these things are. Maybe your values include having some downtime during the day or reserving your weekends for family. Keeping these values front of mind allows you to prioritize them.
- Create safety in advance. Tell safe people you're going to start setting boundaries. This can be a gift to you and to them, speaking to the changes you're making and why. This additionally invites more vulnerability from others, reestablishing the rules of relationship in a spirit of "Can we be all of who we are with one another? I want to hold that space for you, too."
- Look at boundaries from a parts perspective. Part of me wants A, and another part wants B. This can open up more nuance, allowing you to understand why you sometimes struggle with a clear decision.
- Unsubscribe! I could never take my name off email lists. When I started giving myself permission to hit that little button, it felt like FREEDOM! (An additional carrot for those who worry about hurting the sender's feelings: As someone who has an email list and pays per subscriber, I find it a blessing when people who don't want my emails take their name off the list! EVERYBODY WINS!)
- Have a boundaries journal. What are your hard lines in the sand? Often, when people cross a boundary, we are quick to move the line. Seeing our boundaries in black and white can hold us accountable for taking care of ourselves. For example, *If they drink at the party, I will take an Uber home. Or If they criticize my body, I will tell them "This is not okay. If you do it again, I will end the conversation."*
- Imagine an actual boundary around yourself, like a bubble of safety. Is it strong enough, permeable enough? Maybe a fence would be better? Notice what containers allow you to see and to be seen without feeling steamrolled.

- Remember that we aren't looking for people to cosign, understand, or give us permission to set boundaries. We are allowed to take care of ourselves, just because.
- Be curious about a modified yes or no, considering what you are available for and what you would like to qualify. For example, "I would love to go on a hike, but can it be shorter?" Many times, there is a middle ground.

Learning to Trust: *Becoming Vulnerable with Safe People*

After a lifetime of relationships in which we had to become smaller to make room for others, in which we felt perpetually taken advantage of and had to squash our own needs to feel safe, fawners can be cautious when it comes to relationships. Even as we become aware of why we fawned in the past and how we don't need to always accommodate, we can feel like we can't trust ourselves, or others.

I still find it hard to believe that Yancey was the very next person I dated after the Homing Pigeon. These men and our relationships could not have been more different, and yet when Yancey and I first started dating, I was understandably wary. Especially when I found out that he was newly sober.

I had been sober for two decades by this time and did not want a repeat of my marriage to Mark, where he denied his struggles with alcohol and made me feel crazy for insinuating he had a problem. So Yancey's new sobriety was a red flag. But here's where things started to feel vastly different: It was a red flag for Yancey, too. In fact, he was the one who pointed it out. "I know that you're good for me," he said. "But I understand if you don't feel the same." He honored my feelings of hesitation related to his drinking. He wasn't in a rush, and he wanted me to feel safe.

This self-awareness was so different from my past relationships.

He knew what was his, and he was working on it. The overall feeling I got from him was *I'm responsible for my own shit*. He wasn't manipulating me with pretty words or gaslighting me for my concerns. I could feel his honesty and integrity. There was space and mutual respect. This was such a foreign feeling to me, and yet it felt so right. So I leaned in, learning to trust that a man who could take responsibility was a man I might want to partner with.

Over twelve years later, I have never felt unsafe with him, and I have never felt more loved. It's not that we don't have our struggles. It's that we each feel responsible for ourselves *and* for the quality of our relationship. This is what feels so radically different and maintains our strong foundation. It allows us to have an actual partnership where we each take up space.

Safe relationships can be just as foreign to fawners as healthy anger. We never felt safe in our relationships; we felt we needed to perform.

So this is another area where we move out of binary thinking—safe or unsafe, vulnerable or not—and we often have to test the waters. We discover safety in our relationships by wading in a little at a time. As we establish more relational safety, we start to recognize it and move toward that (and away from unsafe relationships), opening up and becoming more vulnerable as we become more secure.

Vulnerability and safety are processes rather than destinations, where we continue attuning to ourselves *and* to the contexts we are in. Each relationship has its own level of safety, and that can change over time. We should be aware of those changes. And while this might sound like hypervigilance, learning to trust is not about anxious monitoring. Rather, it's an honoring, an *honesty*, about what we want to share as well as other people's capacity to receive it.

Being vulnerable doesn't mean offering radical transparency at any cost. We don't owe everyone 100 percent of ourselves. Withholding isn't always avoiding. Learning to be vulnerable might mean our fawn response feels conscious-ish. As we intuitively know, *This is not a safe person. I don't need to make myself vulnerable to them.* We smile, say "Thank you," and move on. But this can feel like we are going backwards, like we are being inauthentic.

In these moments, allow yourself to feel your feelings. Stay curious and take some space. *This is vulnerability.* This is where you will find more information about your sense of safety.

You might find yourself relieved that you didn't do a deeper dive with a particular person. In this case, our work is knowing that *Yeah, I didn't give them all of me, and that makes* sense. Other times, you might feel some regret or a longing to move closer. In that case our work is *I wish I could have been more vulnerable, and I'm going to give it another try.*

We will always live in systems of power, and we will always live in bodies designed to keep us safe. So, again, the goal is not *never* fawning. It's that we don't want to live in full-time fawning survival mode. We don't want to have fixed and rigid rules about safety. We want to bring flexibility and discernment to our relationships.

Vulnerability lies in the gray areas, in the messy middle where there are millions of choices in between.

As we wade into vulnerable waters, we will find there are people we *can* trust with our whole selves. Sadie recently shared about how her therapeutic relationship with me became safer and safer, until it ultimately became the container for her deepest healing: "For years in our relationship, anytime you were soft, showed me physical hugging or a loving gesture, it made me want to vomit. It was scary, I would cry. It was a spike in my nervous system and then a shutdown . . . As uncomfortable as it was, I kept coming back. Whatever little bit of receiving I was able to take in, I wanted more. It felt like needles in my skin and yet, 'I want that, I need that!'"

Over time, Sadie learned she could trust me. This allowed her to finally experience that she didn't need to have all the answers. "I could be a true mess, and you still showed me so much love. So I learned that version of me could be lovable." The safety of our relationship became the container for her to go even deeper into her vulnerability, into the reprocessing that allowed her to hold so much more.

Vulnerability isn't all-or-nothing, and safety happens in degrees. Just as trauma healing is not a linear process, we might feel like we are going two steps forward and one step back. That is okay. Allow yourself to be where you are. Check in with yourself, then turn your attention toward your surroundings and see what wants to happen next.

Taking Up Space: *Being Authentic*

About a year into our working together, Lily had to put all her new-found skills into practice in a way she never saw coming.

She and her best friend, Ava, finished each other's sentences. It was a "she knows me better than I know myself" sort of relationship. But Lily was starting to realize she *had* to like everything her friend liked. Ava's opinion became her own, without any critical thinking or curiosity.

As Lily opened up to dating for the first time in years, she started to become interested in a guy in their mutual friend group. She told her friend about it, but she realized that she didn't want to tell Ava *everything* about this new crush. Lily was leaning into self-trust, keeping parts of this new, exciting experience to herself, rather than sharing every single detail with her friend.

She and her crush, Michael, made a plan to hang out. *She was doing it,* the thing that had been so terrifying for so long! She didn't want to share any details with Ava in advance, but in talking with her friend about other things, the heat began rising on Lily's neck. She felt nervous, *guilty,* as though she'd broken the unwritten rule of

I'm supposed to tell you everything. Their conversation became awkward, and Ava noticed. She started pressing Lily until she eventually caved: "Okay, don't be mad, Michael and I are going to a concert tonight."

While she knew Ava would be upset, Lily had no idea Ava's anger would become so explosive.

Firing off questions of "What? When? and Why?" her friend quickly followed those with accusations. "You are lying by omission. Why would you keep this from the one friend who actually cares about you? You need to fire this new therapist; she is encouraging you to LIE."

Ava had always encouraged Lily to have boundaries. She saw how much of herself she gave away. But she didn't mean Lily should have boundaries with *her*! Ava was interpreting them as an attack on her character.

Lily started shaking. Surprised and terrified, she didn't know how to fix the situation. She'd been paralyzed about dating for so long. Her best friend was like so many people in her world, engaged, married, or having babies. She just wanted access to the same possibilities, and now her friend was furious with her?

Lily backpedaled. She apologized, pledged her adoration, said how much she loved and trusted her friend. She wasn't trying to exclude Ava as much as she was trying to include herself.

Nothing worked. Ava was angry, and after they hung up, she wouldn't return Lily's calls or messages.

The enormity of her reaction had Lily wondering if she really did do something horrible. *Maybe I did lie.* She knew as a fawner she'd told white lies before. But while her process wasn't as graceful as she would have liked, she wasn't lying as much as she was waiting to share more until she felt ready, thinking her friend would support her efforts at growth and healing. She was doing what felt right to her, becoming her own authority.

Lily tried to mend the friendship without abandoning herself. But after another painful two-hour conversation with no resolution, it was clear: Lily's growth was changing the terms of the relationship too much for this friend to tolerate. When we discussed it in session, Lily sighed. "The only way to maintain a relationship with Ava is by being totally submissive. My growth changed the dynamic of our friendship, and she is not okay with it. I had to abandon myself to make sure she didn't feel abandoned. I had to prioritize her feelings instead of tending to my own. I had to excuse her bad behavior because *I made her behave that way*, almost like I deserved it."

Lily was seeing the truth of their dynamic. It was eye-opening, but it also hurt.

While Lily was sorry her personal path felt so disruptive to the friendship, she couldn't agree that what she did was so *wrong*. She couldn't promise to never keep something from her friend again, so Lily stopped apologizing and backpedaling, and the friendship ended.

Ava didn't want the real Lily in her life. She wanted a mirror, a cheerleader, a pledge of allegiance. In the face of such demands, Lily found she could not tolerate it anymore. There are times when she still misses her lifelong friend, but the price of admission isn't worth going back. She and that guy didn't work out, either, but Lily's commitment to herself is going *really well*.

The gift of unfawning is we can be ourselves! Just like Lily learned she doesn't just have to cede authority to her friends, Sadie learned she wasn't only attracted to women, and Liz Gilbert realized she didn't want to give away so much of herself to be loved. The more we let go of our fawning ways, the more we come into our own skin. We feel grounded, real, and embodied.

Becoming authentic is a process of discovery, a culmination of this entire unfawning journey. Another area where strictly cognitive answers leave us half empty.

AA talks about humility as being rightsized, and it's a definition I've always liked. We often interpret being humble to mean becoming smaller. For fawners, it's often about getting bigger. Inhabiting more of ourselves, more of the space we are in. Neither in submission nor in arrogance, we have a true estimation of our worth and can hold it with pride.

Sadie and I were recently talking about how she used to fawn as her ticket to love. It made me wonder: "What is your ticket to love now?"

"I don't have a ticket anymore!" she said. "I used to have a ticket, but now it's just ME."

This made me cry. The ticket was the thing that got the love before. Her body was a ticket—if it was small enough, it would get the love. Her fawning was a ticket. Now, she no longer lives with imposter syndrome, or asks herself *How can I keep performing at this level to keep getting the love?* The acrobatics are gone. Sadie is loveable, and she feels it.

It changes how she offers love, too. Sadie says: "When I am genuinely giving, it takes no toll on me. It brings me joy, and when it's over, that's it. When it's fawning, I feel anxious because I want something in return that I'm not sure I'll get: love, praise, acceptance, etc. and when I don't receive these things, I feel depleted and sometimes resentful."

Sadie remained single for quite a while as she was doing this work. She was grateful for how it changed her life and how it allowed her to finally be herself. But she started to think it would be impossible to find a partner; she didn't think another person could meet her in this new place of unapologetically holding on to herself. "I have this much strength. Who else could hold all of this?"

I just got a message. Sadie is engaged. I have met her fiancé, and they are simply divine as a couple. She sent me a photo of the two of them, out in nature, after he proposed.

As she knew this was likely coming, she had recently asked if I might come to their wedding. My body gave a full-throated "Yes!" . . . but I also shared that I don't think I could be inconspicuous in the corner. I know I would likely be sobbing with joy.

Sadie said, "I know. I wouldn't have it any other way."

This is authenticity, for us both.

Anthony is a literal painter now. He woke up one morning and knew he had to go to the art store. He came home with canvases and paints, and he hasn't stopped. He sends me pictures of his paintings and they are bright, vibrant, full of JOY. Years ago, when we started working together, I suggested he might try to paint. Being a good client, he did, as though it were an assignment. Now he's doing it because he relishes his creativity, connecting him to other realms, and it is magical.

Francis is halfway through graduate school, on her way to becoming a trauma-informed (and trauma-trained) couples therapist. She no longer relies on her sexuality or the perfect performance. She is building her self-awareness and bringing all her healing directly to her studies, to her peers. As someone who has lived through and broken trauma bonds, Francis is a gift to her professors and classmates. She can sometimes wonder in our ongoing work, "Do you think it's crazy that I'm going to be a therapist?" While I want to hold space for the part of her who is worried, allow that part of her to *be with her,* I can't help but say, "Yes, Francis. I think you are going to be the couples therapist I always wished I had. We need you in this field!"

In my most recent session with Davis, we wound our way back to the little boy who was being abused. We connected with him in ways we never had before. Davis was really *with* his childhood self, back in the original box. That little boy is getting close to seeing Davis, too. How hard Davis has worked to come back to find him. We can both feel that this is everything he's been wanting and it's actually happening. All the boxes are open. While Davis still lives within a few of their walls, I can sense that is about to change in big ways, safe ones. Because he's done all the work to make it so.

Lily knew she didn't want to lose herself in a romantic relationship, but she didn't know how much of herself was already lost in her work, in her friendships. The clothespins of her past were still squeezing so many aspects of her true self. Today things are flowing. SHE is flowing. While she doesn't have a boyfriend, she has been dating. Her friendships have shifted in radical and beautiful ways. She is advocating for herself professionally, and her relationship to herself is present and loving. She has become the person *she* needed her to be, and she is one lucky woman, because she is spectacular.

Mia is being a force in her own life, a sustainable one. She is starting a new business, and while the process is scary, she is being *present* throughout all the fears. She knows there is more from her childhood that needs her attention. There are whispers, dreams, callings of more to be revealed, and she is ready for it. Ready to free more of herself, because she knows she is worthy of it and finally can.

Grace is GRACE. The rules, the hats, the tightropes, the fears that ruled her every waking moment have receded to the background, and she is here. She's found a voice, she knows who she is. She is monumentally less concerned with *What will they think?* and she knows what SHE THINKS. We will read more about Grace as our last client story.

Unfawning looks different for each of us, yet there is one universal theme. Unfawning is about welcoming ourselves to the party. We don't compulsively abandon ourselves anymore, or when we do, we recognize it and repair. We remember that we can have a say, that we are allowed a seat at the table. This allows us to exhale, sink into our bodies, and finally be ourselves.

Righting Our Wrongs

. . .

While fawning is about finding safety, coming by our fawning honestly doesn't mean we get a pass for any and all behaviors when we were captured by it, particularly when there was collateral damage. Our shrinking, compulsive caretaking, lying, even choosing our own safety has had consequences. Unfawning means we don't just ask others to be accountable, we become accountable to others as well.

When we are under someone's spell—believing their lies or editing out what doesn't fit our fawning narrative—not only can *we* get hurt, we can hurt others. You can see this through the lens of a high-control group or cult. Although there is typically a charismatic leader at the top—the person who is intentionally manipulative—followers eventually move up the ranks and are made to do the leader's bidding. While these followers believe what they're doing is spiritual, moral, right . . . countless documentaries like *The Vow* and *Breath of Fire* show the harm that is being done, unwittingly.

When one is programmed to fawn, it's common to want everyone below their station to fawn, too. No one calls it fawning in hierarchical organizations. It's referred to as *duty, honor, service,* or *respect.* The same is true in toxic family systems or in corporations. Fawners don't know we are harming people because there is a feeling that *I'm doing it,* too. Or we may sense that harm is being done, but it feels like a sacrifice for the greater good.

Do I think fawners are as culpable as those who are consciously abusing? No. Does that mean we don't need to be held accountable? Also, no. Trauma happens regardless of someone's backstory or intentions. Part of the healing is when we can acknowledge where we have hurt others, whether we meant to or not.

Sometimes becoming accountable means owning your triggers and trauma responses. In our bedroom, my husband and I have a *New Yorker* cartoon by Pat Byrnes in which a man turns to a woman in the kitchen and says, "Is there anything else I can do wrong for you?" Because, well, I'm that woman.

I know my hypervigilance comes from the countless times my brothers and I ran to our rooms as kids, trying to outrun a punishment for doing the most mundane of things *wrong.* In my autopilot mode, the way my husband loads the dishwasher is *wrong.* It feels like *we* are going to get in trouble. My knee-jerk reaction is to criticize, wanting him to do it *right.*

He hates this. I hate this. So I have to practice not saying something. I have to remember that I no longer live in a house with Randy. One of my favorite things Yancey says to me is "There are no shoulds in this family." We won't get in trouble even if we run the dishwasher with one dish placed at a less-than-optimal angle.

I am still so oriented to fixing/helping, it can be hard to stop. And because Yancey doesn't have the big, obvious problems I saw in previous relationships, I can hyperfocus on the smaller stuff. My work here is to release the people who haven't ever harmed me from my critical grasp. Stop believing I know what's best for them and should tell them about it.

Becoming accountable means releasing *everyone* from my critical grasp. In our habituation toward taking care of ourselves through others, fawners tend to think they have *all* the answers for *all* the folks. We've thought long and hard about what each person in our lives needs. What the person in line at the grocery store should be doing. While we've avoided conflict where it was likely necessary, avoided doing our own deeper healing, our opinions for others have leaked out all over the place.

Without asking if someone wants our opinion, we freely give it, often with an air of "Obviously, I know what's best." This is partly to distance ourselves from uncomfortable feelings. If we can't sit with ours, we can't sit with yours, either. Additionally, other people's big feelings and difficulties have pulled us off our center. Rather than setting healthy boundaries, we were still trying to solve for that problem *through them.* "Just do what I suggest, and we'll all be *fine.*"

Glennon Doyle, bestselling author of *Untamed,* once shared on her podcast, *We Can Do Hard Things*, about the metaphorical file folders she has for all her loved ones. They contain all the ideas she has for how they might improve their lives. We genuinely believe we know what's best! When she realized that maybe it was time to let go of all those files, she was like, "Well, now what will I do with my days?" But that is exactly the point. When we let go of managing others, we can start to make a file folder for ourselves.

This is a practice. One I'm not as far into as I'd like to be. But I can see as I continue to heal, this work also releases *me* from my critical grasp. As I let people be themselves, I get to be myself, too.

When we screw up, as we inevitably will, it isn't a moment to feel more shame, but a moment to practice a powerful tool in reciprocal relationships, that of rupture/repair. Coming out of attachment theory, rupture implies a disruption in connection when there's been a misunderstanding, hurt, or harm. Rupture is inevitable. Most of us know this well. What most of us don't know as well is the repair.

That as long as we return to our loved ones after a misstep or blowup, apologize, and assure them our connection still remains, we can be fine. In fact, even better than fine. The repair reinforces our connection. The bad thing can turn into a stronger bond.

For many of my clients, seeing their trauma response has been an opportunity to lean into more vulnerability. It's an opportunity to set new ground rules. How do we want to respect one another as whole people? How can I be a better friend, family member, co-worker? What does actual support look and feel like to you? How can you tell me when I'm overstepping or retreating?

This will be an ongoing process. We will miss the mark! So will others. Unfawning is attempting to hold all the complexity. To enlarge our ability to engage in conflict, because conflict is a natural part of being in relationship. Unfawning means entering a complex world and knowing that we don't have all the answers in advance. We can't soothe others to soothe our own pain. We can't smooth all the edges. There is a sharpness we must confront, and yet it gives the shape of a real life, well and consciously lived.

Grace

Grace was one of my first clients in private practice in 2009. At forty, with a newly adopted baby girl, Grace really wanted to be a good mom. Like many fawners, she went into therapy initially for someone else's benefit. She didn't want to pass down her own relationship to food, her distorted body image, or her low self-worth to her daughter.

At the time, Grace knew her husband was an active alcoholic. She was, in fact, more aware of her husband's drinking than I was of my husband's. It would be another year before I pulled Mark's hidden vodka bottles from our hall closet, seeing the extent of what he'd been hiding and what I did not want to see.

Meanwhile, both Grace and I were doing our best to be *good*, overcompensating for our husbands, undervaluing ourselves, to hold it all together.

Our early work together centered on the classic codependency model—keeping the focus on Grace rather than her husband. While elevating her needs and feelings was important (recall that Grace's mission was to have no needs, to walk a tightrope that told her precisely where to step), I came to see how working on her codepen-dency simultaneously reinforced her dysfunctional relationship. She was trying to be less codependent, to be more lovable. Still bettering herself, not *being* herself.

Grace told me early on, "I will never leave my husband." Setting aside his drinking, she felt like she was living in a romantic fairy tale. As her therapist, I felt the fortress around him. If a problem arose for Grace, but it was behind the fortress walls, we couldn't go there. She would willingly sacrifice pieces of herself if they were ever in conflict with her relationship.

She did not see this as self-abandonment. She saw this as what you do when you are with your soulmate. Grace wore different hats for different relationships, and the hat she wore in her marriage read: *True love, nothing can shake it.*

While I knew pledges of undying love covered in yellow caution tape felt problematic, I didn't yet have the language of relational trauma or fawning. All my training in trauma was still related to acute traumatic events, and I hadn't unpacked any of my own trauma in a meaningful way. So I was in a process parallel to Grace's, de-fended from my own truth and pain. Keeping my own blinders on.

As Grace felt more secure in our relationship, she told me of her recurring nightmares. In one, she was in a big house with beautiful blue and gold wallpaper. She excused herself to find the bathroom and noticed it had several toilets, like a public bathroom, but without the dividers.

"I was bloated and embarrassed to be relieving myself in some-one's home," she said. But in the dream, she had no choice. Hurrying to flush the toilet, she discovered it was clogged.

She watched as the water began to rise, higher and higher, spill-ing onto the floor.

Mortified, Grace saw that it wasn't just the one toilet—ALL of them were spilling into the hallway. Her hands were on her face as she was telling me, "I just knew that all of that overflow was from *me*. It was all of my shit, no one else's—and I couldn't stop it."

Grace was so distressed. It felt so *real*. I felt her anguish as I noticed her attention turn to something just behind my chair.

On a long and low bookshelf in my office sat four potted plants. In the moment Grace finished telling me her nightmare about all her shit—her shame, embarrassment, fears of inadequacy spilling over—a huge worm had worked himself up and over the edge of one of the pots, flopping onto my bookshelf.

"What on earth!" I said as I turned to the fat worm. "Even Carl Jung would be impressed with such a synchronicity." It was a real-time reflection of Grace's dream, of the process we were embarking on. All the things that had been hiding for so long were coming to the surface for Grace and me to both finally acknowledge and deal with.

All Grace's fears, what she perceived as her *grossness,* had to be made visible. She truly believed that *if you really knew her,* you'd see why she had to keep everything so hidden. While she and I didn't know it yet, a lot of that hiding was managed through fawning.

Grace was not a bad person. She had no skeletons in her closet. She was lovely and kind, a brilliant teacher to her students. But on the inside, she believed she was polluted and repulsive, and she was *supposed to be different.* There was no room to exist, and the tension manifested as depression.

Grace managed her depression by bingeing or playing mindless games on her phone—numbing her pain in ways where she might still appear fine. She had to be responsible, put on a happy face, be on for her family and her job.

Her fawning masked her depression. Her depression masked her trauma.

Grace often worried she was like her dad, the one who had literally kicked her out of the house for saying she didn't want onions on her pizza. It's a common worry for my clients, becoming like the person who terrorized us. But then she'd think, He *would never come to therapy—thinking he needed to change.* She saw that he never took responsibility, and she always took too much.

As a child, Grace wasn't aware of her father's alcoholism, and whenever he flew off the handle, her mom would say, "His father was far worse. Your dad is doing much better than how he was raised." Her dad's behavior was excused every time. Her mother never intervened.

Her parents were married for forty-seven years, together for fifty, before her dad's infidelity finally shattered the illusion of their happy family. They divorced just before Grace and I met.

She was the middle child of three, with one older sister and a younger brother her parents adopted when Grace was six. They grew up in a four-bedroom house in Bel Air, one of the most expensive neighborhoods of Los Angeles. Everyone had their own bathroom, and they had a pool out back. But Grace was told they were poor. It was so confusing, another area where she didn't know what was real, what was true; where she learned she couldn't trust herself.

Money was a constant topic of conversation, often conflated with love or worth and held over her head.

Her dad paid for her college, but it came with many strings, including belittling her intellect, saying she'd never get into certain schools.

He paid for her wedding, but he made the guest list, chose the food and venue. Grace had no say in her own wedding plans.

While he could be generous, it was laden with control. She couldn't even invite her brother to her wedding because he was at odds with their dad at the time.

Her brother struggled with mental health and addiction issues, often running away or being placed in juvenile hall. Once in her late teens, her family was on vacation without her brother when her dad said casually by the pool, "You know, I don't really love your brother. But don't get me wrong, I'll always love you and your sister, you are my blood."

Grace was disgusted.

A few years later, her dad called to say, "I might take your brother out of the will. Should I cut him out? If I do, will you promise not to share your money after I'm gone?"

Horrified, Grace suggested, "Why don't you just put his money in a trust so he won't go through it the way you are fearing?"

Meanwhile, she became financially independent as quickly as possible. While this could be seen as cutting the strings tied to her father, Grace said she was trying to be financially literate to prove she was trustworthy, she was smart, she was good with money. She was trying to win him over, to be like him, and it backfired.

Grace's independence was offensive to her dad. Despite all her fawning—*Let me show you how much like you I am, how well you've taught me*—not needing her father was the ultimate slap in the face.

This started an on-again, off-again relationship with her dad. Grace shared his voice mails with me after she'd tried to cut ties with him, and even though I knew they'd be bad, I had no idea. Hostility, rage, vitriol, insanity. I could hardly listen and yet she wondered, "Do you think I'm doing the right thing by not having him in my life?"

Eventually Grace felt like she had no choice. She felt relationally safer managing their relationship than cutting him off. But being with him felt intolerable. On Hanukkah, Grace drove one and a half hours with her infant and a full holiday meal to her dad's house he shared with his new girlfriend. Grace's dad told his daughters not to look this woman up online before they met, saying, "I already know her arrest record, her history with meth and crack. I know she's on disability, and she was a prostitute when we met."

Just a few minutes into their visit, this woman got two inches from Grace's face, talking a mile a minute, shaking, sweating, announcing: "My brother was just arrested for shooting people on the freeway!"

Grace's daughter was sleeping in another room. Her older sister and dad were conversing like nothing was happening. Grace's heart was beating fast, but her face remained neutral. Once again, she responded to insanity with some semblance of sanity, "I'm so sorry that happened. Should we have the appetizer now?"

Although Grace had learned to tolerate so much for so long, she always held a different standard for her daughter. When her husband's drug and alcohol use became dangerous and she got him into rehab, Grace believed they'd still be together when he got home, but things continued to unravel. She did not want the marriage to end, but that's eventually what happened.

It forced Grace into a different relationship with love. She'd always thought, *How can I love myself if someone else doesn't love me?* She believed all the people who could access self-love could do so because they'd received unconditional love from someone else first.

Many fawners feel like self-love is a substitute for the real thing. If *we* love ourselves, we'll be sacrificing the opportunity to experience it from the outside. As though we have finite space for love in our bodies, self-love can feel like a punishment, a consolation prize at best.

But to continue being a good mother, Grace had to turn inward. She began the practice of loving herself the way she naturally loved her daughter. She never saw her daughter as a problem to solve. She never wanted her to hide her humanity, she loved her more for sharing it.

After her husband moved out, Grace looked at pictures they'd taken together. Whereas before, she saw only him, now she saw herself, almost for the first time.

She shared in one session that she was practicing saying her full name, out loud, with love and compassion. She wanted to change the association of the use of her full name with the idea that she was in trouble or there was something fundamentally wrong with her.

She began to practice witnessing herself. Separating herself from what she was doing and her immediate judgment of it. Rather than eating M&M's in bed and thinking, *I'm so fucked up,* she found herself simply noticing her actions: *Hey, look, I'm eating M&M's.* She cultivated curiosity, empathy, a little space. She was seeing and being present to herself, creating internal safety.

We worked with the shame and dysregulation she felt about being a pain or an annoyance anytime she spoke up for herself. She was learning to hold space for her feelings. Although it still felt like she was causing trouble by being a whole person, she was enlarging her capacity to be with herself no matter what.

Co-parenting with a partner who continued to use, she had to create and hold boundaries to keep her daughter safe, establishing written rules related to clean drug tests in their custody agreement. No matter how charming or manipulative her ex-husband would be, Grace found she could hold her boundaries.

Long periods of no contact with her dad were always followed with limited contact. At one point, he expressed his desire to put his girlfriend in his will.

Respecting her dad's wishes while attempting to be levelheaded, Grace advised, "This is someone who might not have your best interest at heart." She reminded her dad that this woman had violent tendencies and suggested he not tell her about the inheritance.

While Grace previously held financial and medical power of attorney, her dad married his girlfriend and took those rights away. He even accused Grace of stealing from him, when his girlfriend had actually sold all his appliances while he was in the hospital.

Upon his death, he gave his new wife half a million dollars.

He gave Grace's brother a quarter of a million dollars.

And he gave Grace and her sister $15,000 each. The rest, likely well over a million, went to charities to which he had no connection or affiliation. In addition, her brother's inheritance had a clause: If he died before he spent it, it could NOT go to anyone other than charity.

Grace was shocked and brokenhearted. Her father's last will and testament felt like a punishment. Like a final declaration: *You aren't worthy.* She didn't care about the inheritance as much as she cared about its message. She was haunted by the question *Did my dad never really love me?*

She'd spent her life trying to regulate his moods and demands, longing to be on his good side. But in his death, he doubled down on every abuse, every slight. No wonder Grace always felt so rotten inside.

The grief that came during this period was the lowest I'd ever seen her. But as she continued to process, take her long walks, take care of her daughter and of herself, Grace was learning to stop pleasing and appeasing. She was holding on to herself. Noticing where she begins and ends, she could start to see that all the overflow from her dream all those years ago *wasn't* all hers. As she saw herself and her humanity, as she saw her dad more clearly than ever before, she realized she was scapegoated to hold so much pain and dysfunction. Made to think that she was too much, and it was all her own making.

Grace is still my client. Our work hasn't been consecutive, but it's been ongoing for sixteen years. We've witnessed each other taking off our wedding rings. Getting into new relationships. Finding more of ourselves along the way.

I've seen her therapy become about her. What she likes and dislikes. What she feels and how she advocates for herself. The old templates and rules are still in the ether, but she can feel them now. She stepped into the work of loving herself, not as a substitute, but as the thing she needed and deserved. A part of her misses the fairy tale of her marriage. A part of her still feels haunted by her father's slight.

But she knows these things don't define her now. She finally knows she is smart. She is fierce. She is worthy.

Grace is and has remained a wonderful mother and a brilliant teacher—even to me.

I am changed by my relationship with Grace. It feels like I'm not supposed to say it, but I learn and grow from my clients as much as I hope they gain from me. Grace and I basically grew up together.

I watched myself go from wearing a therapist's hat when we first met—thinking I had to have all the answers and never wanting my shit to come into the room—to finding that this wasn't an option for me, either.

In my early years as a therapist, I was initially erring too far, as my fawning was apt to do, to where I almost didn't exist. I was over-attuned. My clients' therapy was all about them, but all up to me. In my absence as a whole person, I was robbing them of their ability to become whole themselves.

My clients have now seen me change my last name, get pregnant, and bring in a huge yoga ball to sit on in my office. I was especially terrified when I outed myself as a trauma survivor, sharing my story in my memoir and online, wondering who would want to work with me now.

But I didn't lose any clients with my openness. They felt seen and validated because I've been through this process, too. While I don't think this relational approach is for every therapist, and I don't think it's appropriate for every client, for me and my clients working with complex trauma, I've found it's the only way to be.

I know a lot of people fear that their therapist is judging them. Like we have our internal clipboards, going *Oof, they did* that *again*. Largely, what I've been thinking in countless hours across from that couch is *I'm in awe, inspired; I feel alive and connected*.

So many clients over the years have said, "It must be hard listening to people's problems all day." I've really never experienced it like that. It feels like I'm watching people fall in love with themselves. It feels like we are doing magic together. This doesn't mean every day is a huge aha moment, but that's what the process represents.

I have so much love for my clients. I'm probably not supposed to say that, either. It's not professional. It doesn't have enough therapeutic distance. But I don't know how I could encourage them to be this brave, watch it happen, and witness them step into themselves and love themselves, without loving them myself. Each of my clients has opened up something new in me. By witnessing what has become possible in their lives, I see more of what is possible in mine.

I could not have written this book without my clients. As you've seen, their stories are interwoven with mine. We have worked together to discover what fawning truly is. Their insight and openness have allowed me to name what no one has yet brought to the page this fully. This book is both mine and theirs.

Acknowledgments

I could say that this book came out of the blue, or that I've been writing it for thirty-eight years. Both are true. But what's also true is this book never would have happened if Jan Baumer wasn't such a warm and wonderful person.

I was introduced to Jan by my dear friend Jay Edwards six years before she became my agent. Although our professional paths weren't meant to meld at that time, our connection was such that I never hesitated to reach out for her guidance.

After self-publishing my memoir, I was navigating some tricky waters. Jan's generosity led her to sharing my memoir with her friend and colleague, Lauren Hall. Together, they saw how much of my story was about the fawn response, and they immediately knew I was the one to write a book on the subject.

I wasn't looking for representation or big publishing. I didn't think I had another book in me, either. But when they shared their vision for the book you are now holding, my whole body lit up with excitement and a deep knowing: *I have to write this book.*

This was the first of many synchronistic moments that formed the basis for what is now my dream team. Thank you, Jan and Lauren, for signing me, believing in me, and flat-out handing me what feels like the road map to my greatest calling. From the moment the three of us connected, I have felt the magic of our coven.

I will never forget my first Zoom call with the team at G. P. Putnam's Sons. It was electric. President Ivan Held's cheerful face was front and center, surrounded by the JOY of the imprint's mission statement. When we hung up, I turned to Jan and Lauren, saying, "I want them to adopt me." And that's what they did.

Thank you to my Putnam editor, Michelle Howry. On that call, you said, "You are a storyteller." You appreciated how I wanted to teach through real people's lived experience and were willing to think (and edit) outside the lines of a traditional self-help book. Thank you for allowing me to put my whole heart—and my clients' whole hearts—onto the page. For helping me not only change the conversation, but how we are having it.

The entire team at Putnam is a gift. From the stellar cover design to selling so many international rights, to all the support in marketing and PR—you have amazed me at every turn.

When it came to the writing process, I knew I was endeavoring to do something I'd never done. Weaving so many powerful stories with clinical insight, helping it land for the reader in a way that was accessible and engaging, and doing it on a tight deadline. Thank you once again to Jan and Lauren for introducing me to my collaborator, Cindy DiTiberio, who, simply put, I could not have written this book without.

At the time, Cindy did not know about fawning. But when she read my proposal, she knew, just as I did, that we had to work together.

There is something alchemical when survivors come together with the intention of helping other people. Cindy and I went into the writing cave as former "good girls" who never wanted to ruffle any feathers and came out transformed. She turned my pages around as quickly as I could write them, and we discovered something healing for us both in the process. She held space for me, demanded that I BRING IT, and then asked all the right questions. Working with a fawner who might get pulled from her center, Cindy made sure I stayed true to my vision with as much integrity and truth as humanly possible. She dreamt up the perfect structure for the book—with long-form stories and deep-diving interludes. I didn't put it on the page if it wasn't a YES in my body, and we didn't take anything out if it needed to remain to paint the fullest picture possible. Thank you, Cindy. You have become a forever friend.

To acknowledge my husband, Yancey, and our son, Henry, is an impossible task. Truly, I will find neither the right words nor senti-ment here. The fact of Yancey is a sheer miracle. I have never, I mean ever, felt so loved and supported. He has literally taught me about unconditional love. To see and experience how proud of me he has been in this process is now one of my most favorite things in the world. While Yancey is typically a man of few words, I have contin-ually heard him share about this book while beaming with pride. If that was the only payment I received, I swear . . . it would be enough. He simultaneously stepped up even more as a parent. There were so many things I could not attend to in the way I had previously, and he enthusiastically picked up all the pieces. He is my great love, my best friend, and I could not have done this if he wasn't the true part-ner that he is.

Our son, Henry, is the light of my life. He is known to check out thirty library books at a time, and he's read more in his nine years than I have in my entire life. So to see his mom become an author with Penguin Random House gave me all the street cred a mother could ask for. I marvel at Henry's creativity, his passion—and quite frankly, the way he holds on to himself. I've said it many times, and it bears repeating, Henry does not have a fawning bone in his body.

Acknowledgments

At least not the kind that has captured me. He speaks his mind. He's clear and deliberate. He doesn't do what he doesn't want to do. While my history can make it hard as a parent to honor such a strong commitment to himself, what's also true is that I couldn't be prouder of him. He teaches me—shows me what it's like not to have to appease in order to be loved. And I love him a million times more for it.

To my current therapist, Holly Heath, thank you for your true gift as a clinician, your mentorship, enthusiasm, and belief in me and the power of this book. And to all the therapists who brought their wisdom to my life—with the intention of enabling my own, I thank you.

To Dr. Ramani Durvasula, your contributions to my life and to the field are too numerous to mention, and your generosity and kindness are unmatched. Thank you for lifting me up in ways only you could.

To Patrick Teahan, you are a gift to so many survivors, and I have been comforted by your pure heart behind the scenes. Thank you for doing what you do, for all of us.

Thank you to Dr. David Laramie for helping me step into private practice so many years ago and providing valuable insight on the Medicine to Heal section for this book.

Gialina Morten has covered so many bases, I've lost count! You were sent from the angels and have become one for me. To have you on my team is a dream I never dared to dream.

Everyone needs a right-hand man, and James Rara is the best in the biz. Thank you for all of your support behind the scenes.

To all my friends and family who have continually supported my voice, thank you for seeing me long before I could.

With special thanks to Lori Grant. We've long called each other soul sisters, but the title doesn't suffice. You are mother, friend, sister, godmother to my son . . . you have carried me through my first gig

Acknowledgments

at the Bitter End, through devastating grief and this abundant life. There is no one like you.

To Sara Bollman, for being cut from the same cloth and making something so beautiful of it. Thank you for showing me what's possible.

Stacy Golden, when I grow up, I want to be like you. Thank you for your unwavering support.

Sue Dinner, thank you for being the solid foundation I can always count on, for sharing your journey with me and being a witness to mine. You are family, forever.

Rachel Drews, thank you for holding my whole heart. Your gift at seeing people is profound, and I hope you know—I see you, too. All of you. You've got the good stuff.

To Brittany Olsen and Amy Charters, my friends of almost forty years. You are my chosen family, and the fact that you choose me back is the delight of my life.

Elizabeth Baily, in my next life, I hope to embody a fraction of your magical, creative spirit. Thank you for sharing it with me in this one.

Jennifer Schmidt, thank you for being a force for good, for getting it, and for being the best cheerleader.

Melissa Yaeger, thank you for bringing one of the most important people of my life into the world, and for your friendship over the many mountains we've climbed.

Bill Cusack, you saw this coming long before I could get a glimpse. Thank you for the countless pep talks over frozen yogurt and coffee. Your ability to mirror people's truth changed my life, again and again.

Jillian Shillig, your insight and creativity are like pockets of gold I can't believe I get to mine. Thank you for being YOU.

Kathryn Lubow, for always seeing the thing before I can see it, for guiding me as I find it, and the beautiful walks along the way.

Acknowledgments

To the community I have found (or you found ME) on social media, "Thank you" is wholly insufficient. I thought putting my whole self out there would tank my career, that I'd lose all credibility—but being all of me in one place felt more important than what I feared losing. You all have showed me, every day, that I can be safe and seen without fawning. Thank you for every comment of solidarity, every comforting, beautiful message. You became the net when I jumped and enabled me to get to the place where I could share even more, with even more people.

Notes

CHAPTER 1: THE FOURTH F

7 **"a response to a threat":** Pete Walker, *Complex PTSD: From Surviving to Thriving* (Azure Coyote Publishing, 2013), 109.

7 **"way of harmonizing":** "Martial Arts: What Is Aikido?" National Karate & Kobudo Federation, accessed November 2024, https://www.nkkf.org/blogs/martial-arts-what-is-aikido.

7 **sense their next move:** "What Can Aikido Teach Us About Effective Leadership?" Michigan Ross Sanger Leadership Center, accessed August 2024, https://sanger.umich.edu/news-1-2-19-ema-aikido/.

12 **"a psychologically distressing event":** American Psychiatric Association, *Diagnostic and Statistical Manual of Mental Disorders,* 3rd ed. (American Psychiatric Association, 1980).

12 **70 percent of adults:** C. Benjet et al., "The Epidemiology of Traumatic Event Exposure Worldwide: Results from the World Mental Health Survey Consortium," *Psychological Medicine* 46, no. 2 (2015), 327–43, NIH National Library of Medicine, https://www.ncbi.nlm.nih.gov/pmc/articles/PMC4869975/.

THE FAWNING FAMILY TREE

27 **"A codependent person is":** Melody Beattie, *Codependent No More: How to Stop Controlling Others and Start Caring for Yourself,* 25th anniversary edition (Spiegel & Grau, 2022), 34.

29 **"disease" of codependency:** Beattie, *Codependent No More*, 34.

CHAPTER 2: IT'S NOT YOUR FAULT

45 **"Learning to wear a mask":** bell hooks, *The Will to Change: Men, Masculinity, and Love* (Washington Square Press, 2004), 142.

50 **Watching the film forced:** Sasha Weiss, "The Prince We Never Knew," *New York Times Magazine,* September 8, 2024, https://www.nytimes.com/2024/09/08/magazine/prince-netflix-ezra-edelman-documentary.html.

50 **"white body supremacy":** Resmaa Menakem, *My Grandmother's Hands: Racialized Trauma and the Pathway to Mending Our Hearts and Bodies* (Central Recovery Press, 2017), 10.

51 **"Identifying a narcissistic person":** Ramani Durvasula, *It's Not You: Identifying and Healing from Narcissistic People* (The Open Field, 2024), 83.

51 **"Narcissistic abuse":** Durvasula, *It's Not You,* 42.

51 **"are usually the children":** Pete Walker, "The 4Fs: A Trauma Typology in Complex PTSD," https://pete-walker.com/fourFs_TraumaTypologyComplexPTSD.htm.

54 **"spiritual ideas and practices":** John Welwood, *Toward a Psychology of Awakening: Buddhism, Psychotherapy, and the Path of Personal and Spiritual Transformation* (Shambala, 2002), 207.

CHAPTER 3: WHO, ME?

89 **An issue that comes up:** Onecommune, "Are You Sacrificing Your Authenticity," Dr. Gabor Mate, Instagram Video, September 15, 2024, https://www.instagram.com/reel/C_8o4KQySnM/?igsh=NTc4MTIwNjQ2YQ%3D%3D.

93 **Resentment is:** Alcoholic Anonymous, *The Big Book* (Alcoholic Anonymous World Services, 2002), 64.

SADIE

115 **"the broken maternal relationship":** Kelly McDaniel, *Mother Hunger: How Adult Daughters Can Understand and Heal from Lost Nurturance, Protection, and Guidance* (Hay House, 2021), 189.

CHAPTER 4: THE MERRY-GO-ROUND OF FAWNING

116 **"A definitive symptom of childhood trauma":** Patrick Teahan, *Reality Check with Dr. Ramani,* August 6, 2024.

118 **"We approach experience":** Michael Pollan, *How to Change Your Mind: What the New Science of Psychedelics Teaches Us About Consciousness, Dying, Addiction, Depression, and Transcendence* (Penguin Books, 2018), 16.

119 **"Adults, as well as children":** Bessel van der Kolk, "The Compulsion to Repeat the Trauma," *Psychiatric Clinics of North America* 12, no. 2 (1989): 390–411, https://pubmed.ncbi.nlm.nih.gov/2664732/.

FOR WHAT IT'S WORTH

140 **"such a ferocious":** "To Anyone Feeling Lost or Unhappy in Life, Find Meaning with Liz Gilbert," *The Marie Forleo Podcast,* episode 411, October 1, 2024, https://www.marieforleo.com/blog/elizabeth-gilbert-find-meaning.

TRIGGER CITY

166 **"sudden and often prolonged regressions":** Pete Walker, "Emotional Flashback Management in the Treatment of PTSD," Psychotherapy.net, https://www.psychotherapy.net/article/complex-ptsd.

CHAPTER SIX: BLINDERS OFF

198 *The Me You Can't See*: Executive producers Oprah Winfrey and Prince Harry, Apple TV, 2021.

203 **one study on the effectiveness:** Arafath Mohamed et al., "The Efficacy of Psychedelic-Assisted Therapy in Managing Post-Traumatic Stress Disorder (PTSD): A New Frontier?" *Cureus Journal of Medical Science* 14, no. 10 (2022): e30919, https://pubmed.ncbi.nlm.nih.gov/36465766/.

207 **"There are two kinds of pain":** Menakem, *My Grandmother's Hands,* 19–20.

207 **"Paradoxically, only by walking":** Menakem, *My Grandmother's Hands,* 20.

Index

Index

Index

Index

Index

Index

Index

unfawning (*cont.*)
  therapies (*see* trauma therapies)
  unraveling as, 71–72
unfawning processes
  author's, 152–53, 159–60
  getting back to center, 180–84
  inner attunement and, 156, 162, 180
  noticing the nudges, 161–63
  orienting and, 153–54
  reprocessing trauma, 185–88
  resourcing and, 155–59
  Somatic Experiencing, 192–97
  taking space, 159–61
unprocessed trauma, 92, 185
unresolved trauma, 19–20, 52–53, 154

validation. *See also* invalidation
  author's need for, 234–37
  external, 34, 97–100, 219–20
  quest for, 34–35, 82–83, 194
  unworthy of, 137–38
van der Kolk, Bessel, 119

visualization, 191–92, 194–96
vulnerability
  assertiveness and, 228
  author sharing her, 114
  example of, 37, 122
  to narcissistic abuse, 52
  reinforcing, 8
  with safe people, 246–48

Walker, Pete, 7, 21, 51–52, 166
walking, 157, 181
Woman of the Hour (film), 42–43
worth
  proving one's, 138
  sexuality tied to, 131
  struggle for, 138–39
  struggle with, 194
  validation of, 137–38

Yancey (author's husband), 91,
  128, 225–26, 237–40,
  245–46, 255

ABOUT THE AUTHOR

© ELAINE REID

Dr. Ingrid Clayton is a licensed clinical psychologist with a master's in transpersonal psychology and a PhD in clinical psychology. She has had a thriving private practice for more than sixteen years and is a regular contributor to *Psychology Today*, where her blog *Emotional Sobriety* has received more than one million views. She lives in Los Angeles.

VISIT DR. INGRID CLAYTON ONLINE

ingridclayton.com
substack.com/@ingridclaytonphd
🅕 🅞 ▶️ YouTube IngridClaytonPhD